KU-796-612

Amadio	**Systems Development: A Practical Approach** 558072-1
Amadio/Amadio	**Systems Development Projects** 540813-9
Davis/Olsen	**Management Information Systems: Conceptual Foundations, Structure, and Development,** 2/e 015828-2
Grauer/Sugrue	**Microcomputer Applications,** 2/e 024142-2
Gray	**Guide to IFPS,** 2/e 024394-8 **Guide to IFPS/Personal** 831426-7
Gremillion/Pyburn	**Computers and Information Systems in Business: An Introduction** 051007-5
Kozar	**Information Systems Analysis and Design,** 2/e 056236-9
Kroenke	**Management Information Systems** 557997-9 (accompanied by Kroenke **Project Casebook to Accompany Management Information Systems)**
Kroenke/Dolan	**Business Computer Systems: An Introduction,** 4/e 035604-1 (accompanied by Dolan/Pitter **Using Application Software in Business)**
Liebowitz	**An Introduction to Expert Systems** 554252-8
Lucas	**Information Systems Concepts for Management,** 4/e 038971-3
Lucas	**The Analysis, Design, and Implementation of Information Systems,** 3/e 038929-2
Luce	**Computer Hardware, System Software, and Architecture** 557772-0
Munshi	**Management Information Systems: Cases in Action** 044026-3
Parker	**Management Information Systems: Strategy and Action** 048542-9
Rohm/Stewart	**Essentials of Information Systems** 555448-8
Ruth/Ruth	**Developing Expert Systems Using 1st-CLASS** 556432-7
Sanders	**Computers Today,** 3/e 054850-4 w/BASIC 054847-1
Senn	**Analysis and Design of Information Systems,** 2/e 056236-9
Sprague/Ruth	**Using Expert Systems Using EXSYS** 556430-0
Stamper/Price	**Database Design and Management: An Applied Approach** 557994-X
Trainor/Krasnewich	**Computers!** 2/e 557974-X

For Gus

<u>**Software Tool Kit**</u>

An IBM PC or compatible computer diskette pertaining to topics covered in this volume is available from McGraw-Hill Book Co., Singapore. When ordering the diskette please quote Part No. 0-07-100669-D.

CONTENTS

R.T.C. LIBRARY, LETTERKENNY

PREFACE

This book is a sequel to *Systems Development: A Practical Approach,* also published by Mitchell/McGraw-Hill. *Systems Development Projects* emphasizes the use of computer-aided software engineering (CASE) and fourth-generation language (4GL) tools for systems development and is designed to be used as either:

▶ the core text or supplement in a first systems analysis and design course with a project orientation; or

▶ the core text in a second systems development project course.

Suggestions for tailoring *Systems Development Projects* to your particular time and resource constraints are presented in the accompanying Instructor's Manual.

Purpose

The primary purpose of *Systems Development Projects* is to guide students through their first application of systems development concepts to a real-world, comprehensive project.

Comprehensive Case Study or "Live" Project?

It's your choice. This book is comprehensive and flexible enough to be used either way. You can use it to guide your students through a project that involves a "live" client with out-of-class users; or you can use the written case study presented in Chapter 10. Guidelines for supplementing the written case with out-of-class activities are included in the Instructor's Manual.

Organization of the Text

The organization of this book is based on the Kolb Experiential Learning Model, which suggests that experiential learning should follow four phases: concrete experience, reflective observation, abstract conceptualization, and active experimentation.

Each chapter of this book is divided into three sections. The Horatio & Co. Cost Control System (CCS) section of each chapter follows the development of the computer-based cost control system that accompanies this text. This section of each chapter introduces the material of the chapter with a concrete, hands-on experience.

The What, How, and Why section presents observations about the concrete experience and general concepts based upon the concrete experience. The You Do It section provides guidelines, exercises, and action documents that allow students to apply the concepts of each chapter to their own projects.

The Project Experience

In developing the project course, the instructor faces many decisions. How much conceptual material (new and review) do I present and where do I get it? Do I use a written case study or a live project? Should each team work on a unique project or should all teams work on the same project? Implement projects or stop projects after delivery of an acceptable design? And so on.

We believe that a project experience should:

1. Be governed by a comprehensive and flexible life cycle that recognizes alternative software development methodologies
2. Allow for the use of CASE technology throughout the life cycle
3. Highlight the need for effective client/developer communication and creative problem-solving skills

One of the best analyses of the project experience we have seen appeared as a teaching tip in a recent newsletter. The authors, John Eatman and Wanda Theis, recommend that the project experience should:

4. Encompass a semester-long project
5. Include an implementation phase
6. Be based on a real world business problem

7. Include interfacing with existing systems

8. Be a team project including elements of project management

9. Require all supporting materials and documentation

10. Be deadline driven

Users of *Systems Development Projects* will find support for all of these recommendations.

Other Highlights

Several features of this text deserve special mention.

▶ **Comprehensive Treatment of Software Acquisition/Development.**   In this book, traditional evaluation of alternatives is expanded to include choice of software development methodologies. Prewritten software packages, prototyping, and detailed design are presented as alternatives to be used according to the needs and circumstances of the specific project.

▶ **Your Software "Toolkit."**   Several CASE/4GL options are available to adopters. The self-contained, menu-driven system for the Horatio & Co. CCS, which contains the first prototype of the software for the system, was developed using a CASE tool and a 4GL. Please read about the software options we've developed for using this system with CASE tools at every stage of the life cycle, including implementation, in the section entitled Instructor's Supporting Materials later in this Preface.

▶ **Communication and Problem-Solving Skills.**   Chapter 3 presents effective client/developer communication and creative problem-solving as systems development process skills. A set of comprehensive practice exercises are designed to strengthen students' real interview, reporting, and presentation skills. Detailed guidelines for using this material in class are presented in the Instructor's Manual.

▶ **Interface with Existing Systems.**   The integration of a new system with the existing infrastructure of a company is first considered in Chapter 2, with the development of a global entity-relationship model. The major deliverable of Chapter 9 is the completion of the interface. The question of how to interface with an existing system receives ongoing consideration throughout the intervening chapters.

▶ **Project Management.**   Students will plan, organize, staff, and control the project according to the principles of project management covered throughout the text. Project management topics receiving special coverage include network modeling, Critical Path Analysis, Gantt Charts, budgeting, and team review meetings. Guidelines for working with and monitoring student teams are included in the Instructor's Manual.

▶ **Deliverables.** This book contains tear-out forms and worksheets for a comprehensive list of deliverables, including: statement of business objectives, business tactics, system objectives, cost-benefit analysis, set of analysis DFDs, set of analysis E-R models, sets of design DFDs and E-R models, Designer's Tradeoff Chart, complete data dictionary entries, data structure diagram, system structure chart, detailed program specifications, and structured English descriptions of all supporting procedures. Guidelines for determining your choice of deliverables are included in the Instructor's Manual.

Instructor's Supporting Materials

Systems Development Projects is accompanied by a wealth of software and a comprehensive Instructor's Manual. The complete textbook package is designed to maximize the options available to you in terms of content, emphasis, and delivery method. The package includes:

Software "Toolkit"

Systems Development Projects is supported by an extensive array of *free* software. Adopters are eligible for:

1. Horatio & Co. Cost Control System diskette
2. Educational version of dBASE III PLUS (1 of 2)
3. Educational version of dBASE III PLUS (2 of 2)
4. Full-power version of GENIFER 2.0 (1 of 3)
5. Full-power version of GENIFER 2.0 (2 of 3)
6. Full-power version of GENIFER 2.0 (3 of 3)
7. GENIFER specifications and custom templates for the Horatio & Co. Cost Control System
8. EXCELERATOR and BriefCASE models and dictionary specifications for the Horatio & Co. Cost Control System

The Horatio & Co. Cost Control System diskette (#1) comes shrinkwrapped with each copy of *Systems Development Projects.* The CCS is

SUMMARY OF YOUR SOFTWARE "TOOLKIT"

Disk	Description of Disk	Retail Price	Adopter's Price
Horatio & Co. Cost Control System (CCS)	working, self-contained system for case study; shrinkwrapped with text	na	FREE
dBASE III PLUS	2 disks that make up educational version; comp ISBN: 047884-8	na	FREE
GENIFER 2.0	full-power, menu-driven applications generator for dBASE environment; order form in back of Instructor's Manual	$395	FREE
GENIFER specs	specifications and custom templates for Horatio & Co. CCS; comes with Instructor's Manual	na	FREE
EXCELERATOR & BriefCASE specs	models and dictionary for Horatio & Co. CCS to be used with EXCELERATOR and/or BriefCASE; comes with Instructor's Manual	na	FREE

a self-contained, menu-driven application. This system runs under dBASE III PLUS in a dual-floppy or hard disk environment and requires 384K of RAM. The cost control system GENIFER specifications diskette (#7) contains the GENIFER specifications used to generate the CSS programs.

The remaining diskettes (#2–8), once again, are available *free to adopters with permission to network or make copies for student/lab use only*. No knowledge of dBASE is assumed and, if you choose, no class time need be spent on the dBASE environment. The discussions are generic and can be applied to any interactive database environment.

GENIFER is a menu-driven applications generator for the dBASE environment and is available ordinarily for $395. Adopters of *Systems Development Projects*, however, are eligible to receive one free master of the full-power software (#4–6). The portion of the documentation necessary for using this text is available for sale from Mitchell/McGraw-Hill for $14.95 (ISBN: 835983-X).

In addition to receiving a full-power version of the commercial product, our GENIFER package contains additional programming templates (#7) developed through our consulting and teaching experiences with the product.

For classes using Microrim's R:base for DOS instead of GENIFER/dBASE, an appendix is provided that points out the section of the R:base for DOS documentation that matches the material in Chapter 8, which is where the details of using GENIFER and dBASE are explained in this text.

The final portion of the software "toolkit" concerns CASE support for the early phases of the life cycle. Adopters are eligible for a free diskette (#8) containing models and dictionary specifications for the Horatio & Co. CCS to be used with Index Technology's EXCELERATOR and/or Southwestern's BriefCASE. Optional guidelines for applying these tools to the student project are included in the text.

Instructor's Manual

The Instructor's Manual is an integral part of our delivery package; each chapter corresponds to one chapter of the text and includes these three sections:

1. Chapter Summary
2. Teaching Tips, Strategies, and Pitfalls
3. Thought Questions

Each chapter summary includes an outline of the chapter plus a discussion of the key concepts covered. Because of the unique nature of the project experience, you will find yourself doing less lecturing than in other courses. For the most part, class time can be spent on helping students apply concepts toward the development of their own projects.

Section II follows with a discussion of strategies and pitfalls common to the chapter material. "Tricks of the trade" and points of emphasis are included to help you guide your students through the life cycle.

Each chapter concludes with thought questions. These questions can be used either to highlight in-class discussions about pertinent chapter material or as test items. Suggested answers to these questions are also included.

The final chapter of the Instructor's Manual is unique; it presents a solution to the written case project that is based upon the deliverables outlined in the You Do It sections of each of the earlier chapters. If you are using the written case project, then this solution can serve as the foundation for your course. If you opt for "live" client projects, then this material can be a source of examples of completed deliverables and action documents throughout the project.

Acknowledgments

Many people have contributed their expertise to the development of this text. Thanks first to the following reviewers:

Fred Augustine, Stetson University

Judy Hall, California University of Pennsylvania

Dick Howell, Lansing Community College

Mohamed Khan, Centennial College

Karen-Ann Kievit, Loyola Marymount University

Thomas Luce, Ohio University

Anne McClannahan, Ohio University

Louise Sellaro, Youngstown State University

Ted Surynt, Stetson University

Wanda Theis, University of North Carolina at Greensboro

Melvyn Weisel, Pace University

We also would like to thank Jim Porzak of Bytel Corporation and Denise Nickeson, Dean Barton, Marianne Taflinger, Raleigh Wilson, Rich DeVitto, and Betty Drury of Mitchell/McGraw-Hill for the important role they each played in the publication of this book.

As always, our editor Erika Berg deserves special thanks. She initiated this project, and she nurtured it along by knowing just when to provide a little control, a little encouragement, a little freedom. In the process, she proved she was our friend as well as our colleague.

We would like to close this section by acknowledging our appreciation of Steve Mitchell and the organization he has built. At Mitchell/McGraw-Hill, no one knows fear, and, hence, no one sees limits to what can be achieved. We believe there are more than a few management lessons to be learned from observing what goes on in Watsonville, California.

Bill Amadio
Camille Amadio

Before You Begin

This book emphasizes the use of computer-aided software engineering (CASE) and fourth-generation language (4GL) tools for systems development. Several CASE/4GL options are available to institutions using this book, and this short introduction describes them. Your instructor has chosen the options that are appropriate for your course. He or she will make the diskettes available to you for copying as they are needed.

The Horatio & Co. Cost Control System

Each chapter of this book begins with an episode from the development of the cost control system of Horatio & Co., an imaginary construction firm. The cost control system was developed to help department managers control resources efficiently and effectively.

The Horatio & Co. Cost Control System diskette contains the first prototype of the software for the system. Follow the instructions below to load and run the software.

1. The Horatio & Co. Cost Control System runs under dBASE III PLUS. Academic versions of dBASE III PLUS are available free of charge to institutions using this book. A printer is required if you intend to print reports.

2. Since you will probably want to experiment with the system, make a backup copy of the cost control system diskette before beginning, so that the database can be easily restored.

3. To load dBASE III PLUS on dual diskette systems, place the dBASE III PLUS disk #1 in drive A and type DBASE at the DOS A> prompt. When prompted, remove the dBASE III PLUS disk #1 from drive A, insert the dBASE III PLUS disk #2 in drive A, and press the Enter key.

   If you are using a hard disk system, copy the files on the dBASE III PLUS diskettes to a hard disk subdirectory reserved for dBASE III PLUS, and include the name of the subdirectory in your DOS PATH command.

   To load dBASE III PLUS on hard disk systems, type DBASE at the hard disk DOS prompt.

   If the dBASE III PLUS menu-driven ASSISTANT comes up on program load, hit the Esc key to exit to the dBASE dot prompt.

4. To run the Horatio & Co. Cost Control System, place the cost control system diskette in your computer's data disk drive. The data disk drive is usually drive B for dual diskette systems and drive A for hard disk systems. Hard disk users can also set up a subdirectory for the cost control system on the hard disk and copy the files from the cost control system diskette into the subdirectory.

   Dual diskette users should now load dBASE III PLUS as described above and type the dBASE III PLUS command SET DEFAULT TO B at the dBASE III PLUS dot prompt. When the dot prompt returns, type DO COST. The system is menu driven from this point on.

   Hard disk users who have not copied the cost control system diskette files to a hard disk subdirectory should load dBASE III PLUS as described above and type the dBASE III PLUS command SET DEFAULT TO A at the dBASE III PLUS dot prompt. When the dot prompt returns, type DO COST. The system is menu driven from this point on.

   Hard disk users who have copied the cost control system diskette files to a hard disk subdirectory should log into that subdirectory, load dBASE III PLUS as described above, and type DO COST. No SET DEFAULT command is necessary.

5. A word about data entry. When prompting for data, the system displays a highlight bar indicating the maximum length of the field requested. If the entry is shorter than the maximum, press the Enter key to complete it. If the entry is equal to the maximum, the entry is complete without pressing the Enter key.

6. When a date is to be entered, two slashes will be displayed in the prompt. It is not necessary to type the slashes with the entry. When numeric data with a decimal point is to be entered, a decimal point will be displayed in the prompt. Unless the length of the entry equals the maximum, the user should type the decimal point as part of the entry.

7. If you ever arrive at an error message that offers the choice to Cancel, Ignore, or Suspend, choose Cancel and type DO COST at the dot prompt to restart the system.

8. Choose option Q, QUIT, from the cost control system's main menu to return to the dBASE III PLUS dot prompt. Type QUIT to exit dBASE III PLUS and return to DOS.

We suggest beginning your work with option 4, REPORTS, from the main menu. The database of the cost control system contains budget and expense records for the months of January 1990 and February 1990.

The Budget versus Actual Reports prompt for a cutoff date. Valid entries are 01/31/90 and 02/28/90. The Expense History Reports prompt for a starting date and an ending date. Valid entries here are any pair of dates that cover some portion of the time from 01/01/90 through 02/28/90.

Option 5, ENGINEERS' ACTIVITY ANALYSIS, prompts for an engineer's name and displays an analysis of his or her activity. Valid engineers' names are LUDWIG, TILDEN, and JONES.

Option 3, INQUIRIES, presents a more sophisticated mechanism for making selections than either the REPORTS option or the ENGINEERS' ACTIVITY ANALYSIS option. INQUIRIES presents a data screen and a menu of options along the bottom of that screen. Choosing option G, Go, immediately displays all expense records in the database. Try it.

Once you have displayed all the expense records, try making a selection. Choose option F, Filter, followed by an S for Set. The data screen is cleared, allowing you to fill in your selection specifications. Hit the Enter key three times, and fill in 4100 in the ACCOUNT field. Hit the PgDn key to signal the end of your entries. When the bottom line menu becomes active again, choose option G, Go, and observe that only expenses for account 4100 are displayed.

Try some other inquiry selections. Set a filter (option F followed by S for Set) for SOURCE = NAL-TECH. Also try an inquiry of all records for which DESCRIPTION = DESIGN. Finally, try an inquiry on all records for which ACCOUNT = 4100 and JOB = B107 (hint: fill in both ACCOUNT with 4100 and JOB with B107 before hitting PgDn to complete your specification entry).

Do not be afraid to experiment; there is no way to damage the system. The other options on the INQUIRIES menu are explained later in this book, but please feel free to try them now.

Option 1, MAINTAIN BUDGETS, and option 2, MAINTAIN EXPENSES, of the cost control system main menu allow you to add, delete, and modify records in the database. The bottom line menu is used again. Choose option H, Help, to see an explanation of each choice. Try performing some maintenance operations, like adding a new record, and observe the effect on the REPORTS and INQUIRIES.

GENIFER

Bytel's GENIFER is a menu-driven applications generator for the dBASE environment. The developer maintains specifications about an application's files, variables, indexes, menus, maintenance processes, reports, and inquiries in GENIFER's dictionary files. GENIFER generates dBASE code from the specifications. System users run the generated code under dBASE, independently of GENIFER. A site license for GENIFER is available free of charge to institutions using this book.

The details of using GENIFER and dBASE III PLUS are presented in Chapter 8 of this book. The Horatio & Co. Cost Control System GENIFER specifications diskette contains the GENIFER specifications used to generate the cost control system programs. Follow the instructions below to load and run GENIFER.

1. Since you will probably want to experiment with GENIFER, make backup copies of the cost control system and GENIFER specifications diskettes before beginning so that files can be easily restored.

2. If you have a dual diskette system or if you have not copied the cost control system diskette files to a subdirectory on the hard disk, copy the files from the cost control system diskette and the cost control system GENIFER specifications diskette to a single 720K, 3½-inch diskette and place this diskette in your computer's data disk drive. The data disk drive is usually drive B for dual diskette systems and drive A for hard disk systems.

    If you have copied the cost control system diskette files to a subdirectory on the hard disk, copy the files from the cost control system GENIFER specifications diskette into the same subdirectory.

3. To load GENIFER on dual diskette systems, copy the GENIFER diskettes 1 and 2 to a single 720K, 3½-inch diskette and place this diskette in drive A. Type GEN at the DOS A> prompt.

    If you are using a hard disk system, copy the files on the GENIFER diskettes 1 and 2 to a hard disk subdirectory reserved for GENIFER.

    To load GENIFER on hard disk systems, change to the directory reserved for GENIFER and type GEN at the hard disk DOS prompt.

4. GENIFER works on one project at a time. To activate the cost control system's specifications, choose option 5, Customizer, from GENIFER's main menu, followed by option 1, Environment.

    Press M for Modify and enter the project code, project name, and developer name of your choice. If you are working from a combined cost control system and GENIFER specifications diskette, enter the letter of your computer's data disk drive for the output directory, data directory, and template directory. If you copied the cost control system and GENIFER specifications diskette files into a hard disk subdirectory, enter the drive and name of the subdirectory for the output directory, data directory, and template directory. See the GENIFER documentation and Chapter 8 of this book for more information about these specifications.

Answer the color question according to the display you are using, and press S for Save when prompted.

All GENIFER processing will be directed toward the cost control system specifications until you change the Environment Customizer settings.

5. To return to DOS, choose option Q, EXIT from GENIFER, from the GENIFER main menu.

RBASE for DOS and dBASEIV

The details of using GENIFER and dBASE are explained in Chapter 8 of this book, so that you can build the software for your project with these tools. For classes using RBASE for DOS or the dBASEIV Applications Generator instead of GENIFER and dBASE, an appendix is provided that points out the sections of the documentation that match the material presented in Chapter 8.

EXCELERATOR and BriefCASE

GENIFER, dBASE, and RBASE support the systems developer primarily in the later phases of the life cycle, namely, design, implementation, and maintenance. For the earlier phases—analysis and design—we have tools like EXCELERATOR from Index Technology and BriefCASE from South-Western Publishing Co.

A diskette containing EXCELERATOR and BriefCASE analysis and design specifications for the Horatio & Co. Cost Control System is available free of charge to institutions using this book. Exercises throughout this book ask you to use these tools to explore and expand these specifications.

CHAPTER 1

Problem and/or Opportunity Analysis

Computer-based information systems (CBISs) are developed to serve the business needs of the people who use them. This book helps guide you through the process of analyzing, designing, and building such a system.

The process of systems development begins with an analysis of the business environment. The result of this analysis is an understanding of problems and/or opportunities facing the business and an evaluation of the usefulness of a CBIS solution.

Each chapter of this book is divided into three sections: the Horatio & Co. Cost Control System section, the What, How, and Why section, and the You Do It section. The role of each section is the same in each chapter.

The Horatio & Co. section of each chapter follows the development of a computer-based cost control system for a construction company. This section introduces the material of each chapter through an appropriate concrete experience. The What, How, and Why section of each chapter presents observations about the concrete experience and general concepts based upon the concrete experience. The You Do It section of each chapter provides guidelines, exercises, and action documents that allow you to apply the concepts of the chapter to your own project. The pages of this book are perforated and punched so that figures and action documents can be removed, used, and stored easily.

The Horatio & Co. section of this chapter looks at the problem and/or opportunity analysis for the cost control system project. This analysis is expressed in terms of business objectives, business tactics, and system objectives.

The participants in this analysis are Sam Tilden, engineering department manager, Frank Chapin, president of Horatio & Co., Dan Klockner, general manager of Horatio & Co., and Pete Willard, information systems consultant. As the cost control system project unfolds, new players will join the project team.

The second section of this chapter, the What, How, and Why section, defines the terms *objectives* and *tactics*, makes observations about the analysis for the cost control system, and presents a general procedure for problem and/or opportunity analysis based upon objectives and tactics.

The final section of this chapter, the You Do It section, provides you with guidelines, exercises, and action documents for analyzing the problems and/or opportunities of your project environment.

After completing this chapter you will

1. Understand a method for analyzing business problems and/or opportunities in terms of objectives and tactics

2. Understand the roles played by the user/management group and information systems professionals in the analysis of business problems and/or opportunities

3. Apply the method of objectives and tactics to the analysis of the problems and/or opportunities facing your project

HORATIO & CO. COST CONTROL SYSTEM

Horatio & Co. is engaged in the construction and management of commercial real estate. The specialty of the firm is office park construction projects.

Horatio & Co. developed this expertise as a result of a boom in business relocations from a nearby city to the suburban communities that Horatio & Co. served. The president of the company, Frank Chapin, likes to say, "We were in the right place at the right time."

The real estate boom that brought so much success to Horatio & Co. is now six years old, and it is beginning to level off. Each season brings fewer and fewer new construction projects.

The explosive growth of the area, however, attracted national publicity, and with the publicity came increased competition. Thus the firm faces the difficult situation of competing with a larger number of companies for a dwindling number of projects in the area.

The market strength of Horatio & Co. has always been high-quality, reliable construction. Frank Chapin reports, "We built our reputation by delivering what we promised on time and within budget. We worked best with developers who were willing to pay a little more for a job that was done right the first time."

Not all of the firm's new competitors are following Horatio's high-quality strategy. Several bids have been lost recently because developers decided to accept admittedly lower-quality proposals on the basis of cost. In response to this situation Frank Chapin and Dan Klockner, the general manager of Horatio & Co., are looking for ways to maintain the high-quality

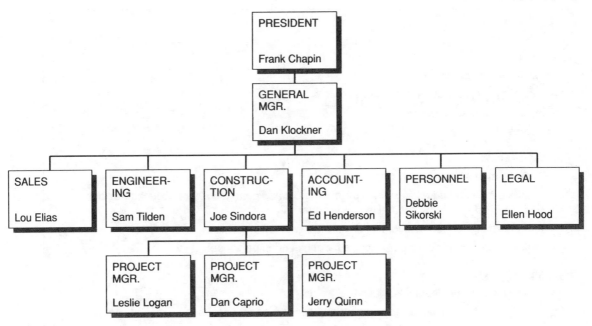

FIGURE 1.1
Horatio & Co. organization chart

position of the firm while cutting the price differential between Horatio and its lower-quality competitors. Chapin and Klockner believe that a 10 percent decrease in Horatio's prices will be enough to sell developers on Horatio's higher-quality projects.

Maintaining current levels of profit in the face of a 10 percent decrease in revenue implies a 10 percent decrease in costs. Chapin and Klockner's short-range plan calls for such a decrease in costs. They realize that the successful implementation of this plan depends heavily upon the business skills of the Horatio & Co. department managers. (Figure 1.1 shows an organization chart for the firm, listing each department and its manager.) Frank Chapin explained the situation and his decisions to the department managers at a special staff meeting.

Plan for the Engineering Department

As part of his effort to decrease costs, Sam Tilden, the manager of the engineering department, is investigating the feasibility of an automated cost

Business Objective

Maintain the current level of profit in the engineering department by

    decreasing clerical costs

    identifying cost overruns within 30 days

    decreasing cost of materials

    decreasing turnover

Business Tactics

1. Eliminate manual preparation of job cost reports
2. Institute a monthly budgeting system by job number and general ledger account to replace the current annual system by general ledger account only
3. Reorganize the vendor base for higher volumes with fewer vendors
4. Institute professional development plans for engineering personnel

System Objective

Reports and inquiries on demand, including

    Budget vs. Actual Reports by job number and general ledger account on a monthly basis

    Job Cost Summary and Detail Reports

    Detail inquiry by source of expense or vendor

FIGURE 1.2
Sam Tilden's plan to maintain current levels of profit in the engineering department

control system. Working with a systems development consultant, Pete Willard, Sam developed the plan presented in Figure 1.2.

How Sam and Pete Developed the Plan

When Sam Tilden thought that a computer-based information system might be of help to him, he called Pete Willard, his former information systems professor, and asked Pete to serve as consultant to Horatio & Co. Pete agreed, and they set up a meeting for 10:00 a.m. on the following Monday at Sam's office.

At this meeting Sam told Pete that Horatio & Co. had undertaken the improvement of the business operations of the departments as a company-wide objective. The purpose of this undertaking was to maintain the current level of profit in the face of declining revenues. Sam and Pete also discussed some specifics of Sam's plan for the engineering department at this first meeting.

Pete said that plans for a systems development project should begin with a statement of business objectives and tactics. He suggested they meet again on Wednesday at 10:00 a.m. to develop such a statement. To prepare for the meeting, Pete suggested that Sam write down "all he knew" about the overall strategy of the firm and the problems and opportunities facing the business operations of the engineering department.

The following dialogue shows what went on at the Wednesday meeting. Pete and Sam began on time.

SAM: Good morning, Pete. How was the trip across town?

PETE: Not bad. Most of the traffic is gone after 9 o'clock.

SAM: I am glad we scheduled for 10 o'clock. That gave me a chance to read my mail and to return a few phone calls.

I tried that exercise you suggested. I wrote down everything I could think of concerning the problems of our business operations. It was more difficult than I expected.

PETE: How so?

SAM: I couldn't decide what was important, and I was reluctant to write down the obvious. I found that talking things over with the other managers helped. In the end, the list was quite long.

PETE: Most people find it challenging to verbalize and write down what they think is obvious. It turns out that these items are not obvious to everyone, and they lead to more important observations later in the process. Let's see what you have.

SAM: Here it is. (Sam's list is shown in Figure 1.3.)

PETE: Well, that's quite a list, Sam. Your comments give me a good first-draft sense of the situation. I'll learn more as we develop specifics from this list.

Today we want to identify the business objectives and tactics of this project. From your writing, we know quite a bit about the problem situation, and it is obvious that these are important issues. Business objectives are basically what we propose to do about that situation, and tactics are how we propose to do it.

(Sensing some confusion on Sam's part) Let me be more specific. You said you are spending money on clerks to prepare job cost reports. Well, decreasing clerical costs might be one of our objectives. That is *what* we want to do. *How* we do it determines our tactics. We could try to get by with fewer clerks or try to find cheaper clerks. We could try

BUSINESS OPERATIONS PROBLEMS

The overall strategy of the firm is to provide high-quality, reliable construction for the commercial markets of the surrounding seven-county area.

Company revenues are expected to fall by 10 percent. We have got to maintain our current level of profit by decreasing costs.

We need better access to job cost information. We spend money for clerks to prepare Job Cost Reports manually. They hate the job, and we have to wait too long for them to prepare the reports. There are also errors and inconsistencies in the reports.

Sometimes the engineers have to prepare the reports themselves. This is a complete waste of time, and it is demoralizing to the engineers. It makes the company look unprofessional, behind the times, and inefficient.

We need more control of expenses. The annual budgeting system is too loose. I can overspend my budget in February and not know about it until August. The system is accurate, and it works well. It is just not tight enough.

We need more organization in our purchasing. We are okay on items purchased by the company as a whole, but for items used only in this department we do not take enough advantage of our buying power. We are spread too thin. If we spent more with fewer vendors, we would have more clout.

Turnover among the engineers is a serious problem. We have more competitors than we used to, and the engineers are more demanding. And it is not only salary. They demand the latest equipment: computers for computer-aided design, and specialized software for mathematical calculations. More importantly, they demand challenging and varied work assignments. As soon as someone learns a particular task, he or she wants to learn something else. I need to be able to plan and make assignments better. I am worried about my own skills with all of the management responsibilities I have. I am losing touch with my profession.

FIGURE 1.3
Sam Tilden's write-down-all-you-know exercise

to get by with fewer reports. We could provide automated tools to prepare the reports more efficiently.

SAM: Aren't we getting into semantics with the difference between objectives and tactics?

PETE: It is easy to get bogged down in systems analysis details. It's sometimes called "analysis paralysis." I want to avoid that as much as you do. Don't worry about the difference between objectives and tactics at this point. Think in terms of solutions to your problem.

SAM: All right.

PETE: Why don't you try to identify some solutions? Look over your problem list and come up with specific ideas about what you want to achieve.

SAM: I agree that decreasing clerical costs should be an objective. I guess I also want to institute professional development plans for the engineers.

PETE: Why?

SAM: Well, because it will help cut down on turnover. If I can make and follow a plan of assignments, I'll do a better job of satisfying the engineers' demand for the assignments they want.

PETE: Is there any other way to cut down on turnover besides instituting professional development plans?

SAM: I see what you were saying about objectives and tactics. My objective is really to reduce turnover. Professional development plans represent one way to do this. In fact, my overriding objective is to maintain the current level of profit in the face of a 10 percent drop in revenue.

PETE: Objectives and tactics together form solutions.

SAM: I understand. Well, I suppose we could let the engineers choose some of their own assignments as an alternative. We could rotate the desirable assignments according to a predetermined schedule. In recruiting, we could look for people willing to specialize, so as to cut down on the demand for varied assignments. There are lots of ways to achieve this objective.

PETE: What about assigning people through some kind of lottery?

SAM: No, I don't think that will work. I would not want the engineers to think they had to be lucky to get desirable assignments.

PETE: Okay. We've covered quite a bit of ground; before we go on, let's backtrack over what we've done so far.

So far we have identified decreasing clerical costs and reducing turnover as objectives, and we have developed quite a long list of tactics to achieve these objectives. What other objectives and tactics can you determine from your list?

SAM: The current budgeting system is not tight enough. I'd like to control costs better in general and I'd like to identify overruns for individual jobs quicker.

PETE: What do you mean by "quicker"?

SAM: If I could have the information in 30 days, I might be able to prevent expenses from running amuck.

PETE: Okay, we'll add the identification of cost overruns within 30 days to the objectives list.

SAM: I think the only way to do this is to replace the current annual budgeting system by general ledger account with a new monthly budgeting system by general ledger account and job number.

PETE: That sounds like a clear tactic to me. Let's add it to the list.

SAM: The item on the list that gave me the most trouble was purchasing. I am not really sure what I need here.

PETE: What are you trying to achieve?

SAM: I want to decrease the cost of the products and services we buy. I am never sure I am paying the best price. Currently I go to vendors for specific items only. I guess I want to take advantage of the volume discounts that I see other firms getting.

PETE: So what is the objective?

SAM: Decrease the cost of products and services.

PETE: How?

SAM: Reorganize our vendor base for high-volume purchases.

Pete and Sam continued their dialogue and ended the session when they had achieved the desired outcome: "identify the business objectives and tactics of this project." You should review the first two parts of Figure 1.2 to see a summary of the business objectives and tactics identified by Pete and Sam.

The third part of Figure 1.2, System Objectives, lists what a new system might do to support the business tactics presented above. These system objectives were developed in a similar dialogue that began with the question, "How can a computer-based information system help with these business tactics?"

Presenting the Plan to Management

Sam was encouraged by the business objectives he uncovered in his analysis with Pete. Decreasing clerical costs, identifying cost overruns within 30 days, decreasing material costs, and decreasing turnover could contribute significantly to maintaining profits in the face of a 10 percent decrease in revenue. He felt that the business tactics of the plan were a viable means to achieve these business objectives. He also felt that the system objectives—reports and inquiries on demand—were critical to the success of the business tactics.

Pete advised Sam that the next step in the systems development process was further analysis of the current situation and of the proposed system. This analysis would include a detailed accounting of the time, money, and other resources needed to develop the proposed system. The analysis would assess the benefits of the proposed system and the likelihood of these benefits being attained. Pete estimated that this analysis would require five days of his and Sam's time.

Sam had to get approval and funding from Frank Chapin in order to undertake the analysis. He knew this would not be easy. Top management was looking to the department managers to cut costs by 10 percent, so any request to fund a new project was sure to meet with close scrutiny.

Sam decided to concentrate on the value represented in his business objectives. If he had to find a 10 percent saving in costs in his department, payroll, cost overruns, turnover, and materials were likely places in which to look. Sam spent 2.6 million dollars per year on these items, so even a small percentage decrease in these costs would be substantial and worth pursuing. In addition, the proposed system was likely to improve the quality of his department's work, another important point in the strategy of top management. Finally, the proposed system would not be restricted to the engineering department. Other departments could use it and realize the same kinds of savings.

Sam summarized these points in a memo. He delivered the memo along with a copy of his plan, Figure 1.2, to Frank Chapin and Dan Klockner.

Sam's proposal was approved. Mr. Chapin agreed with Sam that payroll, cost overruns, turnover, and materials were high-potential areas, but he warned that he was uneasy about the lack of "hard numbers" at this stage of the project. He would be looking for these hard numbers at the end of Sam's analysis.

THE WHAT, HOW, AND WHY

Most companies organize systems development and maintenance activities into a set of phases, commonly called the **systems development life cycle** [1]. Development teams use the life cycle as a blueprint for their activities. In addition, the life cycle can be used as a project management tool, that is, an aid to planning, organizing, and controlling project activities.

The tasks performed during systems development and the outputs produced by these tasks are called the project **deliverables**. By following the systems development life cycle, project team members always know what deliverables should have been completed already, what deliverables should be currently under way, what tasks remain to be done, and how prior work will be used to accomplish future work. The life cycle provides a means of both short-term and long-term planning and control.

The Systems Development Life Cycle

Each phase of the systems development life cycle is made up of procedures and decisions. The version of the life cycle used throughout this book is shown in Figure 1.4.

Problem and/or Opportunity Analysis Phase

The procedures of the **Problem and/or Opportunity Analysis Phase** lead to a decision regarding the usefulness of an information system for the problem and/or opportunity at hand. At this point in the life cycle, it is too early to commit to the development of an information system. A favorable decision at the end of the Problem and/or Opportunity Analysis Phase indicates that an information system solution deserves further study. It represents a commitment to the next two phases of the life cycle.

Systems Analysis Model-Building Phase

In the **Systems Analysis Model-Building Phase** of the life cycle, the development team studies the current means of addressing the problem and/or opportunity at hand. The models serve as a convenient way of describing the present situation and communicating this understanding among development team members.

Once the current situation is modeled, the development team turns its attention toward improving it. The improvements specified at this time become the focus for the rest of the life cycle. To illustrate their importance, the improvements are commonly referred to as requirements.

Evaluation of Alternatives Phase

In the third phase of the life cycle, **Evaluation of Solution Alternatives**, the development team looks for ways to implement the requirements through an information system. Rough estimates of cost are used to decide how many of the requirements will be addressed and the means by which they will be addressed. In doing this, the team considers the five components of a computer-based information system: hardware, software, data, procedures, and personnel [4].

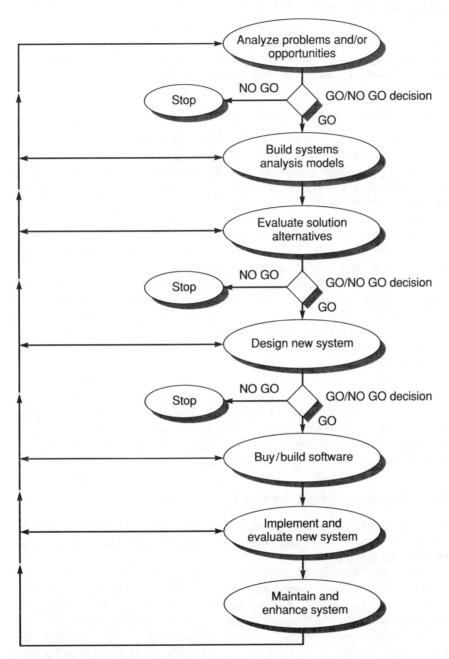

FIGURE 1.4
Systems development life cycle

The development team also evaluates how the new system will be designed and implemented. A decision is made either to proceed with the remaining steps or to abandon an information systems solution in favor of some other way of addressing the problem and/or opportunity.

Design Phase and Beyond

The remaining steps of the life cycle vary, depending upon the choice of software design and implementation methodology. In the **Design New System Phase**, procedures for the new system are designed, operational and management responsibilities are assigned, and the physical layout for the hardware is determined.

The variations arise in connection with the data and software components. If the new system is addressing a common problem, such as accounts receivable processing, then software packages are probably already available to perform the functions [2]. In this case, software and data design activities are minimal. Instead of designing the software, the development team shops for a package that provides an acceptable match with the requirements.

If the problem and/or opportunity at hand is unique, then the software component of the new system is developed instead of purchased. The software design method depends upon the environment available for the development of the system.

Whatever data and software design method is chosen, the development team assembles an estimate of the costs to develop and maintain the proposed system at the end of the design phase. The software and data components are built or bought in the **Buy/Build Software Phase**. They are then combined with the hardware, procedures, and personnel components into a final implementation. A new system is born.

Final Phases of the Life Cycle

During the **Implement and Evaluate New System Phase** of the life cycle, the new system is put into production; it performs the work for which it was designed and built. It lives.

Sometimes, flaws in the design and programming are found and corrected. Sometimes the environment changes, and the system must be changed to stay current. During the **Maintain and Enhance System Phase** of the life cycle, users and systems specialists work together to maintain the system.

Inevitably, changes in the environment and advances in technology push system requirements to the point where the system can no longer handle the work. In this case, the current system is retired, and the life cycle is complete. If the current system needs to be replaced, the development process begins anew.

Performing Problem and/or Opportunity Analysis

The problem and/or opportunity analysis technique presented in this book is based upon identifying objectives and tactics [3]. **Business objectives** are broadly stated, measurable outcomes which are used to guide the activities and decisions of the organization. **Business tactics** are specific actions performed to achieve business objectives. **System objectives** are broadly stated system actions developed to support a set of business tactics. With these definitions in mind, reread Figure 1.2 to understand the difference between business objectives, business tactics, and system objectives.

The development of business objectives and business tactics is really the work of the user/management group. The information systems professional can help guide the development process, but usually does not have enough knowledge of the business to identify objectives and develop effective tactics.

In guiding the process of developing objectives and tactics the analyst often finds that his or her dialogue with the client moves naturally between business objectives, business tactics, and system objectives. It is often necessary to shift the conversation from one topic to another. For example, a discussion may suddenly reveal a business tactic that has no previously defined objective. Discussion of this tactic is meaningless until a reason (objective) for performing it is determined. Figure 1.5 provides questions that the analyst can ask to keep such dialogues on track [3]. Understanding these questions will improve your understanding of the definitions and uses of business objectives, business tactics, and system objectives.

Shift from	To	Guiding question
Business objectives	Business tactics	How would you achieve that?
Business tactics	Business objectives	Why would you do that?
Business tactics	System objectives	What can a system do to help?
System objectives	Business tactics	What would you do with that information?

FIGURE 1.5
Questions to guide the development of business objectives, business tactics, and system objectives

40015568

Once the business objectives and tactics have been determined, however, the information systems professional is responsible for showing how an information system might support the business tactics. Today's information systems work best with business tactics that involve performance quality, performance efficiency, and control mechanisms.

Performance quality refers to how well a job is done. **Performance efficiency** measures the output produced from a given set of inputs. **Control mechanisms** are used to detect substandard performance. Whenever the user/management group develops a set of business tactics that involve these concepts, the potential for an information systems solution is high.

The specific information system functions that support performance and control tactics are shown in Figure 1.6. The more functions that support the business tactics of the problem and/or opportunity analysis, the more likely an information systems solution will be effective. The decision to proceed to the next two phases of the life cycle is based upon an assessment of the appropriateness of these functions for the business tactics of the plan.

A CHECKLIST OF INFORMATION SYSTEM FUNCTIONS

Performance Quality and Efficiency

1. Reduce staff time spent on clerical functions, leading to more productive use or elimination of that time.
2. Organize and present information quickly.
3. Organize and present information in a variety of ways.
4. Select records from a large database and present them in isolation.
5. Summarize the content of a large number of records into a meaningful report or display.
6. Perform compilations and/or analyses which are otherwise impossible.

Control Mechanisms

1. Monitor processes to detect and report substandard performance.
2. Aid in the determination of the cause of substandard performance.
3. Implement actions to correct substandard performance.

FIGURE 1.6

Information system functions that support business tactics involving performance quality and efficiency, and control mechanisms

Measurable is an important term in the definition of objectives. An objective is measurable when it is possible to determine whether or not the objective has been achieved. The business objective of maintaining current levels of profit is measurable because Horatio & Co. management can compare this year's profits to last year's profits and can thus determine whether or not the project has been successful.

An example of a nonmeasurable business objective is "to improve customer satisfaction." Improve it in relation to what? How will we know when it is improved? Improve it by a lot or a little? If a project team cannot answer these questions, then their objectives are not measurable.

The system objectives of the projected cost control system are not completely measurable. At this stage of a project, it is not unusual to work with half-measurable system objectives. The project team can certainly determine whether or not the stated reports and inquiries are available, but the term *on demand* needs more development. "On demand" can mean different things to different people. Refining the system objectives of the plan presented in Figure 1.2 and determining system tactics will be part of the work of the evaluation of alternatives phase of the life cycle.

YOU DO IT

It is now time for you to perform the problem and/or opportunity analysis for your project. Use the cost control system material and the What, How, and Why material, along with the action documents of this section, to guide your efforts; but make the finished product and the process by which it is developed uniquely your own.

Do not be afraid to make choices. If your client is too busy to cover everything presented in this chapter, then you must deal with that reality. Negotiate compromises and work within the constraints of the situation.

Do not be afraid to be creative. Meeting with a client for an interview is one way to collect information. You and your client might also want to consider using written questionnaires, time logs, pocket tape recorders, or other means to collect information.

Try to keep in touch with your own thoughts, feelings, and impressions during this process. Remember, everyone is influenced by his or her own background, experience, and work style. The material and techniques presented here work for us. Try them. If they do not work for you, ask yourself why, and use the experience and the analysis to develop alternatives. You should learn as much about yourself in this project as you do about your client.

PROBLEM AND/OR OPPORTUNITY ANALYSIS DELIVERABLES

1. An understanding of the overall strategy of the firm and the relationship of the current problem and/or opportunity to that strategy

2. A statement of the current problem and/or opportunity in terms of business objectives: *what* should be accomplished

3. A determination of business tactics to support the business objectives: *how* the objectives should be accomplished

4. A determination of the information system functions applicable to the current problem and/or opportunity

5. A decision to study an information system solution further, based upon the previous analysis

ACTION DOCUMENT 1.1
Problem and/or opportunity analysis
deliverables

Deliverable 1: Understanding the overall strategy of the firm

Task	User/Mgt People	IS People	Documents Needed	Documents Produced	Estimated Duration

Deliverable 2: Business objectives

Task	User/Mgt People	IS People	Documents Needed	Documents Produced	Estimated Duration

Deliverable 3: Business tactics

Task	User/Mgt People	IS People	Documents Needed	Documents Produced	Estimated Duration

ACTION DOCUMENT 1.2
Tasks for each deliverable (page 1 of 2)

Deliverable 4: Applicable information system functions

Task	User/Mgt People	IS People	Documents Needed	Documents Produced	Estimated Duration

Deliverable 5: Decision to study information system solution further

Task	User/Mgt People	IS People	Documents Needed	Documents Produced	Estimated Duration

ACTION DOCUMENT 1.2
Tasks for each deliverable (page 2 of 2)

Date _____

To   _____

From _____

Re: Problem and/or opportunity analysis

The following documents are included in this analysis:

☐   Organization chart

☐   Overall strategy of the firm

☐   Plan outlining business objectives, business tactics, supporting information functions, and system objectives

☐   Decision and rationale regarding further study of an information system solution

☐   Other _____

     _____

☐   Other _____

     _____

☐   Other _____

     _____

☐   Other _____

     _____

The following activities were carried out during this analysis:

☐   Interviews with_____

     _____

☐   Write-down-all-you-know with _____

     _____

☐   Other _____

     _____

☐   Other _____

     _____

☐   Other _____

     _____

ACTION DOCUMENT 1.3
Cover sheet for problem and/or opportunity analysis

CHAPTER 2

Getting to Know Your Client

This chapter deals with a set of tools and techniques to collect, organize, and present important background information about your client. If you compare the development of a computer-based information system to the design and construction of a new home, you can see the importance of this information.

We would not give a satisfactory rating to an architect who designs a home with a large library for a family that spends very little time reading. Similarly, an architect who provides elaborate cooking and dining facilities for a working couple who eat most of their meals "on the run" is also probably missing the point.

An architect commissioned to design a home must obtain information about the lifestyle of his or her client—size of the family, recreational interests, aesthetic preferences; in the same way, the systems developer must spend some time getting to know his or her clients and their work.

Client information for a systems development project should be organized into a **client profile**. The Horatio & Co. section of this chapter discusses the development of the client profile for Sam Tilden, manager of the engineering department. In this section, you will observe how Pete Willard, the consultant, collected the information for his profile of Sam.

The What, How, and Why section of this chapter explains the material presented in Sam Tilden's client profile along with the significance of this material for systems development.

The You Do It section of this chapter provides you with the means—guidelines, exercises, and action documents—to develop a client profile for your own project.

After completing this chapter you will

1. understand the roles, activities, and decisions undertaken in administrative and managerial work

2.   understand the various work styles people bring to their work

3.   learn how to develop a graphical model of any work environment

4.   apply these concepts to the development of a client profile for your project

HORATIO & CO. COST CONTROL SYSTEM

The client profile presented in this section concerns Sam Tilden, the manager of the engineering department and initiator of the Horatio & Co. Cost Control System. The cost control system provides access to company-wide accounting data for the purposes of job cost reporting, flexible budgeting, and staff development and assignment.

Roles, Activities, and Decisions

The material for the client profile was collected by Pete Willard. Pete and Sam met to discuss Sam's impressions of his work. To prepare Sam for this meeting, Pete asked Sam to keep a weekly time log and to think about his primary roles in the company. Pete told Sam that this would help Sam focus on how he spent his time at work. Pete asked Sam to bring the completed time log to their meeting.

The following dialogue shows a portion of what went on during this meeting. Pete and Sam began on time.

SAM: Hi, Pete. Thanks for being on time.

PETE: You're welcome. I know you are very busy.

SAM: I have my completed time log.

PETE: How did it go? Did you get anything out of the process of compiling the log?

SAM: Yes, quite a bit. Compiling the log showed me that I spend most of my time allocating resources of one kind or another and communicating information to and from the department.

PETE: Good. At this meeting I would like to compile a profile of your work that includes, among other things, the roles you play, the activities you perform, and the decisions you make. Could you tell me a little more about your roles as resource allocator and information communicator?

SAM: The resources I control are the engineering expertise of the department along with the supporting equipment and materials. I have to make sure that my department meets the needs of the company. I also have to guarantee that the resources are used efficiently and effectively.

In order to communicate effectively, I have to monitor both the internal and external environments of the department. In a sense, I am a spokesman for the department to the external environment and the disseminator of outside information about the company and the market among the engineering staff.

PETE: What activities do these roles involve?

SAM: Well, as a resource allocator, I prepare budget estimates and schedules for the engineering portion of Horatio's projects, and I assign the engineers to staff the projects. I monitor and evaluate activities and expenditures as the projects unfold, and I report performance to the engineers and to senior management. Once in a while, I perform some engineering tasks myself.

PETE: You mentioned that once before.

SAM: I want to stay current with the technical side of my profession, even though I currently hold a management position.

PETE: What other communications do you perform?

SAM: Well, at staff meetings, we discuss the long-range planning for the firm, and I often provide specialized information for planning decisions. With vendors, I negotiate contracts and specify requirements.

PETE: Did all these activities show up on your time log?

SAM: Yes, they did! That's really why these activities are so clear in my mind.

PETE: I'm glad. Many people find the time log or diary helpful in getting a perspective on their workday. We'll come back to the log again a little later. At this point, I would like to discuss the decisions that you make in your work.

SAM: Decisions vary across a wide spectrum. From something formal like,"Which jobs are within budget?" to something totally unstructured like, "Is there a better way to coordinate engineering and construction efforts?"

PETE: What do you mean by "totally unstructured?"

SAM: I call that particular decision totally unstructured because I cannot define coordination. What does it mean specifically? Even if I could define it, how would I evaluate it? What would I hope to achieve through the "better way"? Better in relation to what? And by how much? That sort of thing.

PETE: Can you tell me the percentage breakdown between structured and unstructured decisions in your workday?

SAM: I would say about 75 percent structured and 25 percent unstructured.

PETE: Okay. Let me summarize what we've got so far so that I am sure I understand everything you have told me.

Pete went on to recap Sam's roles as resource allocator and information communicator, his activities as a monitor and controller of the resources and operations of his department, and the range of his decisions from structured to unstructured. This completed the first part of Sam's client profile.

Sam's Work Style

Once Sam and Pete understood each other regarding Sam's roles, activities, and decisions, they turned their attention to Sam's work style. Pete asked Sam to identify some problem or decision that he faces frequently in his work. Sam chose the problem of determining cost estimates for bids on new projects.

Pete showed Sam a list of words (see Figure 2.1). He asked Sam to choose the two words that best described how he (Sam) gathered information for determining costs. Then he asked Sam to choose the two words that best described how he evaluated information for determining costs. Sam told Pete that "analytical" and "thinking" best described his information gathering, and that "systematic" and "think it over" best described his information evaluation style.

Pete responded, "Good; there are no right or wrong answers here. We will use this information whenever we face a choice that involves work style. We now know that you prefer a systematic and analytical approach as opposed to an intuitive, or experimental approach. Do you think that is accurate?" Sam said, "Yes. I have always preferred to think things out before taking any action. I believe most engineers work that way."

People, Units, and Things

The third part of the client profile of Sam Tilden involved the people, units, and things with which Sam must deal in his work. Pete and Sam went back to Sam's weekly time log to identify these entities, and they summarized their findings into the table presented in Figure 2.2.

Information Gathering		Information Evaluation	
conceptual	thinking	systematic	practical
experiential	accepting	intuitive	reserving judgment
analytical	rational	reflective	experimenting
feeling	here and now	active	think it over
		watching	see if it works

FIGURE 2.1
Pete's word list

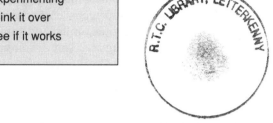

SAM TILDEN'S WORK ENTITIES
(Summarized from weekly time logs)

Work to/from	Desk Work Sessions		Nondesk Work Sessions		Total	
	% of Time	Average Hrs/Wk	% of Time	Average Hrs/Wk	% of Time	Average Hrs/Wk
President	1	.4	1.5	.6	2.5	1.0
General manager	2	.8	7	2.8	9	3.6
Engineers	2.5	1.0	11	4.4	13.5	5.4
Construction project managers	3	1.2	5.5	2.2	8.5	3.4
Administrative assistant	10	4.0	—	—	10	4.0
Files (budgets, schedules, cost ledger)	40	16.0	—	—	40	16.0
Accounting	5	2.0	—	—	5	2.0
Personnel	1.5	.5	—	—	1.5	.5
Legal	1	.4	—	—	1	.4
Sales	1	.4	—	—	1	.4
Vendors	—	—	5	2.0	5	2.0
Unscheduled meetings	—	—	3	1.5	3	1.5
Total	67	26.7	33	13.2	100	39.9

FIGURE 2.2
An analysis of Sam Tilden's work entities

Figure 2.3 presents a model of Sam's work environment and his interactions with it. The model is called a **global-entity relationship (E-R) model.** In Figure 2.3, the boxes represent entities in Sam's environment, such as the accounting department or the president's office; the connecting lines represent essential relationships between entities.

The final figure in this client profile of Sam Tilden, Figure 2.4, shows a percentage breakdown of the communication between Sam and the other people, units, and things identified in the global entity-relationship model. Pete and Sam developed this figure through Sam's estimates of the percentage breakdown of oral and written communication with each entity.

THE WHAT, HOW, AND WHY

The information presented in the previous pages about the cost control system's primary user, Sam Tilden, involves three components:

1. The work Sam does
2. The way Sam chooses to do this work
3. The people and units with which Sam must deal in order to accomplish his work

Before any discussion of hardware, software, problems, opportunities, and solutions takes place, the systems developer should spend some time getting to know his or her clients. Her or she should collect information about the clients and their work into a client profile.

The Work the Client Does

For the first component of the client profile—the work the client does—the developer can call upon three well-known frameworks to collect and organize his or her information. The first framework, proposed by Nobel laureate Herbert A. Simon, is concerned with the manner in which human beings solve problems [7].

Simon's Framework

Simon makes a distinction between programmed and nonprogrammed decisions; in recent years, the terms structured and unstructured have replaced programmed and nonprogrammed in discussions of Simon's work.

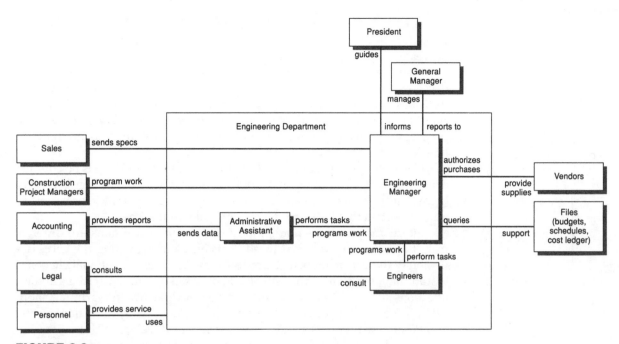

FIGURE 2.3
Global E-R model for the engineering department

PERCENTAGE BREAKDOWN OF COMMUNICATIONS		
Client *Sam Tilden*		
Entity	**% Oral**	**% Written**
President	95	5
General manager	65	35
Engineers	35	65
Construction project managers	35	65
Administrative assistant	35	65
Accounting	5	95
Personnel	50	50
Legal	50	50
Sales	10	90
Vendors	65	35

FIGURE 2.4
Percentage breakdown of Sam Tilden's communications

Structured decisions are "repetitive and routine, to the extent that a definite procedure has been worked out for handling them so that they don't have to be treated *de novo* each time they occur."

Information systems professionals have come to look upon structured decision situations as prime candidates for automation. Typical structured decisions involve questions such as what customers are in default on outstanding invoices, what departments are over budget for year-to-date expenses, and what activities will utilize existing resources to produce the highest profits [2].

Unstructured decisions involve situations in which "there is no cut-and-dried method of handling the problem because it hasn't arisen before, or because its precise nature and structure are elusive or complex, or because it is so important that it deserves a custom-tailored treatment."

Information systems that support unstructured decisions are different from those that support structured decisions, and providing the necessary flexibility to deal with unstructured systems has been a continual challenge to information systems professionals. Typical unstructured decisions involve questions such as What is the best way to schedule jobs in a printing shop? What is the most effective way to synchronize sales and production efforts? and What new products should our company be developing? [2].

A third category, semistructured decisions, has been added to the Simon framework [2]. Semistructured decisions involve both structured and unstructured activities.

Figure 2.5 shows how some of Sam Tilden's typical decisions would be classified according to the Simon framework. Based on Sam's estimates of the

Decision	Type
Which jobs are within budget?	Structured
What was the cost of personnel for job A141?	Structured
Estimate the cost of engineering personnel for a new project.	Semistructured
How much will engineering spend next year?	Semistructured
Assign a staff to a new project.	Semistructured
Is there a better way to coordinate engineering and construction efforts?	Unstructured
Should Horatio & Co. go with a newer, cheaper, but less reliable supplier of steel?	Unstructured

FIGURE 2.5
Some of Sam Tilden's decisions

frequency with which these decisions arise, Pete concluded that Sam's work is dominated by structured and semistructured decisions.

Anthony's Framework

The second framework for analyzing a client's work was proposed by Robert N. Anthony [1]. Anthony chose to consider *activities*, as opposed to the decisions treated in Simon's work. The activities presented in Anthony's framework are operational control, management control, and strategic planning.

Operational control is the process of "assuring that specific tasks are carried out effectively and efficiently." Operational tasks are usually done according to set procedures and logical rules, and hence they are frequently associated with structured decisions. Typical operational control activities include accounts receivable processing, inventory control, and production scheduling [2].

Anthony used the term **management control** to describe the planning and reviewing of operations in terms of the organization's objectives. Through management control, the organization is assured that "resources are obtained and used effectively in the accomplishment of objectives." Workers involved in management control activities go through a continuous cycle of forecasting requirements, budgeting resources, evaluating performance, and reporting results. These activities are usually associated with both structured and unstructured decisions.

The third set of activities in the Anthony model involves **strategic planning**. Strategic planning is the "process of deciding on objectives of the organization, on changes in these objectives, on the resources used to attain these objectives, and on the policies that govern the acquisition, use, and disposition of these resources." For the most part, strategic planning activities involve the "big picture," answering such questions as what business are we in, how do we compete, what are our broad policies, what are our long range plans? These activities are usually associated with unstructured decisions.

The results of strategic planning activities determine management control processes, and these in turn determine operational control tasks. Therefore, the Anthony framework is usually presented in hierarchical form, as shown in Figure 2.6.

Although traces of all types of decisions and activities can usually be found in any one person's job description, most people can point to one type of decision and one level of activity that best characterize their work. A systems developer is interested in the types of decisions and the types of activities faced by clients, because this information provides valuable insight into what kinds of information systems are likely to be of use.

FIGURE 2.6
The Anthony framework as a hierarchy

The more unstructured the client's decisions, the more flexible his or her information systems must be. Operational control systems usually deal with data that is detailed, internal, and concerns the past and the present. Strategic planning systems, on the other hand, usually deal with data that is summarized, from outside the organization, and concerned with the future. Management control systems very often combine the characteristics found in both operational and strategic systems.

Figure 2.7 shows a portion of Pete Willard's notes from his meeting with Sam. In these notes, Pete jotted down phrases from Sam's description of his work activities, and later classified the activities according to the Anthony framework. Based on Sam's estimates of the frequency with which these activities arise, Pete concluded that Sam's work consists primarily of management control and operational control activities.

Mintzberg's Framework

The third framework for studying a client's work was developed by Henry Mintzberg [6]. This framework includes many of the notions represented in the Simon and Anthony models, along with some original ideas. While Simon studied decisions and Anthony studied activities, Mintzberg chose to focus on the variety of *roles* played by the client throughout the day.

The most important roles in the Mintzberg framework for systems development are the so-called **informational roles**. These include the roles of monitor, disseminator, and spokesperson.

As a **monitor** the client "seeks and is bombarded with information that enables him or her to understand what is taking place in the organization and its environment." The monitor gathers information on internal operations in

Activity	Type
Prepare budgets	Management control
Prepare schedules	Operational control
Monitor and evaluate activities	Management control
Report performance	Management control
Long-range planning	Strategic planning
Negotiate contracts	Management control
Specify requirements	Operational control

FIGURE 2.7
Some of Sam Tilden's activities

the form of formal reports and analyses; ad hoc inputs from subordinates, peers, and superiors; and direct observation. The monitor gathers information concerning the external environment from contacts, trade associations, periodicals, gossip, and analyses. Undesirable situations in both the internal and external environment can communicate information to the monitor in the form of pressure.

When the worker's role involves bringing external information into the organization or transferring internal information between units, then Mintzberg says the client is playing the role of **disseminator**. When the work involves informing the external environment of the organization's objectives, plans, policies, and results, then the client is playing the role of **spokesperson**.

In studying the client's informational roles, the systems developer is interested in who is involved (subordinates, peers, superiors, other internal entities, external entities), how they are involved (as sources of information flows, as destinations of information flows), and in what forms the information is conveyed (formal, informal, written, spoken).

Mintzberg organized a second group of roles into what he called the **decisional roles**. These include the roles of entrepreneur, disturbance handler, resource allocator, and negotiator.

The **entrepreneur** is a proactive and innovative role. In this role the client decides which opportunities he or she will exploit or which problems he or she will recognize and attack. Undertaking a systems development project is often the result of an entrepreneurial decision.

When a person confronts situations that are out of his or her control, that person is filling Mintzberg's **disturbance handler** role. The disturbances, such as losing a prominent customer or suffering the loss of a warehouse through fire, are not found in reports; they usually surface through "instant communication."

As **resource allocator**, a client makes decisions regarding the commitment of money, time, materials, equipment, reputation, and other resources. Scheduling resources according to priorities, choosing among competing projects, deciding what work will be done and who will do it, and exercising control over the deployment of resources are all typical resource allocator activities.

The **negotiator** role is closely tied to the resource allocator role. Mintzberg says, "negotiating is resource trading in real time." Some examples of negotiating activities are: negotiating a labor contract or the sale of some asset, acquiring the resources to undertake a systems development effort, and changing company policy to gain access to data that heretofore had been considered confidential.

Systems developers are concerned with the client's decisional roles for two reasons. First, the developer may be able to provide an information system to support one or more of these roles for specific tasks. Second, the developer will face the client in these roles as a systems development project unfolds and decisions about problems and/or opportunities, allocation of resources, and competing projects must be made.

The last set of roles in Mintzberg's framework are the **interpersonal roles:** leader, liaison, and figurehead. As a **leader,** the client supplies his or her organization with unity, purpose, and direction. The **liaison** role deals with the client's connections and reputation outside of his or her own organization. The **figurehead** performs social and legal functions as the person in charge.

Early in their meeting, Sam and Pete determined that Sam's primary roles are those of resource allocator and monitor. The remainder of their dialogue revealed that disseminator, spokesman, leader, and negotiator also apply, but to a lesser extent.

Summary: The Work the Client Does

The Simon, Anthony, and Mintzberg frameworks are important conceptual guides to understanding the work a client does. In getting to know a client, a systems developer weighs what he or she observes about a client's decisions, activities, and roles against his or her experience with specific clients and information systems.

For example, traditional transaction processing and/or reporting systems support structured decisions regarding internal operational control very well. If the developer observes such structured decisions in a client's

work, then the techniques of transaction processing and/or reporting systems development are likely to yield a useful information system, should the need for one be uncovered.

If, on the other hand, the developer observes many unstructured decisions and strategic planning activities in the client's work, then this client will probably not benefit from a transaction processing system. If this client's problems and/or opportunities require information system solutions, then the developer is likely to find these solutions among the more flexible decision support systems and expert systems.

The client's problems and/or opportunities may not require a technological solution at all. For instance, a manufacturer may have a problem with substandard performance. A production quality control system may seem to be the solution, when in fact poor leadership or incompetent management may be at the heart of the problem.

At this early stage of a project, the developer uses the frameworks presented here to evaluate observations about his or her clients and their work. Through this analysis, the developer can gain some perspective on the situation facing him or her, and can gather some early clues about whether an information system solution might be appropriate and what form it might take.

The Client's Work Style

The second component of the client profile involves the client's work style. The ways in which a client works depend upon many factors, such as the task at hand and the client's personality, educational background, and prior experience. The information systems developer is naturally interested in work style because the developer is often called upon to produce a system that will improve the client's work performance. Any knowledge of how the client approaches his or her work will improve the quality of the developer's effort.

The ways in which a client formulates or acquires, analyzes and interprets information when faced with a problem or decision, provide valuable insight into the client's approach to his or her work. The general term used to describe these problem-solving or decision-making behaviors is **cognitive style**.

McKenney and Keen [4] believe that consistent modes of problem-solving and decision-making behavior (cognitive style) develop through training and experience, and that these modes can be classified along two dimensions: information gathering and information evaluation.

Information gathering relates to "the processes by which one's mind organizes the verbal and visual stimuli it encounters." The authors identify two types of individuals:

1. **Preceptive individuals,** who focus on relationships, who use concepts to filter data, and who evaluate new data in terms of their expectations
2. **Receptive thinkers,** who focus on detail and derive information from the data itself rather than from fitting the data to their existing concepts

Information evaluation refers to problem-solving processes. Again, two types of individuals are noted:

1. **Systematic individuals,** who approach a problem by structuring it in terms of some method
2. **Intuitive thinkers,** who use trial-and-error and solution testing

McKenney and Keen define a person's cognitive style as the combination of his or her information evaluation and information gathering styles. Four combinations are possible: (1) systematic-preceptive, (2) systematic-receptive, (3) intuitive-preceptive, (4) intuitive-receptive.

McKenney and Keen claim that each of us has a dominant cognitive style and that our dominant style influences not only the way we solve problems but also our recognition of problems.

Cognitive style is important in systems development because many systems people fall into the systematic-preceptive category. The problems they recognize and the solutions they propose can sometimes reflect their dominant style. A knowledge of the client's decision-making preferences can guide the developer in choosing the most effective design alternatives.

Systems developers should recognize the existence of other styles and realize that no one style is right for all situations. An information system that the developer considers very useful might not be useful at all to the client, and may not even address a problem that the client feels is important.

Entity-Relationship Modeling

The final component of the client profile involves the other units in the internal and external environment with which the client must deal. The model presented in Figure 2.3 is called a global entity-relationship (E-R) model. E-R modeling is a popular means of organizing and presenting this type of information.

An **entity** is any person, unit, object, or event, however concrete or abstract. In the global E-R model, the different people, units, objects, and

events are called **entity types**. The **base entity type** is the one that contains the client.

For a chief executive officer, the base entity type of the global E-R model might be the entire company; the other entity types of the model might represent units of the external environment such as customers, competitors, suppliers, and the government. For a department manager like Sam Tilden, the base entity type of the global E-R model is the engineering department; the other entity types of the model represent units inside and outside of Horatio & Co.

A good way to start the development of the global E-R model is to identify internal entity types from the client's organization chart. In fact, the global E-R model is basically an expanded organization chart that shows external entity types and relationships other than superior-subordinate.

The Horatio & Co. organization chart, Figure 1.1, shows that the engineering department is one of six departments at Horatio & Co. When Sam Tilden was questioned about the relationships between the engineering department and the other five departments, his answers formed the basis for the global E-R model, Figure 2.3. It is usually not possible to show the relationships among the nonbase entity types without cluttering the diagram; these relationships have been eliminated from the global E-R model shown in Figure 2.3.

In representing the relationship between a pair of entity types in the global E-R model, it is advisable to summarize the relationship into a single pair of phrases. For example, in Figure 2.3 the administrative assistant "sends data" to the accounting department, and the accounting department "provides reports" back. Naturally, the relationship is much more complicated and involved than that; but at this stage of the project the developer is not interested in detail beyond what is shown in the global E-R model. The goal of the global E-R model is merely to identify entity and relationship types.

Once the client's peers have been identified and recorded on the global E-R model, the developer turns his or her attention to superiors and subordinates. The Horatio organization chart shows two entity types superior to the engineering department manager: the president's office and the general manager's office. There are two entity types subordinate to the engineering department manager: the engineers and the administrative assistant (not shown in Figure 1.1).

In developing the global E-R model, it is advisable not to identify entity types with a person's name because people change positions and organizations rapidly.

The Horatio organization chart presented in Figure 1.1 does not show the makeup of the engineering department. In deriving the global E-R model, the developer should ask the client to specify the entity subtypes that make up his or her base entity type and to explain the relationships among the subtypes and the existing entity types of the model.

The relationship lines should originate either at the entity types or at the entity subtypes, according to the definition of the relationship. For example, in Figure 2.3 the engineering department as a whole uses the personnel department, but it is the engineering department manager who reports to the general manager.

The development of the global E-R model is brought to a close with the representation of external entity types such as vendors. The client should be able to identify these easily. The same convention of summarizing a complicated relationship into a pair of phrases is observed for the relationships involving external entity types.

YOU DO IT

It is now time for you to construct the client profile for the primary client(s) of your project. You must decide

What you want to collect

How to collect it

How to organize it

How to present it

Use the client profile of Sam Tilden, and the What, How, and Why material, along with the action documents of this section, to guide your efforts; but make the finished product and the process by which it is developed uniquely your own.

Do not be afraid to make choices. If your client is too busy to cover everything presented in this chapter, then you must deal with that reality. Negotiate compromises and work within the constraints of the situation.

If your project involves a "live client," you will collect and organize the information for the profile with your client. If you are using the accompanying written case project (Chapter 10), you will develop the analysis according to the directions provided by your instructor.

Action Documents for the Client Profile

This section contains a set of tables, charts, and forms to use in the preparation of the client profile.

Action Document 2.1 presents a list of deliverables for the profile. Use it as a convenient checklist for what should be included in the final product. Remember that you may have to make choices about what to include, depending upon the availability of your client and his or her receptiveness to this material.

Action Document 2.2 is designed to help you plan and control your client profile activities. For each deliverable listed in Action Document 2.1, you need to list the tasks required, the user/management people involved in each task, the information systems people involved in each task, the documents needed for each task, the documents produced by each task, and the estimated duration of each task.

Key-Word Lists

In collecting information about the client's work decisions, activities, and roles, we have found lists of key words to be useful. If you are interviewing a client, listen for the key words as indicators of the various categories of the frameworks presented in this chapter. If you are using a written questionnaire, you might want to include the key words in the questions or otherwise use them as cues to stimulate the client's response. Both of these techniques are illustrated in the dialogues in the Horatio & Co. section of this chapter. Action Document 2.3 lists key words for analyzing a client's work decisions; Action Document 2.4 lists key words for analyzing a client's work activities; and Action Document 2.5 lists key words for analyzing a client's work roles.

The same key-word technique can be used in gathering information about the client's work style. Action Document 2.6 lists key words that might indicate a person's information-gathering and evaluation preferences [3]. You may choose to listen for these words in an interview, or research and prepare a written questionnaire or evaluation form to collect this information.

E-R Modeling Guidelines

An outline for developing the global entity-relationship model is presented in Action Document 2.7. The purpose of this model is to represent the people, objects, units, and events with which the client must deal in the performance of his or her work. It is difficult to imagine developing the global E-R model without some face-to-face contact with the client. In our experience, we have found the Mintzberg roles and the key words presented in Action Document 2.5 to be useful in articulating the relationships between entity types in the global E-R model.

In developing and using the global E-R model, remember that the terms *base entity type*, *internal environment*, and *external environment* are all dependent upon the client in question. Sam Tilden's responsibility is the engineering

department. For him, the construction project managers and the general manager are external entity types, even though these entity types belong to Horatio & Co. For someone at a higher management level, say the president, these entity types all represent part of the internal environment.

The percentage breakdown between oral and written communication (see Figure 2.4) is essential for determining how important computer support is to your client. Action Document 2.8 shows typical forms of oral and written communication [5]. All of the terms are self-explanatory, with the exception of *tours*. A tour takes place when the client leaves his or her office or workplace to collect information.

With these definitions, your client should be able to provide the oral and written percentage breakdowns. The manner in which the percentages are determined and collected is, of course, up to you.

Use the figures, activities, and documents presented in this chapter as you see fit, but do not hesitate to use other activities or documents that you think might be helpful. When you have completed your client profile analysis, collect all of your documentation and use the cover sheet (Action Document 2.9) to submit your documentation as a progress report to your instructor. Check all items that apply to your progress report and add any items that are not listed.

References

1. Anthony, R. N. *Planning and Control Systems: A Framework for Analysis.* Boston: Harvard University, 1965.

2. Gorry, G. A., and M. S. Scott Morton. "A Framework for Management Information Systems." *Sloan Management Review* Volume 13, Number 1 (Fall 1971): pp. 55–70.

3. Kolb, D., I. Rubin, and J. McIntyre. *Organizational Psychology.* Englewood Cliffs, N J.: Prentice-Hall, 1974.

4. McKenney, J. L., and P. Keen. "How Managers' Minds Work." *Harvard Business Review* Volume 52, Number 3 (May-June 1974): pp. 79–90.

5. McLeod, R., and J. W. Jones. "A Framework for Office Automation." *MIS Quarterly* Volume 11, Number 1 (March 1987): pp. 87–104.

6. Mintzberg, H. *The Nature of Managerial Work.* New York: Harper & Row, 1973.

7. Simon, H. A. *The New Science of Management Decisions.* New York: Harper & Row, 1960.

CLIENT PROFILE DELIVERABLES

1. An analysis of the client's work roles according to the Mintzberg framework
2. An analysis of the client's work activities according to the Anthony framework
3. An analysis of the client's work decisions according to the Simon framework
4. An analysis of the client's cognitive style
5. A global entity-relationship model for the client's work environment

ACTION DOCUMENT 2.1
Client profile deliverables

Deliverable 1: Client work roles analysis

Task	User/Mgt People	IS People	Documents Needed	Documents Produced	Estimated Duration

Deliverable 2: Client work activities analysis

Task	User/Mgt People	IS People	Documents Needed	Documents Produced	Estimated Duration

Deliverable 3: Client work decisions analysis

Task	User/Mgt People	IS People	Documents Needed	Documents Produced	Estimated Duration

ACTION DOCUMENT 2.2
Tasks for each deliverable (page 1 of 2)

Deliverable 4: Client cognitive style analysis

Task	User/Mgt People	IS People	Documents Needed	Documents Produced	Estimated Duration

Deliverable 5: Global entity-relationship model

Task	User/Mgt People	IS People	Documents Needed	Documents Produced	Estimated Duration

ACTION DOCUMENT 2.2
Tasks for each deliverable (page 2 of 2)

**KEY WORDS FOR SIMON'S
FRAMEWORK OF DECISIONS**

Structured Decision

repetitive

routine

standard

definite procedure

prescribed method

Unstructured Decision

novel

nonstandard

intuitive

requires judgment

requires instinct

requires insight

ACTION DOCUMENT 2.3
**Key words to be used in analyzing a client's
decisions**

KEY WORDS FOR ANTHONY'S FRAMEWORK OF ACTIVITIES

Operational Control	Management Control	Strategic Planning
tasks	resources	objectives
jobs	budgets	goals
production	evaluation	policies
operations	tactics	the future
procedures	summaries	the big picture
schedules	effectiveness	fundamentals
day-to-day activities	control	the market
day-to-day business of the firm	review	competitors
transaction processing	respond	long-term
efficiency	optimize	external environment
tangible work	staff	
	organize	

ACTION DOCUMENT 2.4
Key words to be used in analyzing a client's activities

KEY WORDS FOR MINTZBERG'S FRAMEWORK OF ROLES

Informational Roles

Monitor	**Disseminator**	**Spokesperson**
monitor	disseminate	speaks for
seek	external to internal	internal to external
observe	internal to internal	report
analyze	report	inform
question	transmit	
gather		
inspect		

Decisional Roles

Entrepreneur	**Disturbance Handler**	**Resource Allocator**	**Negotiator**
exploit opportunities	handle situations	allocate resources	negotiate
initiate change	buy time	schedule	represent
innovate	fight fires	program	trade
		report priorities	settle
		authorize actions	
		exercise control	
		make commitments	

Interpersonal Roles

Leader	**Liaison**	**Figurehead**
lead	represent organization	attend social functions
provide purpose	make contacts	provide symbol of authority
provide unity		
provide direction		
lend enthusiasm		
support		

ACTION DOCUMENT 2.5
Key words to be used in analyzing a client's roles

KEY WORDS FOR MCKENNEY AND KEEN'S FRAMEWORK OF COGNITIVE STYLE

Information Evaluation

Systematic	Intuitive
reflective	active
watching	practical
observant	pragmatic
reserved	experimenting
think it over	see if it works

Information Gathering

Preceptive	Receptive
conceptual	experiential
analytical	feeling
thinking	accepting
logical	here and now
rational	

R.T.C. LIBRARY, LETTERKENNY

ACTION DOCUMENT 2.6
Key words to be used in analyzing a client's cognitive style

DEVELOPING THE GLOBAL E-R MODEL

I. From the organization chart,

    a) identify the base entity type

    b) identify subtypes of the base, including the client

2. From the organization chart,

    a) identify peers of the base entity type

    b) identify superiors of the base entity type

    c) identify other entity types from within the organization

3. Identify entity types external to the organization.

4. Express the relationships between the base and all other entity types as pairs of phrases.

ACTION DOCUMENT 2.7
**An outline of the global E-R model
development process**

TYPICAL FORMS OF COMMUNICATION

Oral

business meals

scheduled meetings

social activity

telephone calls

tours

unscheduled meetings

Written

computer reports

letters

memos

noncomputer reports

periodicals

ACTION DOCUMENT 2.8
**A checklist to be used in analyzing oral
versus written communication**

Date _____

To _____

From _____

Re: Client profile analysis

The following documents are included in this analysis:

☐ Client work roles analysis

☐ Client work activities analysis

☐ Client work decisions analysis

☐ Client cognitive style analysis

☐ Global entity-relationship analysis

☐ Other _____

_____

☐ Other _____

_____

☐ Other _____

_____

☐ Other _____

_____

The following activities were carried out during this analysis:

☐ Interviews with _____

_____

☐ Other _____

_____

☐ Other _____

_____

☐ Other _____

_____

☐ Other _____

_____

ACTION DOCUMENT 2.9
Cover sheet for client profile analysis

CHAPTER 3

Effective Communication and Creative Problem Solving

At this point in your project you have already experienced the need for the material presented in this chapter. Your communication and problem-solving skills were just as important to your success with Chapters 1 and 2 as your mastery of the concepts of objectives and tactics and the client profile.

Your work in this chapter will not produce any deliverables for your project; rather, it will introduce you to knowledge and skills that you can practice throughout this course and throughout your career as a systems developer.

What skills make a good systems developer is a question that has intrigued authors and researchers for quite some time. Naturally, a good systems developer must possess a certain amount of technical expertise, but experience has shown that technical expertise alone is not enough. The successful systems developer is one who combines his or her technical expertise with other skills that support the process of developing systems.

This chapter concentrates on two critical systems development process skills: effective client/developer communication, and creative problem solving. Effective communication is listed first because the systems developer cannot work alone; effective communication must begin and end the problem-solving (systems development) process. It must begin the process in order to guarantee the accurate identification of problems and/or opportunities; and it must end the process because without effective client/developer communication, no solution can be implemented properly.

The Horatio & Co. section of this chapter repeats the dialogue between Sam Tilden and Pete Willard from Chapter 1. In that session, Sam and Pete began to develop the business objectives and tactics for the project. In this chapter, the dialogue is examined in terms of communication and problem-solving processes.

In the What, How, and Why section of this chapter you will find background material on the communication and problem-solving processes and behaviors presented in the first section.

The You Do It section of this chapter provides a set of exercises and action documents to develop your communication and problem-solving skills. Your instructor will provide guidelines for doing the exercises throughout this course. You should continue practicing some of them, on your own, when the course is finished.

After completing this chapter you will have

1. understood the significance of effective communication and creative problem solving as systems development process skills

2. practiced a set of exercises designed to develop your competence in effective communication and creative problem solving

3. learned to use a set of action documents that can be applied to the remaining interactions of your project

HORATIO & CO. COST CONTROL SYSTEM

When Sam Tilden thought that a computer-based information system might be of help to him, he called Pete Willard, his former information systems professor, and asked Pete to serve as consultant to Horatio & Co. Pete agreed, and they set up a meeting for 10:00 a.m. on the following Monday at Sam's office.

At this meeting Sam told Pete that Horatio & Co. had undertaken the improvement of the business operations of the departments as a company-wide objective. The purpose of this undertaking was to maintain the current level of profit in the face of declining revenues. Sam and Pete also discussed some specifics of Sam's plan for the engineering department at this first meeting.

Pete said that plans for a systems development project should begin with a statement of business objectives and tactics. He suggested they meet again on Wednesday at 10:00 a.m. to develop such a statement. To prepare for the meeting, Pete suggested that Sam write down "all he knew" about the problems and opportunities facing the business operations of the engineering department.

The following dialogue shows what went on at the Wednesday meeting. Pete and Sam began on time.

SAM: Good morning, Pete. How was the trip across town?

PETE: Not bad. Most of the traffic is gone after 9 o'clock.

SAM: I am glad we scheduled for 10 o'clock. That gave me a chance to read my mail and to return a few phone calls. I tried that exercise you suggested. I wrote down everything I could think of concerning the

problems of our business operations. It was more difficult than I expected.

PETE: How so?

SAM: I couldn't decide what was important, and I was reluctant to write down the obvious. I found that talking things over with the other managers helped. In the end, the list was quite long.

PETE: Most people find it challenging to verbalize and write down what they think is obvious. It turns out that these items are not obvious to everyone, and they lead to more important observations later in the process. Let's see what you have.

SAM: Here it is. (Sam's list is shown in Figure 3.1.)

BUSINESS OPERATIONS PROBLEMS

The overall strategy of the firm is to provide high-quality, reliable construction for the commercial markets of the surrounding seven-county area.

Company revenues are expected to fall by 10 percent. We have got to maintain our current level of profit by decreasing costs.

We need better access to job cost information. We spend money for clerks to prepare job cost reports manually. They hate the job, and we have to wait too long for them to prepare the reports. There are also errors and inconsistencies in the reports.

Sometimes the engineers have to prepare the reports themselves. This is a complete waste of time, and it is demoralizing to the engineers. It makes the company look unprofessional, behind the times, and inefficient.

We need more control of expenses. The annual budgeting system is too loose. I can overspend my budget in February and not know about it until August. The system is accurate, and it works well. It is just not tight enough.

We need more organization in our purchasing. We are okay on items purchased by the company as a whole, but for items used only in this department we do not take enough advantage of our buying power. We are spread too thin. If we spent more with fewer vendors, we would have more clout.

Turnover among the engineers is a serious problem. We have more competitors than we used to and the engineers are more demanding. And it is not only salary. They demand the latest equipment: computers for computer-aided design, and specialized software for mathematical calculations. More importantly, they demand challenging and varied work assignments. As soon as someone learns a particular task, he or she wants to learn something else. I need to be able to plan and make assignments better. I am worried about my own skills with all of the management responsibilities I have. I am losing touch with my profession.

**FIGURE 3.1
Sam Tilden's write-down-all-you-know
exercise**

PETE: Well, that's quite a list, Sam. Your comments give me a good first-draft sense of the situation. I'll learn more as we develop specifics from this list.

Today we want to identify the business objectives and tactics of this project. From your writing, we know quite a bit about the problem situation, and it is obvious that these are important issues. Business objectives are basically what we propose to do about that situation, and tactics are how we propose to do it.

(Sensing some confusion on Sam's part) Let me be more specific. You said you are spending money on clerks to prepare job cost reports. Well, decreasing clerical costs might be one of our objectives. That is *what* we want to do. *How* we do it determines our tactics. We could try to get by with fewer clerks, or try to find cheaper clerks. We could try to get by with fewer reports. We could provide automated tools to prepare the reports more efficiently.

SAM: Aren't we getting into semantics with the difference between objectives and tactics?

PETE: It is easy to get bogged down in systems analysis details. It's sometimes called "analysis paralysis." I want to avoid that as much as you do. Don't worry about the difference between objectives and tactics at this point. Think in terms of solutions to your problem.

SAM: All right.

PETE: Why don't you try to identify some solutions? Look over your problem list and come up with specific ideas about what you want to achieve.

SAM: I agree that decreasing clerical costs should be an objective. I guess I also want to institute professional development plans for the engineers.

PETE: Why?

SAM: Well, because it will help cut down on turnover. If I can make and follow a plan of assignments, I'll do a better job of satisfying the engineers' demand for the assignments they want.

PETE: Is there any other way to cut down on turnover besides instituting professional development plans?

SAM: I see what you were saying about objectives and tactics. My objective is really to reduce turnover. Professional development plans represent one way to do this. In fact, my overriding objective is to maintain the current level of profit in the face of a 10 percent drop in revenue.

PETE: Objectives and tactics together form solutions.

SAM: I understand. Well, I suppose we could let the engineers choose some of their own assignments as an alternative. We could rotate the

desirable assignments according to a predetermined schedule. In recruiting, we could look for people willing to specialize, so as to cut down on the demand for varied assignments. There are lots of ways to achieve this objective.

PETE: What about assigning people through some kind of lottery?

SAM: No, I don't think that will work. I would not want the engineers to think they had to be lucky to get desirable assignments.

PETE: Okay. We've covered quite a bit of ground; before we go on, let's backtrack over what we've done so far.

So far we have identified decreasing clerical costs and reducing turnover as objectives, and we have developed quite a long list of tactics to achieve these objectives. What other objectives and tactics can you determine from your list?

SAM: The current budgeting system is not tight enough. I'd like to control costs better in general and I'd like to identify overruns for individual jobs quicker.

PETE: What do you mean by "quicker"?

SAM: If I could have the information in 30 days, I might be able to prevent expenses from running amuck.

PETE: Okay, we'll add the identification of cost overruns within 30 days to the objectives list.

SAM: I think the only way to do this is to replace the current annual budgeting system by general ledger account with a new monthly budgeting system by general ledger account and job number.

PETE: That sounds like a clear tactic to me. Let's add it to the list.

SAM: The item on the list that gave me the most trouble was purchasing. I am not really sure what I need here.

PETE: What are you trying to achieve?

SAM: I want to decrease the cost of the products and services we buy. I am never sure I am paying the best price. Currently I go to vendors for specific items only. I guess I want to take advantage of the volume discounts that I see other firms getting.

PETE: So what is the objective?

SAM: Decrease the cost of products and services.

PETE: How?

SAM: Reorganize our vendor base for high-volume purchases.

Pete and Sam continued their dialogue and ended the session when they had achieved the desired outcome: "identify the business objectives and tactics of this project." Figure 3.2 summarizes the results of the session.

Business Objectives

Maintain the current level of profit in the engineering department by

decreasing clerical costs

identifying cost overruns within 30 days

decreasing cost of materials

decreasing turnover

Business Tactics

1. Eliminate manual preparation of job cost reports
2. Institute a monthly budgeting system by job number and general ledger account to replace the current annual system by general ledger account only
3. Reorganize the vendor base for higher volumes with fewer vendors
4. Institute professional development plans for engineering personnel

FIGURE 3.2
Sam and Pete's business objectives and tactics

THE WHAT, HOW, AND WHY

Current research [2,5,8,12,13] into systems development process skills has shown that

1. Effective communication and creative problem solving are critical for systems development
2. Successful developers employ common communication and problem-solving techniques

Vitalari and Dickson [13] studied 18 systems developers from nine different corporations. Each corporation was represented by a highly rated developer and a low-rated developer (in the opinion of the developers' managers).

The researchers presented the developers with the problem of determining the information requirements for a new accounts receivable system for a large consumer retail company. The developers were asked to verbalize their thought processes as they solved the problem, and their comments were recorded and analyzed. Several specific problem-solving processes and behaviors were found to be associated with the highly rated group.

Guinan's research [5] continued with the idea of studying highly rated versus low-rated developers. In her experiment, she observed and analyzed 58 interviews between clients and developers. Her analysis revealed several

specific communication processes and behaviors associated with the highly rated group. Dr. Guinan's experiment was based upon many of the ideas of her teacher, Robert Bostrom [2].

Koberg and Bagnall published their work on creativity and problem solving in an imaginative book entitled *The All New Universal Traveler: A Soft-Systems Guide to Creativity, Problem-solving, and the Process of Reaching Goals* [8]. The book represents the authors' experiences in seminars, workshops, research, and experimentation on design and creative problem solving.

Effective Client/Developer Communication

The goal of client/developer communication in systems development is a shared, complete, and accurate model of the current and desired systems [2]. When client/developer communication achieves this goal, it is effective; when it does not achieve this goal, it is not effective. Every interaction between client and developer should make progress toward this goal.

On most systems projects the developer is viewed as the expert in the process of developing systems. As a result, the developer must take the lead in achieving effective communication with the client.

Rapport

In *The Random House Dictionary* [3], two of the definitions for the word *understand* are: "to be thoroughly familiar with; apprehend clearly the character, nature, or subtleties of," and "to grasp the significance, implications, or importance of."

These definitions of understanding closely match the goal of client/developer communication stated above: a shared, complete, and accurate model of the current and desired systems. A systems developer can guide his or her communication efforts by keeping in mind certain key phrases from the dictionary definition of understanding, namely, "to apprehend clearly the nature and character of" and "to grasp the significance or importance of."

When a developer seeks to apprehend the nature and character of the client's work and to grasp its significance and importance, he shows the client that he understands and accepts the client's views and perceptions of the world. In a sense, the developer and the client are communicating within the same context. The developer shows himself or herself to be attentive and responsive, and the client is likely to feel that the developer is trustworthy and competent.

Researchers in client/developer communication say that a good developer establishes a **rapport** with his or her client [2]. The extent of such rapport

can determine the developer's success in achieving a shared, complete, and accurate model of the current and desired systems.

Pete Willard established rapport with Sam Tilden during their meeting by channeling his questions toward a deeper understanding of Sam's business problems. For example, Pete asked Sam to look over his problem list and to think of specific ideas about what he wanted to achieve. By the end of the meeting, Sam believed that Pete was able to help him solve his problem.

Communication Processes

Communication processes are internal activities that affect external actions. This section discusses two communication processes, calibration and frame flexibility, that can help establish rapport with the client and lead to a shared, complete, and accurate model of the current and desired systems. Several exercises presented in the You Do It section of the chapter are designed to improve your calibration and frame flexibility skills.

Calibration   In addition to speaking and writing, effective client/developer communication involves listening, observing, responding to cues, and adapting to results as they unfold. **Calibration** is the process of evaluating the client's verbal and nonverbal cues and modifying one's behavior accordingly. A simple example should clarify this definition.

Suppose a developer knows that his or her client is intimidated by the technical aspects of using a computer. In an effort to put the client at ease, the developer uses a set of cartoons showing user-friendly computers complete with smiling faces. Upon seeing the cartoons, the client stiffens in his seat, folds his arms, looks away for a few seconds, and then casts a glance at the developer that says, loud and clear, "Are you serious?" The perceptive developer admits his or her mistake, removes the offending material, and begins again with a new approach.

The above example is not meant to discourage the use of humor and metaphors in communicating with clients. It is meant to illustrate the need to be sensitive to the cues generated by the client and to respond accordingly.

An example of calibration occurred in Sam and Pete's dialogue when Pete responded to Sam's question, "Aren't we getting into semantics with the difference between objectives and tactics?" Pete told Sam, "Don't worry about the difference . . . at this point. Think in terms of solutions to your problem." Pete calibrated his presentation, acknowledging Sam's impatience with the terms and turning toward a different point of view.

Frame Flexibility   **Frame flexibility** is the ability to look at a situation from multiple perspectives [5]. Since systems developers design and build products that other people need and use, frame flexibility is a crucial skill.

The client's frame of reference is the most important frame for a developer to understand. The developer must know the problems of the client's business and recognize them to be important (rapport). For example, a developer of accounting systems must recognize the importance of collecting and maintaining accurate data. A person who wants to concentrate on the big picture and ignore boring details will not be successful as a developer of accounting systems unless he or she moves away from that particular frame of reference.

Sometimes the developer must look beyond his or her own experiences to find an effective frame of reference. Early business computers were installed in corporations to process internal accounting data, and access to these machines and the rooms in which they were located was severely restricted. Somewhere in the past, someone asked, "What if our customers could access our computers directly from their sites?" The result: automated teller machines and worldwide airline reservations, along with banking, shopping, and library research at home.

Pete demonstrated frame flexibility in his dialogue with Sam by the way he used the write-down-all-you-know exercise. Pete let Sam's comments define the frame of reference, and he committed himself to finding effective solutions within this frame. Pete made suggestions, but he did not try to impose his own personal frame of reference upon Sam.

Communication Behaviors

Communication behaviors are external actions carried out during an interaction. The relationship between these external behaviors and the internal processes of calibration and frame flexibility is one of cause and effect; that is, internal processes spark external behaviors. For example, if a developer sees his or her client getting lost in a discussion of system requirements, the developer should give the client a chance to catch up with the discussion (calibration). This might be accomplished through commenting that some things still seem unclear, and suggesting a review of the discussion up to this point (external action).

Guinan [5] identified five communication behaviors that can help establish rapport and lead to shared, complete, and accurate models. These are:

Outcome frames

Backtrack frames

Pointers

Metacommunication

Reframes

Outcome Frames Guinan's research showed that effective developers specify an **outcome frame** at the start of a meeting or interview. Through the outcome frame, the developer establishes the goals and controls the processes of the interaction.

Pete established the outcome frame for his interview with Sam when he said, "Today we want to identify the business objectives and tactics of this project." This set the agenda for the interview.

Outcome frames can be used to evaluate the relevance of various activities. When the conversation strays from the stated outcome frame, the developer can say, "These are important points, but we really cannot discuss them effectively until we settle . . ."

At times, the client is responsible for establishing the outcome frame. As a listener, the developer is responsible for identifying the outcome frame from the client's remarks. If the outcome frame is not established, the developer can ask a guiding question, such as "What would you like to accomplish in this meeting?"

Formulating the outcome frame should be the first step in preparing for a meeting or interview. The outcome statement should be written during preparation and explained to the participants early in the meeting. If many people are participating in the interaction, the developer might want to distribute a written outcome statement before the event takes place.

Backtrack Frames Periodic progress reviews or **backtrack frames** help to promote shared understanding during meetings. The developer should backtrack to clarify and repeat important information or to steer a meandering interview back toward the stated outcome frame.

Naturally, the most important backtrack in an interview comes at the end of the dialogue. By reviewing the proceedings, participants can assess their progress and identify agreed-upon policies or actions. The final backtrack is also useful in identifying issues that remain unresolved and that require further attention.

Pete Willard used a backtrack frame about halfway through his dialogue with Sam. He reviewed the objectives and tactics developed so far, and he set the stage to continue the process. It is safe to assume that Pete ended the meeting with a comprehensive backtrack session over the entire day's results.

Pointers The effective developer learns to use both vague and specific language. A vague question allows the listener to be spontaneous, to fill in details, and to reveal vocabulary, attitudes, values, and further avenues of questioning [7].

Pete's suggestion to Sam, "Write down all you know," is deliberately vague. Sam filled in many details, and Pete learned about Sam's work, his environment, and the problems he faces.

Vague language that invites a listener to fill in is appropriate when the developer is encouraging discussion or creativity. Some systems development tasks, however, need specific language. If vague language is used to articulate the requirements of a system, then the client and the developer will each fill in their own meanings; the result is bound to be disappointment on both sides.

Rather than filling in, the effective developer presses for more specific information when it is required. Specific questions or **pointers** help elicit additional information and avoid filling in. Pete's suggestion to Sam about identifying specific solutions is an attempt to refine Sam's vague comments, "We need more control of expenses," and "We need more organization in our purchasing," into more detailed statements.

Pointers may be used at any time during an interview or meeting. Used early on, they provide a foundation upon which a more general discussion may be built. Used later in an interview, pointers can provide the necessary focus and detail for the session.

Metacommunication   Metacommunication is communication about the communication taking place in an interaction. Phrases such as "I understand you" or "I am not sure I follow what you're saying" are examples of metacommunication.

Metacommunication provides feedback to the client and encourages him or her to continue along productive lines or to abandon nonproductive lines. Metacommunication also indicates when one topic ends and another begins.

Metacommunication is crucial to the development of rapport and shared understanding between client and developer. To judge the importance of metacommunication, imagine what it would be like to converse with a developer about something very important to you—your work—while the developer sits stone-faced, the entire time, never indicating that what you are saying is having any impact on his or her understanding of the situation. What would your reaction be?

Metacommunication can also break down barriers caused by differences in rank within the organization, differences in specialties, or anxiety over the systems development process. Metacommunication lets the client know that the developer is engaged in the interaction.

Several times during their dialogue, Pete let Sam know that he was following the discussion. He did this directly with phrases like those quoted above, and he did it in more indirect ways. Rather than say "I understand you," Pete often repeated Sam's phrases to confirm to Sam that he (Pete) had received the message.

Reframes   Reframes provide alternative points of view in an interaction; they are especially useful in discussing client problems. Through

reframing, the developer provides a fresh perspective on the problem at hand, which in turn stimulates the client to develop new responses to familiar circumstances [5].

When Sam's impatience with the difference between objectives and tactics threatened the discussion, Pete used a reframe. First he did some meta-communication about appreciating the problems of getting bogged down in semantics, to let Sam know that his concerns were heard; then he suggested that Sam think in terms of solutions, to redirect the interaction toward productive work.

Creative Problem Solving

Systems developers produce systems in response to client problems and/or opportunities. The problem-solving process is often presented as a series of steps:

1. Recognize and accept the problem or opportunity.
2. Gather information about the context within which the problem or opportunity exists.
3. Determine the objectives of a solution effort (what the solution should do).
4. Determine possible tactics for the solution (how we should achieve our objectives).
5. Choose a course of action.
6. Implement the solution.
7. Evaluate the results.

The systems development life cycle, Figure 1.4, is a particular version of this general problem-solving process.

Creative problem solvers are not necessarily born with that talent. The skills presented in this section can be mastered with practice. Several exercises included in the You Do It section of this chapter are designed to improve your creative problem-solving skills.

Flexibility

Earlier in this chapter, frame flexibility was identified as a desirable communication process. If the research presented here has a common theme, it is that systems developers, like all creative problem solvers, must be flexible in their

thinking. The concepts discussed below identify other areas of the problem-solving process that require flexibility.

In the Vitalari and Dickson experiment [13], all of the developers formed opinions and made guesses about the problem and its solution as they worked through the problem-solving process. The highly rated developers, however, were much more willing to discard the ideas that new evidence proved to be unworkable. The researchers found this to be the most significant difference between highly rated and low-rated developers.

The iterative process of developing, testing, and modifying ideas during the problem-solving process is called **hypothesis management.** The more flexible a developer can be in discarding low-probability hypotheses and retaining a small number of valid hypotheses, the more effective he or she can be in problem solving.

Pete Willard demonstrated good hypothesis management when he discarded the suggestion of a lottery for engineer assignments. This action allowed Sam and Pete to focus on other options that showed more promise of success.

Vitalari and Dickson also found that highly rated developers thought in terms of **flexible strategies** more often than the low-rated developers. The highly rated group set goals and formulated plans to achieve these goals. The most significant difference observed in strategic behavior was the willingness of the highly rated developers to modify strategies in the face of changes in information or the environment.

Analogical Reasoning

Both Vitalari and Dickson [13] and Koberg and Bagnall [8] suggest that successful developers should employ **analogical reasoning**. Analogical reasoning involves classifying problems according to common characteristics and relating them to previous experience. Comparing and contrasting with other problems can help to structure the current problem, search for additional information, and suggest solutions.

The danger of analogical reasoning lies in over-reliance on a limited set of analogies. This can lead to forced solutions that are inappropriate for the problem at hand. Several exercises in the You Do It section are designed to counteract this type of bias by expanding your ability to create varied analogies.

The client profile developed in Chapter 2 illustrates the use of analogical reasoning. By noting similarities and differences between the current client and other clients, the developer gets a sense of perspective on the current situation. Using the key-word lists of Chapter 2 as cues to relevant frames of reference is also an example of analogical reasoning.

YOU DO IT

This chapter presents effective communication and creative problem solving as critical systems development skills. These skills cannot be learned passively; they must be practiced. This section presents a set of exercises for you to do alone and with your classmates. If these exercises are practiced regularly over time, your systems development process skills will improve.

Effective Communication Exercises

Earlier in this chapter, calibration and frame flexibility were presented as desirable internal processes. Five external behaviors were also identified: outcome frames, backtrack frames, pointers, metacommunication, and reframes.

Recall the relationship between internal processes and external behaviors. Internal processing sparks external behaviors; that is, external behaviors are employed to achieve the results dictated by the developer's internal processing of the communication.

1. Writing a Dialogue

Your first exercise in effective communication is to write a dialogue similar to the one that opened this chapter. Work on this alone. Use either a real or an imaginary situation, but be specific.

Before beginning to write the dialogue, answer each of the following questions (the nine Ws) for each participant [6]. Remember that the goal of effective communication with a client is a shared, complete, and accurate understanding of the current and desired systems, achieved through rapport. Use questions 7 through 9 to narrow the objective of the interaction down to something that can be achieved in a single client/developer session (the outcome frame).

1. Who am I?
2. What time is it?
3. Where am I?
4. What surrounds me?
5. What are the circumstances? (past, present, future)
6. What is my relationship to the circumstances, to the other participant, and to the other things surrounding me?

7. What do I want from this interaction?
8. What is in my way?
9. What should I do to get what I want?

Once you have established the background specifics of the interaction, write a dialogue that establishes rapport between the participants and that includes instances of calibration and frame flexibility. The internal processes should involve several of the effective communication behaviors cited above: outcome frames, backtrack frames, pointers, metacommunication, and reframes. Use the dialogue at the beginning of this chapter as a guide; identify instances of calibration, frame flexibility, and the resulting external communication behaviors. Your dialogue should be about the same length as Sam and Pete's dialogue.

2. Enacting a Dialogue

Choose a partner and read your dialogue aloud. Take the role of the client first. Review the specifics you developed in response to the nine Ws. Your partner should do the same for his or her role.

Live in the moment of the reading and observe your partner's behavior. After the reading, discuss the presence and effect of calibration, frame flexibility, and the communication behaviors written into the dialogue. Decide if the objectives of the session were achieved.

Repeat this exercise, taking the role of the developer instead of the client. As you are reading, live in the moment. Observe the client and his or her behavior. Make your communication behaviors work toward the objective you stated in your response to the seventh W (What do I want from this interaction?). After the reading, discuss the effectiveness of the communication.

Repeat the readings outlined above, using your partner's dialogue as the script.

3. Improvising a Dialogue

For this exercise, select either your dialogue or your partner's dialogue, and decide who plays what role. Begin reading the dialogue, but about halfway through, put down your scripts and improvise the rest of the interaction.

Remember the objective of the interaction (the seventh W) and what you need to do to achieve it (the ninth W). During the improvisation, live in the moment. Do not think about what you are going to say next. Listen to your partner, observe his or her behavior, and respond truthfully and naturally. The exercise ends when you have both achieved your objectives.

After the exercise, write down three verbs that describe your actions during the dialogue and three verbs that describe your partner's actions. Your partner should do the same. Use only transitive verbs, for example, she *ignored* me, I *reassured* him. Review these verbs in light of your answers to the seventh and ninth Ws. Discuss the compatibility of your actions with your objectives.

4. Listening Exercise

It has been estimated that most people operate at only a 25 percent level of efficiency when they are listening. This exercise is designed to increase your listening ability, your observational skill, and your analogical reasoning [11]. It can be done alone or with your classmates. Repeat the exercise regularly over a period of time, and observe the changes in your performance.

1. Listen carefully for two minutes and make a list of the sounds you hear.
2. Think of as many classifications of each sound as you can, for example, pleasant-unpleasant, loud-soft, strange-familiar. Also, imagine the source of the sound, that is, identify what is causing the sound.
3. Listen carefully for two minutes with your eyes closed and make a list of the sounds you hear.
4. Repeat step 2 for the new list of sounds.
5. Compare the two lists.

5. Observing Yourself and Others

Earlier in this chapter, calibration was identified as an important process in effective communication; and several communication behaviors, such as backtracking, were suggested to facilitate calibration.

Basically, calibration is being attentive and responsive to the client. This exercise provides practice in observing and responding to behavior in others and in yourself. It is often called the repeating game. It can be done in front of the class, in front of one observer, or without observers.

1. Choose a partner. Sit facing each other. Relax.
2. Player 1 makes an observation about player 2, for example, player 1 says, "Your hands are folded."
3. Player 2 acknowledges the observation by repeating the phrase: "My hands are folded." Player 2 then makes an observation about player 1, for example, "You are smiling."
4. Player 1 acknowledges player 2's call and makes a new call about player 2, and so on.
5. Continue for three minutes.

It is not necessary to make explicit motions when you are being observed; your partner will find more than enough to call. Take your time when it is your turn to call and stick to observations about your partner's behavior.

After the exercise is performed, try to recall specific reactions you had to your partner's calls and specific reactions your partner had to your calls. If this exercise is performed regularly over a period of time, you will notice an increase in your powers of observation regarding others and yourself.

You can extend your observational activities beyond the repeating game to include public places. Pick out someone in a crowd, watch them, and make silent calls of the behaviors you observe. Expand the exercise to include mirroring the behaviors you observe. Walk like them, sit like them, breathe like them. Try to get a sense of how the person feels by imitating their behaviors.

6. Observing the Environment

For a systems developer, the need to observe extends beyond the client and his or her behavior to the surrounding environment [7]. The storage equipment in a client's office—file cabinets, bookshelves, computer diskette files—indicates the volume of information stored by the client personally. The processing equipment—microcomputer, terminal, calculator, pens, pencils, and paper—indicates the amount of processing and analysis work done by the client personally. The publications kept in the office can indicate the type of information used by the client. An abundance of computer reports and memos may indicate a preference for internal information; an abundance of trade journals and news publications may indicate a need to be aware of the external environment.

This simple exercise is designed to improve your competence in making quick and accurate observations of the surrounding environment. It must be done in a group. As usual, frequent practice over a period of time is recommended.

To perform the exercise, each person in the group should observe the room for 30 seconds. After the observation, one person leaves the room, and while he or she is out, the group makes a basic change in the room. The person returns and has to tell what he or she observes to be different. Repeat, choosing a different person to leave the room [9].

Creative Problem Solving Exercises

Earlier in this chapter, the notions of hypothesis management, strategy modification, and analogical reasoning were presented as distinguishing characteristics of the problem-solving processes of highly rated systems developers. Research into expertise in other disciplines has also identified the ability to recognize patterns and to discriminate between irrelevant and critical patterns as essential to expert behavior [12].

7. Chunking

The process of recognizing and reacting to patterns is sometimes called chunking. The creative problem solver is one who sees that all problems are not new and independent of each other. The creative problem solver groups relevant patterns together as a chunk of understanding and links that chunk to others, so that patterns in a problem invoke chunks, which activate other chunks, and so on.

This simple exercise is designed to improve your chunking ability, that is, your ability to see patterns and relationships. One of the authors learned this exercise from Robert Bostrom.

Choose a partner. One person thinks of a noun, tells it to the other person, and directs the other person to chunk up to a less specific, larger frame, or down to a more specific, smaller frame, or sideways to another item on the same level. The other person responds according to the directions. Repeat the exercise reversing the roles.

For example, A gives B the noun "word" and directs B to chunk up. B responds with "communication," and gives A the word "apple" with the direction to chunk down. A responds with "Macintosh," and gives B the noun "book," along with the direction to chunk sideways. B responds with "newspaper," and gives A the word "newspaper," with the direction to chunk down. A responds with "New York Times." And so on.

8. Idea Dump

The ability to generate ideas is critical to effective hypothesis management, strategic thinking, and creative problem solving. A person is not likely to reject an unworkable idea or hypothesis if he or she does not have an alternative with which to replace it [8].

For this exercise, identify and accept the importance of a specific problem that is real to you; for example, my swimming pool leaks, threatening to collapse if all the water drains out (a real problem for the authors). Write down as many solutions about your problem as possible, for example, patch the leak, replace the missing water each day, replace the pool, fill in the pool, sell the land on which the pool is located, sell the house and move. Compare this exercise to Pete's generation of tactics to decrease clerical costs in the dialogue at the beginning of this chapter.

Share your ideas with others in the class. Be critical; think about why they will or will not work. Determine what this analysis tells you about the problem. Determine how well each idea matches your prior expression of the importance of the problem. Did this analysis change your acceptance of the problem or your notion of why the problem is important? Decide which ideas or parts of ideas should be saved for further analysis.

Relaxation and Concentration

Relaxation, a return to equilibrium in both body and mind, and concentration, maintaining a one-pointed mind, are recognized performance enhancers in a wide range of activities from business management to athletics [1,4]. Relaxation and concentration can focus the systems developer's mind and expand his or her awareness beyond the suggestions he or she normally accepts.

The exercises presented here were developed by Dr. Phil Nuernberger [10]. They were designed to help you relax and to eliminate "chatter"—the stream of thoughts inside the mind that prevents and interferes with concentration. We experience chatter when, for example, we keep on thinking when we listen to someone talk—when we answer them mentally or think about something else altogether. By halting this flow of thoughts, the developer can pay more attention to the wealth of perceptual data that bombards everyone during any problem-solving communication process.

9. Diaphragmatic Breathing

Breathing with the diaphragm instead of the chest has long been associated with healthy and relaxed functioning [10]. This exercise is designed to restore diaphragmatic breathing as your normal, moment-to-moment, resting breathing pattern.

To practice diaphragmatic breathing, lie on a firm, padded surface, with your feet 12 to 18 inches apart, your arms slightly away from your body with your palms up, and a small pillow under your head to support the curve of your neck. This is called the relaxation posture.

Place your right hand on your upper abdomen and your left hand on your upper chest. Concentrate on the air moving down into the upper abdomen. Your right hand should rise with the inhalation and fall with the exhalation. There should be no movement in the left hand at all. Within a few moments, you will become more rested and quiet.

When you are sure of the movement, place your left hand back down, slightly away from your body with the palm up. Keep your right hand on your stomach for a few more moments, then put it back down, away from your body with the palm up. Continue concentrating on the air moving down into the upper abdomen, with no movement in the upper chest, until the end of the exercise.

At the beginning, this exercise should be practiced three times a day for about ten minutes. (As soon as you wake up in the morning, at the end of your work day, and right before you go to sleep are good times.) Also, try to pay attention to your breathing during the day. Eventually, you will establish the habit of breathing from the diaphragm.

This exercise can also be done sitting up, if you find it difficult to practice in the relaxation posture. Sit on the edge of a chair with your back straight, your knees bent at slightly more than a 90-degree angle, and your hands resting on your thighs.

10. Breath Awareness

To perform breath awareness, relax, breathe from the diaphragm, focus your attention inside the bridge of the nose between the two nostrils, and concentrate on the feeling of the cool air on the inhalation and the warm air on the exhalation. Do not think; just concentrate on the feeling of the breath.

Do not worry if you do not feel the temperature change at first; it will come with practice. When first practicing this exercise, it is sufficient to concentrate on the feeling of the breath—the pressure inside the bridge of the nose as you inhale and exhale.

Try this exercise the next time you are listening to someone talk. If you concentrate on the feeling of the breath, the "chatter" will cease and you will be surprised at how much more of the person's voice you will hear.

You can also do this exercise for a few minutes before you begin working on a particularly difficult problem. You will find that the exercise clears your mind of extraneous thoughts and helps focus your attention on the problem. In fact, anytime you change tasks or you find your mind wandering, you can use breath awareness to refocus your attention.

Action Documents

This section contains checklists to help you with the remaining interactions of your project.

Preparing for an Interaction

A systems developer must prepare for every interaction, no matter how insignificant it might seem. Use the items listed in Action Document 3.1 to prepare for an interaction with your client if your project involves an outside user, or to prepare for an interaction with Carol Bodnar if you are using the accompanying written case project.

Be specific in filling in the details about the interaction. Your first preparation step should be to answer the nine Ws for your role as developer. As
you continue your preparation, fill in alternative ways to accomplish each
item in the checklist. Make a choice for each item, and indicate why you chose
the alternative you did.

For example, item 3: Prepare the agenda for the interaction. An agenda
could be an outline of topics or a list of specific questions. For this interaction,
ask yourself if you prefer to use a topic outline or a list of specific questions.
What factors led to your decision? What change in the situation would cause
you to change your decision? Repeat this analysis for each item on the
checklist.

The dialogue presented at the start of this chapter can provide some
guidance concerning alternatives. The discussions of the communication and
problem-solving processes presented in this chapter can also be of help.

Doing an Interaction

Earlier in this chapter, rapport was presented as a fundamental requirement
for effective communication. Only when rapport is established can the developer hope to arrive at a shared, complete, and accurate understanding of the
current and desired systems. When the developer establishes rapport with
the client, the client trusts the developer to help the client achieve his or her
goals.

Action Document 3.2 summarizes, in a list of key phrases, the results of
the communication research presented in this chapter. Apply this list to your
interactions with your instructors, superiors, or subordinates. Choose someone with whom you feel you have developed rapport. Identify the *dos* and *do
nots* you both follow. Repeat with someone with whom you have not established rapport.

To apply Action Document 3.2 to your project, review the dialogue
presented at the start of this chapter in light of the key phrases. Identify
successes and missed opportunities. For missed opportunities, suggest an
alternative, more satisfactory course of action. Carry your observations as
reminders into the interactions with your client(s).

Reviewing an Interaction

Communication researchers have long used an instrument called the Anderson and Anderson Interview Rating Scale to measure communication effectiveness [5]. Usually, the instrument is administered as a questionnaire to
clients and developers. Respondents are asked to indicate to what extent
specific behaviors occurred during an interaction. Responses are specified on
a five-point scale that ranges from *always* through *never*.

The Anderson and Anderson Interview Rating Scale will be used as an action document in two ways. Action Document 3.3 presents a selection of questions from the instrument. You can ask your client to evaluate interactions with you, or you can use the questions to evaluate yourself and identify your strengths and weaknesses in establishing rapport. For practice, answer the questions as if you were Sam Tilden and you were asked to evaluate the dialogue presented at the beginning of this chapter.

Monitoring Your Progress

How will you know your communication and problem-solving skills are improving? Each week you should review your recent activities in light of the following list. Every experience that matches one of these items is another step toward improving your communication and problem-solving skills. Feel free to add to the list any further items that you feel are appropriate.

1. I noticed something new about an environment in which I have been many times.
2. I noticed something new about a person whom I have known for a long time.
3. I developed a new way to perform a familiar task.
4. I saw someone doing something, and recalled a situation in which I behaved in the same way.
5. I had a successful interaction with someone who has always been difficult to deal with.
6. I took a risk.
7. The words to a familiar song took on a new meaning for me.
8. I changed my mind about something important.
9. I finally understood the meaning of a word or phrase I have been using for a long time.

References

1. Benson, H. *The Relaxation Response*. New York: Avon Books, 1976.
2. Bostrom, R. "Successful Application of Communication Techniques to Improve the Systems Development Process." *Indiana University Working Paper*, 1987.

3. Flexner, S., ed. *The Random House Dictionary of the English Language.* New York: Random House, 1987.

4. Galway, W. *The Inner Game of Tennis.* New York: Random House, 1974.

5. Guinan, P. *Patterns of Excellence for IS Professionals.* Washington, D.C.: ICIT Press, 1988.

6. Hagen, U. *Respect for Acting.* New York: Macmillan Publishing Co., 1973.

7. Kendall, K., and J. Kendall. *Systems Analysis and Design.* Englewood Cliffs, N.J.: Prentice-Hall, 1988.

8. Koberg, D., and J. Bagnall. *The All New Universal Traveler.* Los Altos, Calif.: William Kaufmann, 1981.

9. Moore, S. *Training an Actor.* Harmondsworth, England: Penguin Books, 1979.

10. Nuernberger, P. *Freedom from Stress.* Honesdale, Pa.: Himalayan International Institute of Yoga Science and Philosophy, 1981.

11. Polsky, M. E. *Let's Improvise.* Englewood Cliffs, N.J.: Prentice-Hall, 1980.

12. Prietula, M. and H. A. Simon. "The Experts in Your Midst." *Harvard Business Review* Volume 67, Number 1 (January-February 1989): pp. 120–124.

13. Vitalari, N. and G. Dickson, "Problem Solving for Effective Systems Analysis: An Experimental Exploration." *Communications of the ACM* Volume 26, Number 11 (November 1983): pp. 948–956.

INTERACTION PREPARATION CHECKLIST

1.   The nine Ws.
2.   Collect background information.
3.   Prepare the agenda for the interaction.
4.   Decide how to record the interaction.
5.   Identify needed materials, equipment, aides.
6.   Choose a date, time, and place.
7.   Notify the client.
8.   Direct the client in his or her preparation.

**ACTION DOCUMENT 3.1
Interaction preparation checklist**

KEY PHRASES FOR RAPPORT

Do	Do Not
listen	insist on always being right
inspire confidence	act artificially
desire to be of service	set solitary goals
make things clear	block and frustrate
use an encouraging tone	condescend
act as co-worker	use technical jargon
command respect	remain aloof
gain trust	lie

ACTION DOCUMENT 3.2
Key phrases for establishing rapport

ANDERSON AND ANDERSON INTERVIEW RATING SCALE (SELECTED ITEMS)

Answer each item using the following five-point scale:

Always		Occasionally		Never
(1)	(2)	(3)	(4)	(5)

1. The developer insisted on always being right.
2. I had confidence in the developer.
3. The developer was artificial in his or her behavior.
4. The developer acted as if he or she had a job to do and did not care how it was accomplished.
5. I felt blocked and frustrated in my attempt to relate to the developer.
6. I felt the developer had a genuine desire to be of service.
7. The developer's remarks made things clearer for me.
8. The developer's tone of voice encouraged me.
9. The developer could be a co-worker with me on a common problem.
10. I respected the developer's ability.

R.T.C. LIBRARY, LETTERKENNY

ACTION DOCUMENT 3.3
**Selected items from the Anderson and
Anderson Interview Rating Scale**

CHAPTER 4

Systems Analysis Models

Since we have covered quite a bit of ground, let's backtrack for a moment so that we all understand what has been done so far. Chapter 1 introduced the systems development life cycle and helped guide you through the Problem and/or Opportunity Analysis Phase of your project. Chapter 2 helped you develop your client profile, including the global entity-relationship model. These were the first steps of the Systems Analysis Model-Building Phase of your project. Chapter 3 interrupted your work on your project to discuss the important topics of effective communication and creative problem-solving—systems development skills that are used throughout the life cycle.

In this chapter, you will continue the work of the Systems Analysis Model-Building Phase that you began in Chapter 2. The models developed in Chapter 2 were general and comprehensive in nature. The models of this chapter narrow the focus down to the computer-based information system you identified in the problem and/or opportunity analysis for your project.

The Horatio & Co. section of this chapter provides concrete experience by presenting the actual models that were developed during the cost control system project. These models are called the Context Data Flow Diagram, the Final Analysis Data Flow Diagram, and the Requirements Model.

The What, How, and Why section of this chapter begins with an explanation of the terminology and conventions of data flow diagramming. The section concludes with a review of all of the models of the model-building phase and an analysis of the strengths and weaknesses of each model.

The final section, You Do It, provides exercises, guidelines, and action documents to help you build the models presented in this chapter for your own project.

After completing this chapter you will

1. understand data flow diagramming and requirements modeling and their role in the systems development life cycle

2.   know how to develop the Context Data Flow Diagram, the Final Analysis Data Flow Diagram, and the Requirements Model for any system

3.   build the Context Data Flow Diagram, the Final Analysis Data Flow Diagram, and the Requirements Model for your project

HORATIO & CO. COST CONTROL SYSTEM

Sam and Pete produced three models during this phase of the cost control system development project. Two of these models represented the current manual system for processing costs in the engineering department. This manual system was eventually replaced by the automated system developed during the project.

The third model dealt directly with the proposed new system. At this point in the project, no one knew enough about the new system to call it by its eventual name. The three models developed for the cost control system project are described in this section.

The Context DFD

The first model of the current manual system for processing costs in the engineering department is shown in Figure 4.1. The model is called a Context Data Flow Diagram or Context DFD.

The models presented in this chapter were drawn with EXCELERATOR and BriefCASE. Two different tools were used so that you could judge the strengths and weaknesses of each. Normally, only a single systems analysis modeling tool is used on a given project.

The Context DFD for the manual cost system shows the system as a single process, represented by the circle at the center of the model. The model also shows four entities external to the manual cost system: the accounting department, engineers, vendors, and construction project managers. Finally, the model shows the system connected to the external entities by 17 paths upon which data and information flow. The four external entities and the 17 paths connecting the current manual system to the external entities comprise the context within which the current manual cost system operates.

The Context DFD was developed through a dialogue between Sam and Pete. The success of the session depended upon the principles of good

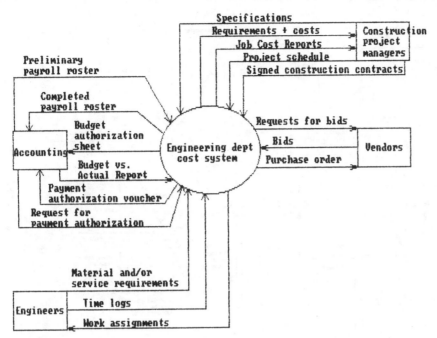

FIGURE 4.1
Context DFD for the cost control system project (produced on a dot matrix printer using BriefCASE)

communication that were presented in Chapter 3. The outcome frame for the Context DFD session was:

1. To establish the boundary of the current manual system for processing costs in the engineering department
2. To identify the external entities that interact with the current system
3. To identify the paths that cross the boundary of the current system to and from the external entities

The Final Analysis DFD

The second model of the current manual system for processing costs in the engineering department is shown in Figure 4.2. The model is called a Final Analysis Data Flow Diagram or Final Analysis DFD. The word *final* refers to

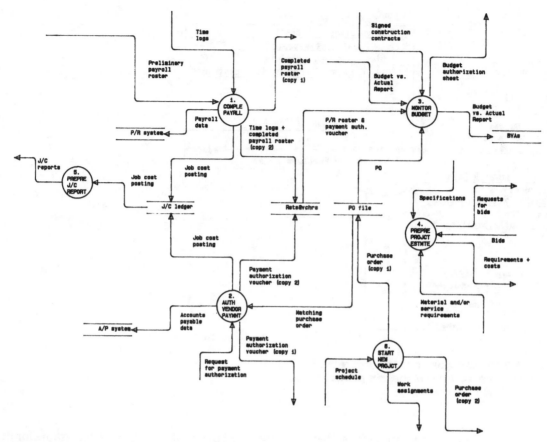

FIGURE 4.2
Final Analysis DFD for the cost control system project (produced on a pen plotter using EXCELERATOR)

the process of developing this diagram through a series of revisions. This process is described in the You Do It section of this chapter.

The Final Analysis DFD represents what goes on inside the circle labeled "Engineering dept cost system" in the Context DFD. The system of processing costs in the engineering department is made up of six processes, represented by six circles in Figure 4.2. These processes are:

1. Compile payroll

2. Authorize vendor payments

3. Monitor annual budgets

4. Prepare project estimates
5. Prepare job cost reports
6. Initiate new projects

For drawing convenience, the external entities shown in the Context DFD are not shown in the Final Analysis DFD. However, the 17 paths between the system and the external entities are shown in the Final Analysis DFD. These paths are the data flows that seem to come from or go to nowhere in the Final Analysis DFD. Whenever you encounter such a data flow in a Final Analysis DFD, you can identify the relevant external entity by finding that data flow in the corresponding Context DFD, which shows all of the external entities.

The Final Analysis DFD presented in Figure 4.2 also shows six places where data and information are held or stored. A storage place is represented by a pair of parallel lines. The storage places of the current manual system of processing costs in the engineering department are:

Payroll system

Accounts Payable system

Job Cost ledger

Completed rosters and payment authorization vouchers

Purchase Order file

Budget versus Actual report file

In the Final Analysis DFD, the data storage places are connected to the processes by paths. There are 12 such paths in Figure 4.2. Since these paths begin and end within the current manual system, they are not shown in the Context DFD. The Final Analysis DFD shows both internal and external paths, whereas the Context DFD shows only those paths that cross the boundary of the system to or from the external entities.

The Requirements Model

The third model developed during the model-building phase of the systems development life cycle is called the Requirements Model. The Requirements Model deals directly with the proposed new system. The Requirements Model for the Horatio & Co. Cost Control System is presented in Figure 4.3.

The Requirements Model presented in Figure 4.3 reflects the ability or lack of ability of the current manual system to support the business tactics and system objectives of the problem and/or opportunity analysis (Figure 1.2). The first requirement of Figure 4.3 implies that all the processes

Cost System Requirements

1. Continue to perform the functions and maintain the data of the Final Analysis DFD.
2. Provide a convenient access mechanism for the data of the Job Cost Detail Reports and Job Cost Summary Reports.
3. Provide for the maintenance and use of monthly budget data by job number and general ledger account.
4. Provide the analysis required for the reorganization of the vendor base. Provide a control mechanism for choice of vendor.
5. Provide for the maintenance and use of professional development plan data for engineering department personnel.

FIGURE 4.3
The Requirements Model for the cost system

of the current manual system serve a useful purpose and must be continued in the new system.

The second requirement implies that the current access mechanism for job cost data is inadequate. At present, job cost data is kept in a ledger, and all job cost reports are prepared by assembling the necessary information by hand from the ledger. In their dialogue on new system requirements, Sam and Pete decided to improve the process of compiling Job Cost Reports.

Requirement 3 of Figure 4.3 calls for the creation and maintenance of new data. Current budget data is maintained and used on an annual basis. Sam's tactic of identifying cost overruns within 30 days requires monthly budget data, so new data must be created and maintained by the new system.

Requirement 4 calls for new uses of the data maintained and stored in the file for completed rosters and payment authorization vouchers and in the purchase order file. Manual access to this data will prove to be inadequate for the proposed analyses.

The fifth requirement of Figure 4.3 is like the third. Data on the professional development of engineering department personnel must be created and maintained by the new system.

THE WHAT, HOW, AND WHY

The Systems Analysis Model-Building Phase of the project was undertaken as a result of the decision made at the end of the Problem and/or Opportunity

Analysis Phase (Chapter 1). The decision committed the resources to study the usefulness of an information systems solution further. The model-building phase will be followed by the Evaluation of Alternatives Phase of the life cycle (see Figure 1.4) before another go/no go decision is made [1].

Data flow diagramming is probably the most popular method of system analysis modeling in use today. The DFDs presented in the previous section represent the current manual system for processing costs in the engineering department; in later chapters, DFDs will be used again to represent the design of the new automated cost control system.

DFD Symbols, Terminology, and Conventions

All data flow diagrams represent processes. A **process** is the method by which inputs are transformed into outputs. In Figure 4.2, process 2, Authorize Vendor Payments, has two input paths and four output paths. The data flowing in from the accounting department and from the Purchase Order file is transformed into data flowing out to the accounting department, to the accounts payable system, to the job cost ledger, and to the file of completed rosters and payment authorization vouchers.

The data flow diagramming style presented in this book was developed by Edward Yourdon [2,4]. In Yourdon DFDs, processes are represented by circles. In another popular diagramming style, developed by Gane and Sarson [3], processes are represented by round-cornered rectangles. Figure 4.4 shows the Final Analysis DFD for the cost control system drawn in the Gane and Sarson style.

External entities are represented by rectangles in Yourdon diagrams and by squares in Gane and Sarson DFDs. External entities in data flow diagrams are sometimes called **terminators**. They always appear at the beginning or end of the paths that cross the boundary of the system in question.

The purpose of the Context DFD is to represent the terminators of a system and the paths that connect the terminators to the system. Terminators must appear in a system's Context DFD; however, as the level of detail in a set of DFDs increases, the terminators are dropped from the diagrams for drawing convenience.

In DFD terminology, the places where data collects in a system are called **data stores**. Data stores can be as simple as a spike on a clerk's desk for collecting sales receipts, or as complex as a computer-based accounts payable system. A data store is represented in Yourdon DFDs by a pair of parallel lines, and in Gane and Sarson diagrams by a rectangle with its horizontal sides extended to the right.

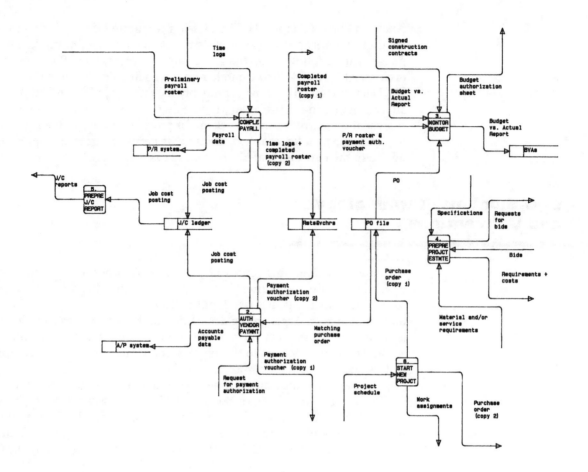

FIGURE 4.4
**Final Analysis DFD for the cost control
system project, Gane and Sarson style
(produced on a pen plotter using
EXCELERATOR)**

The primary purpose of developing a Final Analysis DFD is to identify the current system's central data stores. The current manual system of processing costs in the engineering department, shown in Figure 4.2, has six central data stores located in file cabinets, ledger books, and computer systems.

In data flow diagrams, processes, data stores, and terminators are connected to other processes by paths, called **data flows**, upon which data and information travel. Both Yourdon and Gane and Sarson use arrows to represent data flows.

Every data flow must either begin or end with a process. A data flow cannot connect a data store to another data store or a terminator to a data store. If such a connection appears, further analysis is required to uncover the process which enables the connection to be made.

The interpretation of a data flow as a path upon which data and information travel can cause some confusion when one is first learning to read DFDs. The arrows of the model do not imply sequencing of the processes, so data flow diagrams are not read like flow charts. Data flow diagrams are read like road maps. They show all possible destinations and all possible paths to the destinations.

Since the Context DFD (Figure 4.1) and the Final Analysis DFD (Figure 4.2) represent the current manual system at two levels of detail, they form what is called a **leveled** set of data flow diagrams. Sometimes the process of moving from one level of detail to the next is called **exploding** the processes of a DFD. The six processes shown in Figure 4.2 represent an explosion of the single process, the engineering department cost system, shown in Figure 4.1.

In developing a leveled set of data flow diagrams, the developer must be careful to conserve each process's data flows. This means that all data flows that cross the boundary of a process must appear in the next-level diagram, if any, and in the previous-level diagram, if any.

In the Context DFD for the current manual system, Figure 4.1, there are 17 data flows that cross the boundary of the system to or from the terminators. In the Final Analysis DFD, Figure 4.2, these same 17 data flows cross the boundary of the system. Every data flow that crosses the boundary of the system in Figure 4.1 crosses the boundary of the system in Figure 4.2, and no new data flows cross the boundary of the system in Figure 4.2. There are additional data flows in the Final Analysis DFD, but these data flows are internal to the process labeled "Engineering dept cost system" in Figure 4.1. The presence of these internal data flows does not violate the principle of conservation of data flows.

The Context DFD shown in Figure 4.1 represents a good deal of the physical processing characteristics of the manual engineering department system. For example, the terminators and the data flows are identified by the actual names used in day-to-day practice. In this regard, the Context DFD accurately represents how costs are actually processed in the engineering department.

By contrast, the processes of the Final Analysis DFD do not correspond to actual processes in the engineering department. The processes of the Final Analysis DFD represent logical groupings of many distinct operations. In essence, the Final Analysis DFD represents what is done rather than how it is done.

In systems analysis modeling, the term **physical model** refers to a model that accurately represents how processes are carried out. The term **logical model** refers to a model that represents what is done rather than how it is done.

Data Modeling versus Function Modeling

Data flow diagrams represent the processing functions of a system; they are called **process-oriented models** or **function-oriented models.** The global entity-relationship model introduced in Chapter 2 is an example of a **data-oriented model.** Data-oriented models represent the data requirements of a system or represent the things about which data is stored in the system, rather than representing how the data is processed in the system. Some authors say that data-oriented models represent data at rest in the system, whereas process-oriented models represent data in motion.

The systems development methodology presented in this book calls for the use of both data- and process-oriented models. The various perspectives supplied by the different types of models enhance the developer's understanding of the current and proposed systems.

For example, the global entity-relationship model for the engineering department, Figure 2.3, shows the engineering department related to accounting, vendors, engineers, and construction project managers. These entities comprise the entire context of the cost control system, Figure 4.1. By comparing the global entity-relationship model for the engineering department with the Context DFD for the cost control system, the developer can understand the extent to which the cost control system will affect the engineering department.

The global E-R model shows the engineers performing tasks for the engineering manager. The data flow diagrams fill in many specifics about this relationship. From the DFDs, the developer sees that some of the engineers' tasks involve identifying material and/or service requirements for project estimates, receiving work assignments when a new project is initiated, and supplying time logs that are used in the compilation of payroll.

In general, the developer shifts his or her attention from the E-R model to the DFDs to fill in details about the processing requirements of the system. Shifting attention from the DFDs to the entity-relationship models of the system usually improves understanding of the big picture. Of course, preparing two sets of models also improves the accuracy and completeness of the modeling process. Inaccuracies and omissions in one type of model are often uncovered in the development of the second type of model.

YOU DO IT

Use the cost control system models, the what, how, and why section material, and the action documents of this section to guide your efforts in developing the systems analysis models for your project. As always, make the final product and the process by which it is developed uniquely your own.

If your project involves a "live client," you will develop the models with your client. If you are using the accompanying written case project (Chapter 10), you will develop the models according to the directions provided by your instructor.

DFD Exercises

These exercises are designed to be done with a classmate before you attempt to develop data flow diagrams with your client. Practice as many as time permits.

1. Leveled DFDs

The first exercise requires you to develop a set of leveled DFDs to represent some system that you control. Your checkbook or perhaps some operation you perform at work are possible systems. Stick to something you control so that your understanding of how the system works is accurate and complete. Be creative.

Once you have developed the set of leveled DFDs, show them to a classmate and ask him or her to develop a written description of the system you modeled. Evaluate this description for *accuracy*, *completeness*, and *understanding*, and feed your comments back to your classmate. Continue the process until you are satisfied that your classmate has described your system accurately and completely.

2. Analogical Reasoning with DFDs

For the second exercise, choose any of the DFD patterns presented in Action Document 4.3, the key-word list for expanding level zero processes. Choose a partner and each of you write a description of some operation that might have the pattern as its model. Exchange descriptions with your partner and talk about the accuracies and inaccuracies, differences and similarities in your descriptions.

3. A Simulated DFD Session

For the third exercise, work with a classmate to simulate the DFD development sessions with your client. Your classmate should have some system in mind, and you should interview him or her to develop a set of leveled DFDs. Remember, the DFDs represent a shared, complete, and accurate understanding of the system in question. Use these words to evaluate your progress and to decide when you are done.

4. EXCELERATOR

The fourth exercise is for those of you who know EXCELERATOR and who have the EXCELERATOR data disk that accompanies this book. The data disk contains the Context DFD, the Final Analysis DFD, and the level 1 DFD for process 2 for the Horatio & Co. Cost Control System project. The single process of the Context DFD explodes to the Final Analysis DFD, and process 2 of the Final Analysis DFD explodes to the level 1 DFD for process 2.

In the level 1 diagram, process 2.2 explodes to a structure chart whose description screen contains the structured English specifications for the process. In the Final Analysis DFD, both the Job cost ledger data store and the Job cost posting data flow explode to the same record in the XLDictionary.

For practice, bring the graphical models up on the screen, and print them out if you wish. Use the Explode and Return options to navigate from one model to another. Examine the accompanying documentation for accuracy and completeness through the XLDICTIONARY and DOCUMENTATION modules. Run the options of the ANALYSIS module to evaluate accuracy and completeness further.

Imagine you are the project manager for the cost control system project. Prepare a written report of your EXCELERATOR review for the person responsible for using EXCELERATOR on the project. Identify missing models and documentation along with models and documentation that seem incomplete or inaccurate.

5. BriefCASE

The fifth exercise is for those of you who know BriefCASE and who have the BriefCASE data disk that accompanies this book. The data disk contains the Context DFD, the Final Analysis DFD, and the level 1 DFD for process 2 for the Horatio & Co. Cost Control System project. The single process of the Context DFD explodes to the Final Analysis DFD, and process 2 of the Final Analysis DFD explodes to the level 1 DFD for process 2.

In the level 1 diagram, process 2.2 is linked to a process specification in the data dictionary. In the Final Analysis DFD, the Job cost ledger data store is linked to a data store specification, and the Job cost posting data flow is linked to a data structure specification.

For practice, bring the graphical models up on the screen, and print them out if you wish. Use the Explode and Implode options to navigate from one model to another. Examine the accompanying documentation for accuracy and completeness through the data dictionary option.

Imagine you are the project manager for the cost control system project. Prepare a written report of your BriefCASE review for the person responsible for using BriefCASE on the project. Identify missing models and documentation along with models and documentation that seem incomplete or inaccurate.

Action Documents for Systems Analysis Model Building

The deliverables of the Systems Analysis Model-Building Phase of the life cycle are summarized in Action Document 4.1. Guidelines for developing each deliverable are presented in Action Documents 4.2, 4.5, and 4.6. Action Document 4.7 will help with planning and scheduling model-building tasks and identifying the necessary inputs and outputs. Other action documents will help you develop these deliverables, as explained below.

The Context DFD

Developing the Context DFD is a straightforward process, summarized in the steps of Action Document 4.2. The Context DFD development process delivers, besides the model, a complete set of documents used in the current system. Whenever a document is mentioned in the discussion of the Context DFD, ask your client for a copy of the document and mark the document with the name given to it by the client. Always include the copies of the documents with the Context DFD model.

The Final Analysis DFD

The Final Analysis DFD is developed through a series of steps that produce a set of leveled data flow diagrams.

Grouping Context Data Flows   The leveling process begins with the Context DFD. The developer separates the data flows of the Context DFD into logical groups and represents each group by a process. Each process is named with a phrase that describes the logic of the grouping.

Figure 4.5 shows the grouping of the Context DFD data flows for the Horatio & Co. Cost Control System. The process names, Compile payroll, Authorize vendor payments, and so on, were supplied by Pete Willard and Sam Tilden to describe the underlying logic of the grouping of data flows. Figure 4.5 represents the Level 0 Analysis DFD.

Exploding the Processes   The next step in developing the Final Analysis DFD is the expansion of the processes of the level 0 model into greater

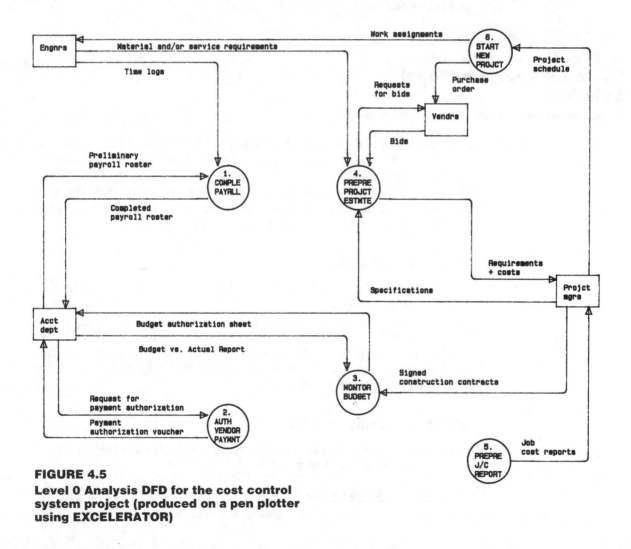

FIGURE 4.5

Level 0 Analysis DFD for the cost control system project (produced on a pen plotter using EXCELERATOR)

detail (level 1, level 2, etc.). One of the developer's objectives in discussing the details of each process with the client is the identification of the data stores involved in each process. The developer explodes each process of the level 0 diagram and fills in details regarding data and processing until satisfactory representation and understanding are achieved.

Figure 4.6 shows the explosion to level 1, of process 2, Authorize Vendor Payments, from the cost control system project.

The explosion of a level 0 process involves the identification of details and subprocesses. The developer finds clues to the details and subprocesses in the verbs that the client uses in describing the functions of each process.

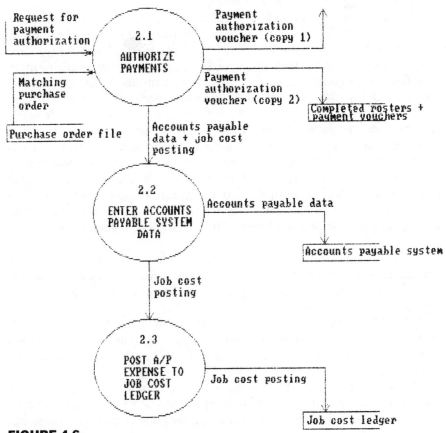

FIGURE 4.6
Level 1 Analysis DFD for process 2,
AUTHORIZE VENDOR PAYMENTS
(produced on a dot matrix printer using
BriefCASE)

For example, Sam Tilden might describe the process of authorizing vendor payments as follows. Pay attention to the verbs shown in italics.

> When Accounting receives an invoice from a vendor, they send it to me to *authorize* payment. I *check* the purchase order and *return* a payment authorization voucher. The expense is *entered* into the accounts payable system and *posted* in the job cost ledger. We *file* a copy of the invoice and the voucher.

When an experienced developer hears a client use verbs like *check, enter,* and *post,* the developer recalls familiar patterns of DFD symbols (using analogical reasoning). The key-word list in Action Document 4.3 is designed to help you associate some DFD patterns with the verbs you hear your client use in describing his or her level 0 processes.

Alongside each group of key words, a simple DFD pattern is shown. In each group the first key word, which defines the DFD pattern, is printed in boldface type. Use the patterns only as a guide; the actual details may vary. For example, the *enter* pattern in Action Document 4.3 shows only one input data flow. Your entry process may involve two inputs instead of one, and perhaps one data flow comes from a data store instead of a terminator.

Recording Procedures with Structured English   As more and more detail is added, the leveled set of DFDs moves further from the logical (what is done) and closer to the physical (how it is done). Sometimes a developer decides that an abundance of physical information is important to his or her understanding of the logic of the current system. In this case, he or she completes the leveled set of data flow diagrams by describing each process in the most detailed DFDs with a shorthand notation called structured English.

Structured English is a combination of English and the language of structured programming. The procedure is presented as a series of sequential steps. Decisions are represented by the "case" structure, and repetitions are represented by loop structures.

Figure 4.6 represents the most detailed DFD in the series that represents process 2, Authorize vendor payments. Figure 4.7 shows the structured English description of process 2.2, Enter accounts payable system data, from Figure 4.6.

In deciding whether to develop structured English descriptions, the resources required to develop the descriptions should be weighed against the descriptions' contribution to understanding the logic of the current system.

Connecting Data Stores and Processes   The Final Analysis DFD is produced by copying the data stores uncovered during the explosion process onto the level 0 diagram and connecting these data stores to the appropriate processes by data flows (see Figure 4.2).

I. COLLECT THE FOLDER MARKED "VOUCHERS TO BE ENTERED" FROM THE DEPARTMENT MANAGER'S "APPROVED TRANSACTIONS" FILE.

II. FOR EACH VOUCHER IN THE FOLDER DO THE FOLLOWING:

   A. Use the Accounts Payable Code Lookup Program to determine the identification code for the voucher's vendor, G/L accounts, and job cost distribution descriptions.

   B. Select the appropriate case.

      Case 1 (all identification codes found by the lookup):

         Record identification codes on the voucher. Hold voucher for entry into Accounts Payable.

      Case 2 (one or more identification codes not found):

         Prepare "Request for Master Change" Form. Leave unsigned form and voucher in department manager's "IN" basket.

III. FOR EACH CODED VOUCHER ENTER THE VOUCHER THROUGH ACCOUNTS PAYABLE VOUCHER MAINTENANCE PROGRAM. COMPLETE THREE SCREENS:

  HEADER, G/L DISTRIBUTION, AND J/C DISTRIBUTION. NOTE: G/L Distribution Total and J/C Distribution Total must match the amount of the voucher entered at the header screen.

IV. DO THE FOLLOWING UNTIL AN ERROR-FREE PROOF LIST IS OBTAINED:

   A. Print the proof list from the Accounts Payable Voucher Maintenance Program.

   B. Compare the printed record count to the actual count of the vouchers.

   C. Compare the printed dollar total to the actual total of the vouchers.

   D. Proofread the G/L and J/C Distribution lines.

   E. If batch contains errors, correct erroneous voucher through the change option of the Accounts Payable Voucher Maintenance Program.

V. RUN THE ACCOUNTS PAYABLE VOUCHER UPDATE PROGRAM. VERIFY BATCH RECORD COUNT AND DOLLAR TOTAL ON SCREEN.

VI. PHOTOCOPY VOUCHER AND FILE COPIES WITH LAST PROOF LIST IN ACCOUNTS PAYABLE JOURNAL OF ORIGINAL ENTRY.

VII. SEND ORIGINALS TO ACCOUNTING DEPARTMENT VIA INTEROFFICE MAIL.

FIGURE 4.7
Structured English description for accounts payable transaction entry

Action Document 4.4 summarizes the steps in the construction of the Final Analysis Data Flow Diagram.

The Requirements Model

The Requirements Model for the new system focuses on both data and processing requirements. The guidelines presented in Action Document 4.5

break the development tasks down into manageable steps. Make your own choices about the means of collecting the information for this model from your client: face-to-face interviews, written materials, or both.

Use Action Document 4.6 to plan and control your modeling-building activities. At the end of this phase, collect all relevant models, documents, and other materials, and use the cover sheet, Action Document 4.7, to submit your work as a progress report to your instructor.

References

1. Amadio, W. *Systems Development: A Practical Approach*. Watsonville, Calif.: Mitchell Publishing, 1989.

2. DeMarco, T. *Structured Analysis and System Specification*. Englewood Cliffs, N.J.: Yourdon Press, 1978.

3. Gane, C., and T. Sarson. *Structured Systems Analysis Tools and Techniques*. New York: Improved System Technologies, 1977.

4. Yourdon, E. *Modern Structured Analysis*. Englewood Cliffs, N.J.: Yourdon Press, 1989.

SYSTEMS ANALYSIS MODEL-BUILDING DELIVERABLES

1. A Context DFD for the current system showing the boundary of the current system, the terminators, and the paths that cross the boundary of the current system to and from the terminators

2. A Final Analysis DFD for the current system, showing its central data stores

3. A Requirements Model listing the data and processing requirements of the new system

ACTION DOCUMENT 4.1
Model-building phase deliverables

DEVELOPING A CONTEXT DFD

1. Draw the Context DFD with the user(s). Since the objectives of the process are simple, all members of the development team can participate in a single session.

2. Hold the session in a space which encourages free exchange and movement. Use a chalkboard or other medium which allows easy access and modification.

3. Start the session with a naive representation of the current system. This will introduce the Context DFD symbols and begin the discussion by giving the group something to shoot at.

4. Stick to the goals of establishing the boundary of the current system, identifying terminators, and identifying data flows that cross the system's boundary.

5. Stick to rough sketches to avoid any trauma associated with discarding a diagram and starting over. Plan to throw several diagrams away.

6. Adopt the user's terminology. Refer to documents by their correct name. Take copies of all documents and mark them with the names used in everyday practice.

ACTION DOCUMENT 4.2
Guidelines for developing the Context DFD

KEY WORDS FOR EXPANDING LEVEL 0 PROCESSES

Key Word   **DFD Pattern**

enter
maintain
collect
compile
add
file
tabulate

match
check
authorize
monitor
review
decide
determine
reconcile
release
identify
verify
analyze

update
change
revise
modify
post
apply

generate
prepare
produce
print
notify
contact

ACTION DOCUMENT 4.3
Key words for expanding level 0 processes

CONSTRUCTING A FINAL ANALYSIS DFD

1. Draw the Level 0 Analysis DFD by separating the data flows of the Context DFD into logical groups. Connect each group of data flows to a process. Name each process with a transitive verb and a direct object.

2. Expand each of the Level 0 processes into subprocesses. Conserve the Level 0 data flows and use data stores to introduce new data flows. Continue expanding the subprocesses until an adequate level of detail is achieved.

3. Combine the data stores and the Level 0 Analysis DFD into the final version of the Analysis DFD. Observe the connections between processes established by the inclusion of the data stores in the diagram.

ACTION DOCUMENT 4.4
**Steps in the construction of the Final
Analysis DFD**

CONSTRUCTING A REQUIREMENTS MODEL

1. Examine the processes and context data flows of the Analysis DFD to determine if any of them no longer serve a useful purpose.

2. Examine each business tactic developed in the Problem and/or Opportunity Phase. Determine the availability of required data in the Analysis DFD data stores. Be concerned only with the existence of the data, not with the means by which it is stored.

3. For each business tactic, judge the adequacy of existing access and control mechanisms.

4. Examine each system objective developed in the Problem and/or Opportunity Analysis Phase for new system requirements regarding data and processes.

ACTION DOCUMENT 4.5
Steps in the construction of the Requirements Model

Deliverable 1: Context DFD for the current system

Task	User/Mgt People	IS People	Documents Needed	Documents Produced	Estimated Duration

Deliverable 2: Level 0 Analysis DFD for the current system

Task	User/Mgt People	IS People	Documents Needed	Documents Produced	Estimated Duration

Deliverable 3: Level 1 and beyond Analysis DFDs for the current system

Task	User/Mgt People	IS People	Documents Needed	Documents Produced	Estimated Duration

ACTION DOCUMENT 4.6
Tasks for each deliverable (page 1 of 2)

Deliverable 4: Structured English descriptions of most detailed processes

Task	User/Mgt People	IS People	Documents Needed	Documents Produced	Estimated Duration

Deliverable 5: Final Analysis DFD for the current system

Task	User/Mgt People	IS People	Documents Needed	Documents Produced	Estimated Duration

Deliverable 6: Requirements model for the new system

Task	User/Mgt People	IS People	Documents Needed	Documents Produced	Estimated Duration

ACTION DOCUMENT 4.6
Tasks for each deliverable (page 2 of 2)

Date _____

To _____

From _____

Re: Systems analysis models

The following documents are included in this analysis:

☐   Context DFD

☐   Final Analysis DFD with level 0 through level _____ DFDs preceding

☐   Structured English procedure descriptions

☐   Requirements Model

☐   Other _____

_____

☐   Other _____

_____

☐   Other _____

_____

☐   Other _____

_____

The following activities were carried out during this analysis:

☐   Interviews with _____

_____

☐   Written exercises with _____

_____

☐   Other _____

_____

☐   Other _____

_____

☐   Other _____

_____

ACTION DOCUMENT 4.7
Cover sheet for systems analysis models

CHAPTER 5

The Evaluation of Alternatives Phase

The Evaluation of Alternatives Phase of the systems development life cycle follows the Systems Analysis Model-Building Phase. Completion of this work fulfills the commitment made in the first go/no go decision of the life cycle.

Evaluation of alternatives concentrates on the new system and brings a development project to the second go/no go decision of the life cycle (see Figure 1.4). This chapter presents the logical and physical models of the new system that support this decision.

If the second go/no go decision of the life cycle is positive, the project proceeds to the Design New System Phase. If the decision is negative, the development team abandons an information system solution to the problem and/or opportunity at hand and seeks another way to address the situation.

The Horatio & Co. section of this chapter presents the evaluation of alternatives for the cost control system project. You will recognize data flow diagramming and entity-relationship modeling from previous chapters. The Designer's Tradeoff Chart represents a new modeling technique that is used for the final physical form of the new system.

The What, How, and Why section of this chapter provides detailed explanations of how to develop the deliverables presented in the previous section. The section also explains how these deliverables are used in the subsequent go/no go decision.

The final section, You Do It, provides guidelines, exercises, and action documents to help you to evaluate alternatives for your own project and to begin preparing materials for the presentation to management regarding the next phase of the life cycle.

After completing this chapter you will

1. know how to decide which new system requirements should be automated and which should not

2. know how to quantify the benefits of automation
3. know how to develop useful logical models of the new system
4. understand how to tradeoff new system features, responsibilities, and costs to arrive at a feasible physical form for the new system
5. apply these tools and techniques to the preparation of the second go/no go decision for your project

HORATIO & CO. COST CONTROL SYSTEM

The deliverables of the Evaluation of Alternatives Phase of the cost control system project are presented in this section. Detailed information about the preparation of these deliverables is covered, as usual, in the What, How, and Why section of this chapter.

In the last chapter, Pete and Sam completed the Context DFD and the Final Analysis DFD for the current manual system for processing costs in the engineering department, and the Requirements Model for the new system. Their first task in the Evaluation of Alternatives Phase was to assess the boundary of the new system. The new system incorporated the six processes of the Final Analysis DFD (Figure 4.2), and the three new processes of the Requirements Model (Figure 4.3): monthly budgets, reorganization of the vendor base, and professional development plans.

Understanding the New Processes

In order to understand more about the new processes, Pete and Sam developed a leveled set of DFDs for these processes. They named the processes: 7, MAINTAIN PROFESSIONAL DEVELOPMENT Plans; 8, MAINTAIN MONTHLY BUDGETS; and 9, MAINTAIN VENDOR CONTROL DATA STORE. The Level 1 DFD for the MAINTAIN PROFESSIONAL DEVELOPMENT PLANS process is shown in Figure 5.1.

The Role of Automation

Pete and Sam's second task in the Evaluation of Alternatives Phase was to determine the role of automation in the new system, that is, the mix of work

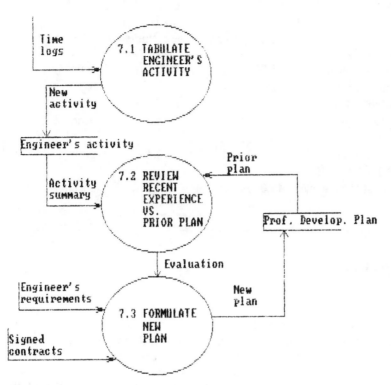

FIGURE 5.1
Level 1 of process 7, MAINTAIN
PROFESSIONAL DEVELOPMENT PLANS
(produced on a dot matrix printer using
BriefCASE)

assigned to the computer and work assigned to humans. Their determination was based upon the concept of value [6].

Pete asked Sam to imagine an ideal automated system and to identify which of the nine processes within the new system boundary would benefit most from automation. He also asked Sam to state the value of the benefits, the likelihood these benefits will occur, and the specific forms these benefits will take.

A summary of Sam and Pete's analysis appears in Figure 5.2. Sam and Pete decided to call the proposed new system a cost control system when they realized that all of the benefits involved decreasing costs.

In addition to listing the dollar values of the benefits, Sam and Pete expressed the values of the benefits as percentages of the engineering department's annual budget. The engineering department spends $1 million

Requirement (see Figure 4.3)	Benefit	Value ($/year)	% of Annual Dept. Budget	Likelihood
2. Job Cost Reports	Replace report preparer	18,000	0.7	certain
	Save 1 hour per day of each engineer's time	125,000	4.8	high
3. Monthly budgets	Eliminate 4% average cost overrun	104,000	4.0	even
5. Professional development plans	Avoid resignations in the engineering department	10,800 each	0.4	even
4. Reorganization of vendor base	Decrease cost of materials by 1%	16,000	0.6	uncertain

FIGURE 5.2
Summary of the benefits of automation

per year on payroll, another $1.1 million on subcontractors, and $0.5 million on equipment and materials, for a total of $2.6 million per year. Sam was happy to see that the percentages totaled to 10.5 percent, slightly above the company-wide objective of a 10 percent reduction in costs.

Compare Figure 5.2 to the Final Analysis DFD, Figure 4.2, and the Requirements Model, Figure 4.3, to determine the extent of the automated portion of the new system. Observe the processes that were included in the automated portion and the processes that were excluded.

The Design DFD

Pete began the design of the automated portion of the new system by focusing his attention on its central data stores. He began by identifying the new system outputs implied by each requirement listed in Figure 5.2. He then determined the data stores needed to support these outputs. Finally, Pete identified the sources of these data stores' contents and collected his findings into a data flow diagram called the Design DFD.

To understand the design method, consider Job Cost Reports, the first requirement listed in Figure 5.2. Automated Job Cost Reports require a data store similar to the job cost ledger maintained by the current manual system. The sources of this data store's contents are the time logs, completed payroll rosters, and payment authorization vouchers (see Figure 4.2, the Final Analysis DFD).

Figure 5.3 shows the Design DFD for the automated portion of the Horatio & Co. Cost Control System. Pete made a note about vendor control at the bottom of the diagram, because the data stores required by that process bore no logical connection to the data stores required by the other three processes, and because of the uncertain benefits associated with vendor control. When he discussed the matter with Sam, they decided to drop vendor control from the new system for the moment and to proceed with only the three requirements represented in Figure 5.3: Job Cost Reports, monthly budgets, and professional development plans.

The Physical Form of the New System

Sam and Pete examined several alternatives for the automated portion of the new system. They finally decided to develop their own software and run it on the local area network that the engineering department used for word processing and computer-aided design (CAD). The software would provide pre-programmed reports that users could select from a menu, and more flexible ad hoc reporting that would allow users to formulate and answer one-of-a-kind questions.

The decision to develop the software for the new system and to use the local area network brought Betsy Klein onto the cost control system project team. Betsy started at Horatio & Co. as Sam's administrative assistant. She educated herself in microcomputer technology and quickly became the most knowledgeable person in the firm. Betsy agreed to work on the development of the software for the cost control system and to manage the system once it was implemented.

In estimating the costs of developing the new system, the project team considered five components: hardware, software, data, procedures, and personnel [8]. Cost estimates for the design and development of the cost control system are shown in Figure 5.4. The method by which these costs are derived is explained in the What, How, and Why section of this chapter.

Horatio & Co. management will weigh these costs against the value of the benefits shown in Figure 5.2 to make their second go/no go decision. This decision will commit the resources to pursue the next phase of the systems development life cycle.

When Sam Tilden weighed the cost control system's benefits against the estimated costs, he decided in favor of pursuing the project. The benefits were in line with the company-wide objective of a 10 percent decrease in

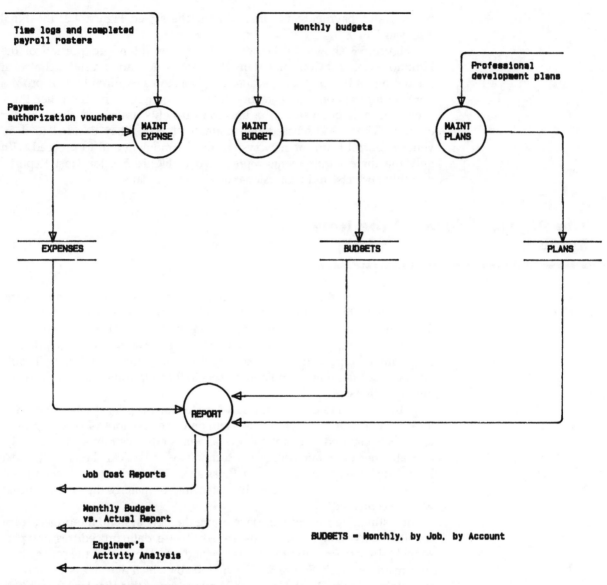

FIGURE 5.3
The Design DFD for the automated portion
of the cost control system (produced with a
pen plotter using EXCELERATOR)

Additional network station	$ 2,000	
Minicomputer to PC line	negligible	
dBASE III PLUS network version	1,500	
Software development (Sam and Betsy)	4,000	
System manager	3,000	per year
Minicomputer data entry programming	2,500	
Minicomputer to PC communication software	250	
Integrate manual and automated procedures	400	
Conversion of job cost ledger entries	900	
Preparation of monthly budgets	600	
Training (menu system)	500	
Training (ad hoc reporting)	5,000	
Software development (Pete)	4,000	
Totals: New system startup	$24,650	
Ongoing	$ 3,000	per year
This analysis	$ 4,000	

FIGURE 5.4
Cost estimates to design and develop the new cost control system

expenses, and the costs were such that the system would pay for itself in a short time.

In order to get the necessary funding, he would have to convince the Horatio & Co. president, Frank Chapin, of the value of the investment. Mr. Chapin was expecting a written report and a formal presentation on the results of the systems analysis phase and the Evaluation of Alternatives Phase.

THE WHAT, HOW, AND WHY

In the Evaluation of Alternatives Phase of the systems development life cycle (see Figure 1.4), developers use the models constructed in the previous model-building phase to support decisions and analyses. These decisions and analyses lead to the go/no go decision that is made at the end of the Evaluation of Alternatives Phase.

The path to the go/no go decision begins with the identification of the **boundary** of the new system. This boundary is constructed by combining the processes of the Final Analysis DFD that are included in the Requirements Model with the new processes specified in the Requirements Model.

At this point in the life cycle, the developers do not know any details of the new processes specified in the Requirements Model. In order to bring their understanding of these new processes to the point where intelligent decisions can be made, the developers expand the new processes of the Requirements Model through a set of leveled data flow diagrams. This leveling provides insight into the processing functions and the data store requirements of these new and, as yet, nonexistent processes.

Once the boundary of the new system has been determined and modeled, the developers turn their attention toward automation. They decide which of the processes within the boundary of the new system are the best candidates for automation. The decision is based upon an assessment of the benefits and costs of automation.

Quantifying the Benefits of Automation

Computer-based information systems provide benefits by improving either company revenues or costs. Usually improvement is considered to be increased revenues or decreased costs, but this is not always the case. Keeping revenues from decreasing or keeping costs from increasing may very well be the benefit provided by a computer-based information system.

A system development project may also be initiated in response to a change in competition or government regulation that has implications for the continued existence of the firm. It is difficult to imagine a bank competing in today's market without providing automated teller machines (ATMs) for its customers. ATMs very likely increase the cost of doing business, but when the alternative is the failure of the business, the project is undertaken despite the cost.

Decreasing Costs

Almost all early computer-based information systems were implemented to decrease costs, in particular clerical costs. Tasks formerly done by people are now carried out by the computer. The term **cost displacement** was coined to describe this phenomenon.

Cost displacement benefits are the easiest to quantify. The time required for a person to perform a task can be estimated, and a dollar value, based upon that person's rate of pay, can be assigned. This **how long–how much analysis** was applied to the benefits accruing from automated job cost reports, as you can see from Figure 5.2.

The report preparer's annual salary is $18,000 per year. If he or she is no longer assigned to prepare Job Cost Reports, then the $18,000 cost is saved or displaced by the automated system.

The $125,000 saving in engineers' time is a little more difficult to estimate. Sam estimated that one hour per day was spent or wasted by each engineer on manual Job Cost Reports. Sam used an average annual salary of $50,000, an eight-hour average work day, and an average work force of 20 people to arrive at the $125,000 figure. The calculation is:

$$\frac{1 \text{ hour wasted}}{8 \text{ hours in workday}} \times \$50,000 \text{ per year} \times 20 \text{ engineers} = \$125,000$$

The analysis of the saving of engineers' time raises the critical issue of the likelihood of achieving proposed benefits. If the report preparer is assigned elsewhere, then his or her salary is not spent by the engineering department, and cost saving is definite. If the engineers save one hour per day, however, they must use that time on productive work in order for the benefit to accrue to the company. This may not happen automatically, and it is the responsibility of the development team to assess the likelihood that these benefits will, indeed, be achieved.

Only the members of the user/management group can assess the likelihood that benefits will occur. Specific statements are to be encouraged, and vague language is to be avoided. In assessing the likelihood that benefits will occur, the information systems professional relies on the techniques of good developer/client communication presented in Chapter 3. The use of pointers to elicit specific information and to avoid "filling in" is probably the most important communication behavior for these kinds of sessions.

The benefits associated with the monthly budgets and the reorganization of the vendor base were not presented as cost displacement benefits; consequently, they were not calculated by the how long–how much method. Monthly budgets were developed to help Sam control cost overruns more effectively, and the reorganization of the vendor base was proposed to help Sam acquire materials more efficiently.

Benefits accruing from the improved effectiveness of the user/management group can be quantified using the **percentage effectiveness** method. Sam Tilden estimated a 4 percent average cost overrun in the engineering department, and he felt that monthly budgets would eliminate 100 percent of the overruns. His percentage effectiveness for monthly budgets was therefore 4 percent.

Once the developers decide on the percentage effectiveness they think the new system will provide, they must estimate the likelihood that this percentage will be achieved. Sam felt he had an even chance (fifty-fifty) of eliminating 100 percent of the cost overruns in the engineering department through the institution of monthly budgets (see Figure 5.2).

For the reorganization of the vendor base, Sam was very specific about the percentage effectiveness. He stated his goal as the reduction of the cost of materials by 1 percent (see Figure 5.2). However, he could not judge how likely he was to achieve this goal. In such a situation, the development team should study the projected benefits further to provide more specifics; or they should drop the process from consideration for the automated portion of the system. Without a specific benefit value and an informed estimate of the likelihood that the benefit will be achieved, the development team *cannot* consider a candidate for the automated portion of the new system past this point in the life cycle.

Increasing Revenues

The use of computer-based technology to increase revenues is more recent than the use of such technology to decrease costs. There are basically two ways to increase an organization's revenues. The organization can sell more goods or services, or it can sell essentially the same amount of goods or services at a higher price.

Selling more goods or services might involve introducing new products, or it might involve selling larger quantities of existing products. It could also mean finding new customers, or selling larger quantities to existing customers.

Quantifying the benefits of proposed revenue-increasing systems is more complicated than quantifying the benefits of cost-decreasing systems. Acquiring hard numbers for the benefits of a system designed to improve sales or market share can be difficult and expensive.

The percentage effectiveness method of quantifying benefits can be used for systems designed to increase revenues. As Sam did for the reorganization of the vendor base, the developers estimate the value of a percentage point increase in market share or sales volume, and then they assess the likelihood of achieving this goal via the proposed system.

Benefits that are difficult to quantify without specific experience are sometimes called **intangible benefits**, while benefits that are easy to quantify without experience are called **tangible benefits**. The technique of identifying the specific form of the benefits and the likelihood the benefits will occur measures the value of the benefits; it also provides some safeguards against committing resources to "soft" proposals, that is, those whose benefits are mostly intangible [3]. The technique relies upon the expertise of the user/ management group to identify those problems and/or opportunities worthy of commitment [9].

If a system proposal identifies significant intangible benefits, then a **pilot project** may be undertaken before a full-fledged commitment is made. A pilot project is a smaller, less expensive project whose purpose is to provide the experience necessary to quantify the intangible benefits of a larger proposed system.

The Design DFD

The process of developing the Design DFD starts with the outputs necessary to support the proposed automated process. It proceeds to the data stores that will support the outputs and then to the inputs that will be used to maintain the data stores [4]. In addition to identifying the central data stores, the Design DFD also identifies the entities represented by the database of the system.

Examine the data flows, data stores, and notes of Figure 5.3. The following list summarizes the entity types, that is, the things about which data is stored:

Expense

Budget

Job

Account

Vendor

Material and/or service

Engineer

Activity

Plan

The technique of generating pairs of relationship types was explained in Chapter 2 for the Global E-R model. Applying this technique to the entity types listed above, we obtain the system entity-relationship model or **system E-R model** shown in Figure 5.5.

Because the scope of the system E-R model is smaller and because it is developed later in the life cycle, the system E-R model shows more detail than the global E-R model. This detail is communicated in three system E-R modeling symbols: the arrowhead, the solid circle, and the hollow circle [1].

An arrowhead indicates that the entity the arrow points to can have many instances related to each instance of the entity that the arrow points away from. For example, the arrowhead pointing from BUDGET to EXPENSE indicates that many expenses can be charged to a single budget.

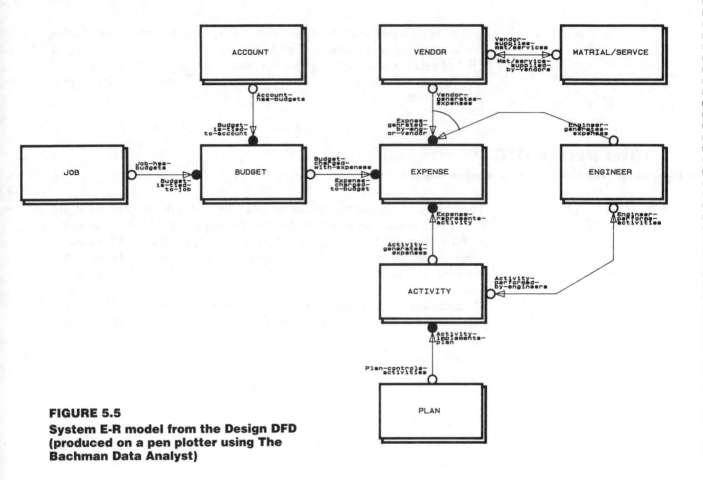

FIGURE 5.5
**System E-R model from the Design DFD
(produced on a pen plotter using The
Bachman Data Analyst)**

The absence of the arrowhead indicates that the entity can have a maximum of one instance related to each instance of the entity at the other end of the relationship. For example, the absence of an arrowhead pointing from EXPENSE to BUDGET indicates that only one budget may be charged with a particular expense.

A relationship on a system E-R model can be **one-to-many, many-to-many,** or **one-to-one**. For example, the relationship between BUDGET and EXPENSE is one-to-many, that is, each expense is charged to one, and only one, budget, while each budget can be charged with many expenses. The relationship between ACTIVITY and ENGINEER is many-to-many, that is, each activity can be performed by many engineers, and each engineer can perform many activities. Figure 5.5 does not contain a one-to-one relationship.

A solid circle on a system E-R model indicates a **mandatory relationship** between the entity next to the solid circle and the entity it is joined to. A hollow circle indicates an **optional relationship** between the entity next to the hollow circle and the entity it is joined to. For example, the relationship from EXPENSE to BUDGET is mandatory; that is, every expense must be charged to a budget. The relationship from BUDGET to EXPENSE, however, is optional; a budget might exist for which no expenses have been generated yet.

Both the Design DFD and the system E-R model provide insight into the data requirements of the automated portion of the new system. The procedures of the new system will be developed to support these data requirements. Since each model presents a different perspective of the data requirements, it is advisable to develop both the Design DFD and the system E-R model at this point in the life cycle.

The Designer's Tradeoff Chart

With the completion of the Design DFD and the system E-R model, the development team considers the final physical form of the new system. The technique presented in this book relies upon the **Designer's Tradeoff Chart** [2].

Tradeoff is the most important word in the systems developer's vocabulary [10]. The Designer's Tradeoff Chart is designed to help the development team choose the proper mix of features, responsibilities, and costs. For example, a development team may choose to lower the cost of a proposal by giving up some feature of the system, or they may choose to lessen their responsibilities by buying a more sophisticated hardware configuration.

The Chart should be used iteratively. The development team should indicate the mix of features and responsibilities that they desire, and then the mix should be evaluated for technical, operational, and economic feasibility. If the current mix proves to be infeasible, then it should be revised and the evaluation repeated.

Technical feasibility refers to the ability of the organization's technical resources to support a given mix. **Operational feasibility** refers to the match between the features and responsibilities of a given mix and the people in the user/management group. **Economic feasibility** refers to the match between the proposed system's benefits and costs.

Figure 5.6 presents the final tradeoff chart for the cost control system. An X beside a feature or responsibility indicates that it is desired or required. The word NOW indicates that a feature or responsibility already exists in the current manual system for processing costs in the engineering department.

The cost estimates presented in Figure 5.4 were derived from the final Tradeoff Chart. The development team examines each line of the chart that is marked with an X and identifies the costs of implementing that line. For

DESIGNER'S TRADEOFF CHART

Access

X		Direct access points on desks
X		Shared direct access points near desks
	NOW	One shared direct access point
	NOW	Access through intermediary

Flexibility of Output

X	NOW	Ad hoc reporting (selection of presentation and data)
X		Several predetermined presentations with selection of data
		One predetermined presentation with selection of data
		Several predetermined presentations with no selection of data
		One predetermined presentation with no selection of data

Turnaround Time on Output

X		While you wait (seconds)
		While you wait (minutes)
		Come back later (hours)
	NOW	Come back later (days)

Timeliness of Data*

		Up to the minute	* Note: With the current system, some data is updated daily and some is updated only monthly. The specification calls for daily updates of *all* data and reports.
X	NOW	One day old	
		One week old	
	NOW	One month old or more	

System Responsibilities

X		Responsible for hardware and software
		Responsible for hardware
		Responsible for software
	NOW	Responsible for neither hardware nor software

Data Responsibilities

X		Responsible for initial data conversion
X	NOW	Responsible for source documents
X	NOW	Responsible for data entry
X		Responsible for updating and purging
X		Responsible for backup and restore
X		Responsible for match with other company systems
X	NOW	Responsible for security and confidentiality

Learning

		Everyone must learn everything
X		Someone must learn everything; everyone must learn something
		No one need learn everything; everyone must learn something
		Someone must learn something; others need learn nothing
	NOW	No one need learn anything significant

FIGURE 5.6
Final Tradeoff Chart for the cost control system

instance, Sam and Pete determined that the access requirements listed in Figure 5.6 would require the purchase of one additional network station, and they placed the cost of this station at $2,000.

Software Development Methods

The issue of software acquisition and/or development crosses several boundaries of the Tradeoff Chart [5]. Systems developers face two basic options in regard to software: buy it or build it. If the development team chooses to build the software, they face an additional choice: use prototyping or use the traditional detailed design method.

The analysis of software acquisition/development methods should examine prewritten software packages first. If a satisfactory package is not available, then the project team considers developing the software. If a 4GL/CASE environment is feasible and the user/management group is willing to commit the necessary time, prototyping should be used. If prototyping is not feasible, then the detailed design approach should be used.

Prototyping relies on modern software development tools to create a quick working model of the proposed system. Users experiment with the working model, and provide feedback that is incorporated into the model. The process stops when the user is satisfied with the system that has evolved.

The **detailed design method** relies on specifying requirements completely before any programming begins. Once the user/management group signs off on a detailed design, it is "frozen," programmed, and delivered back to the user. Guidelines for the software acquisition/development decision are presented in the You Do It section of this chapter.

YOU DO IT

Use the cost control system material, the what, how, and why section material, and the action documents of this section to guide your efforts in developing the systems analysis models for your project.

If your project involves a "live client," you will evaluate alternatives with your client. If you are using the accompanying written case project (Chapter 10), you will evaluate alternatives according to the directions provided by your instructor.

Action Documents for Evaluation of Alternatives

The deliverables of the evaluation of alternatives phase of the life cycle are summarized in Action Document 5.1. An action document for planning and scheduling evaluation of alternative tasks, and identifying the necessary inputs and outputs appears at the end of this section (Action Document 5.6).

New Processes

At this point in the life cycle, you are asking your client to use DFDs to design the new processes specified in the Requirements Model. The guidelines and action documents presented in Chapter 4 should be used again to develop the leveled set of DFDs for these new processes. The only difference between the DFDs of this chapter and those of the previous chapter is that the models of this chapter represent proposed new processes rather than existing processes.

Benefits of Automation

Action Document 5.2 presents a decision tree for quantifying the benefits of automation. Each node (question) in the tree represents a question to be answered by your client. Each branch (line segment) in the tree represents a specific answer to the preceding question. The end of each path (box) represents the method that should be used to quantify the benefits.

For example, the first question the client must answer is whether the benefits of the new system will accrue from decreased costs or increased revenues or both. If benefits are expected from decreased costs, then the client should identify whether these will result from cost displacement or improved effectiveness. If cost displacement is expected, then the how long–how much quantification method should be employed. Keep in mind that one can follow both paths from a decision; for example, a system may provide both cost displacement and improved effectiveness.

Use Action Document 5.2 as you see fit. You might want to use it to prepare questions for an interview, or you might want to construct a written questionnaire for your client based upon the tree.

Design DFD and System E-R Model

The Design DFD represents the database of the new system. After you have decided which Requirements Model processes will be automated, the Design DFD is developed by

1. identifying automated outputs
2. determining the data stores to support the outputs
3. identifying the sources of the data stores' contents

The System E-R Model depicts the entities represented in the database of the new system. Use the techniques presented in Chapter 2 and in the What, How, and Why section of this chapter to develop your System E-R Model.

The Design DFD and the System E-R Model for the Horatio & Co. Cost Control System are included on the EXCELERATOR and BriefCASE diskette that accompanies this book. If you are using this diskette, examine the cost control system models and use either EXCELERATOR or BriefCASE to develop your own models.

Designer's Tradeoff Chart

The final physical form of the new system strikes a balance between system features, responsibilities, and costs. Action Document 5.3 presents a blank Designer's Tradeoff Chart. Let your client assess the current system by placing NOW beside the features and responsibilities of the current system. Then let the client specify the features and responsibilities of the new system by placing Xs. You should evaluate the specifications for technical, operational, and economic feasibility, and repeat the process until a satisfactory and feasible physical form for the new system evolves.

Economic feasibility is determined by reviewing each line of the Tradeoff Chart and identifying the associated costs. (Figure 5.4 shows the results of the review process for the Tradeoff Chart presented in Figure 5.6.) Total costs are compared to the value of benefits identified earlier and the likelihood these benefits will occur. The go/no go decision is then made whether or not to proceed to the next phase of the life cycle.

Action Document 5.4 is provided to help with the evaluation of the technical and operational feasibility [7] of your project system. As usual, you should use the questions presented in Action Document 5.4 to guide and support your efforts in whatever way you see fit.

Software Acquisition or Development

Use Action Document 5.5 to guide you and your client to a decision regarding software acquisition/development. The most common candidates for prewritten software packages are accounting systems. If you are considering prototyping, be sure your client understands the process and the time commitment he or she is making.

Use Action Document 5.6 to plan and control your evaluation of alternatives activities. At the end of this phase, collect all relevant models, documents, and other materials, and use the cover sheet, Action Document 5.7, to submit your work as a progress report to your instructor.

References

1. *Bachman Data Analyst Reference Manual.* Cambridge, Mass.: Bachman Information Systems, 1988.

2. Amadio, W. *Systems Development: A Practical Approach.* Watsonville, Calif.: Mitchell Publishing, 1989.

3. Davenport, T. "The Case of the Soft Software Proposal." *Harvard Business Review* (May-June, 1989): pp. 12–24.

4. Gane, C., and T. Sarson. *Structured Systems Analysis Tools and Techniques.* New York: Improved System Technologies, 1977.

5. Gremillion, L., and P. Pyburn. "Breaking the Systems Development Bottleneck." *Harvard Business Review* (March-April 1983): pp. 130–137.

6. Keen, P. "Value Analysis: Justifying Decision Support Systems." *MIS Quarterly* Volume 5, Number 1 (March 1981): pp. 1–15.

7. Kozar, K. *Humanized Information Systems Analysis and Design.* New York: McGraw-Hill, 1989.

8. Kroenke, D., and K. Dolan *Business Computer Systems.* Watsonville, Calif.: Mitchell Publishing, 1990.

9. Prietula, M., and H. Simon. "The Experts in your Midst." *Harvard Business Review* (January-February 1989): pp. 120–124.

10. Weinberg, G. *Rethinking Systems Analysis and Design.* Boston, Mass.: Little, Brown and Company, 1985.

EVALUATION OF ALTERNATIVES DELIVERABLES

1. A leveled set of DFDs for the new processes specified in the Requirements Model
2. A list of the Requirements Model items that would benefit most from automation, including the specific form of the benefits, the value of the benefits, and the likelihood of achieving the benefits
3. A Design DFD for the automated portion of the new system
4. A System E-R Model
5. A completed Designer's Tradeoff Chart, evaluated for technical, operational, and economic feasibility
6. A decision regarding the method of software acquisition/development
7. A recommendation regarding the second go/no go decision of the systems development life cycle

ACTION DOCUMENT 5.1
**Deliverables for the Evaluation of
Alternatives Phase**

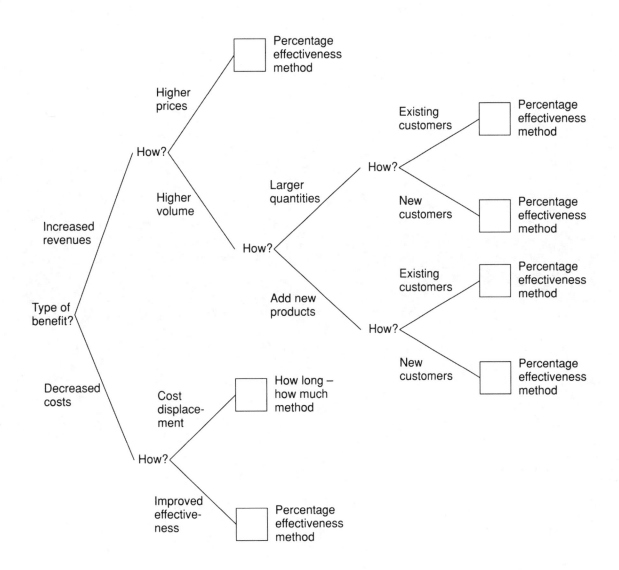

ACTION DOCUMENT 5.2
Decision tree for quantifying the benefits of automation

DESIGNER'S TRADEOFF CHART

Access
Direct access points on desks
Shared direct access points near desks
One shared direct access point
Access through intermediary

Flexibility of Output
Ad hoc reporting (selection of presentation and data)
Several predetermined presentations with selection of data
One predetermined presentation with selection of data
Several predetermined presentations with no selection of data
One predetermined presentation with no selection of data

Turnaround Time on Output
While you wait (seconds)
While you wait (minutes)
Come back later (hours)
Come back later (days)

Timeliness of Data
Up to the minute
One day old
One week old
One month old or more

System Responsibilities
Responsible for hardware and software
Responsible for hardware
Responsible for software
Responsible for neither hardware nor software

Data Responsibilities
Responsible for initial data conversion
Responsible for source documents
Responsible for data entry
Responsible for updating and purging
Responsible for backup and restore
Responsible for match with other company systems
Responsible for security and confidentiality

Learning
Everyone must learn everything
Someone must learn everything; everyone must learn something
No one need learn everything; everyone must learn something
Someone must learn something; others need learn nothing
No one need learn anything significant

ACTION DOCUMENT 5.3
The Designer's Tradeoff Chart

FEASIBILITY EVALUATION

Technical Feasibility

Is the specified technology available?

How many other organizations are using the specified technology? What has been their experience?

Is it practical for us to get involved in the specified technology?

Do we currently possess the specified technology?

Do we possess the technical expertise to use the specified technology? If we do not, can we acquire it in a reasonable way?

Operational Feasibility

Will some users have to work harder?

Will some users lose subordinates, authority, or responsibility?

Will some users lose freedom?

Will some users lose contact with other workers?

Will some users have to be trained?

Will some users lose the fun of their jobs?

Will some users lose earnings such as overtime?

Are there any threats to the status of some users?

Are there any threats to promotion for some users?

ACTION DOCUMENT 5.4
**Guides for evaluating technical and
operational feasibility**

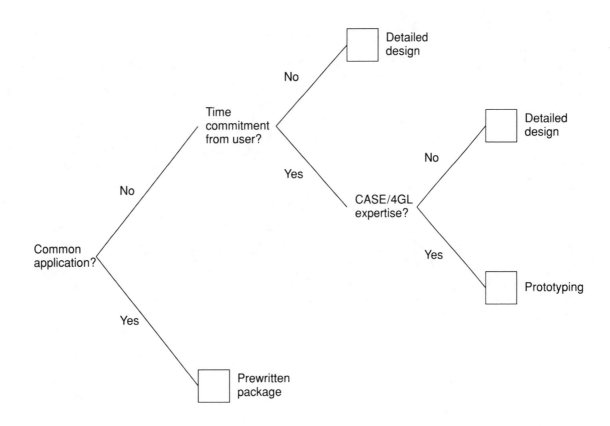

ACTION DOCUMENT 5.5
**Decision tree for software acquisition/
development**

Deliverable 1: Leveled set of DFDs for new processes

Task	User/Mgt People	IS People	Documents Needed	Documents Produced	Estimated Duration

Deliverable 2: Benefits of automation in the new system

Task	User/Mgt People	IS People	Documents Needed	Documents Produced	Estimated Duration

Deliverable 3: Design DFD for the automated portion of the new system

Task	User/Mgt People	IS People	Documents Needed	Documents Produced	Estimated Duration

**ACTION DOCUMENT 5.6
Tasks for each deliverable (page 1 of 3)**

Deliverable 4: System E-R Model

Task	User/Mgt People	IS People	Documents Needed	Documents Produced	Estimated Duration

Deliverable 5: Designer's Tradeoff Chart

Task	User/Mgt People	IS People	Documents Needed	Documents Produced	Estimated Duration

Deliverable 6: Software acquisition/development decision

Task	User/Mgt People	IS People	Documents Needed	Documents Produced	Estimated Duration

**ACTION DOCUMENT 5.6
Tasks for each deliverable (page 2 of 3)**

Deliverable 7: Recommendation for the go/no go decision

Task	User/Mgt People	IS People	Documents Needed	Documents Produced	Estimated Duration

ACTION DOCUMENT 5.6
Tasks for each deliverable (page 3 of 3)

Date _____

To _____

From _____

Re: Evaluation of alternatives

The following documents are included in this analysis:

☐ DFDs for new processes

☐ Benefits of automation

☐ Design DFD

☐ System E-R Model

☐ Designer's Tradeoff Chart

☐ Software acquisition/development decision

☐ Recommendation for go/no go decision

☐ Other _____
_____

☐ Other _____
_____

☐ Other _____
_____

The following activities were carried out during this analysis:

☐ Interviews with _____
_____

☐ Written exercises with _____
_____

☐ Other _____
_____

☐ Other _____
_____

☐ Other _____
_____

ACTION DOCUMENT 5.7
Cover sheet for evaluation of alternatives

The You Do It section provides guidelines, exercises, and action documents to help you and your client with the second go/no go decision for your project.

After completing this chapter you will have

1. learned how to develop a comprehensive set of project planning and control documents

2. learned how to combine these documents with the prior systems analysis and evaluation of alternatives to deliver an effective presentation to management regarding the second go/no go decision of the systems development life cycle

3. applied these tools and techniques to the second go/no go decision for your own project

HORATIO & CO. COST CONTROL SYSTEM

On the basis of his systems analysis and evaluation of alternatives, Sam Tilden decided to recommend continuation of the cost control system project. The go/no go decision to proceed to the Design New System Phase of the life cycle was the responsibility of the top managers at Horatio & Co., Frank Chapin and Dan Klockner. Sam arranged a meeting at which he would make a formal presentation concerning his recommendations to Chapin and Klockner. Pete Willard also attended this meeting.

Gaining Management Approval

Three days before his presentation, Sam distributed a packet of written material to Frank Chapin and Dan Klockner. The written material consisted of an executive summary of Sam and Pete's systems analysis, evaluation of alternatives, and recommendation to proceed to the next phase, along with supporting detail documents.

The written material for Sam's presentation to management is presented on the following pages.

Executive Summary

This project was undertaken in support of the company-wide objective to reduce costs by 10 percent. The project analysts were Sam Tilden, engineering department manager, and Pete Willard, consultant.

The project analysts propose a computer-based information system, referred to hereafter as the cost control system, for collecting and maintaining expense, budget, and engineers' professional development plan data.

Reports showing expenses by job, and reports showing actual expenses versus budget, will be available upon demand. Various inquiries regarding expenses will also be available, along with analyses of professional staff activities.

In addition to predefined reports and inquiries chosen from a menu, the project analysts recommend the capability and training to produce one-of-a-kind reports and inquiries to answer specific questions on demand.

The estimated benefits accruing from the cost control system are shown in Figure 6.1.

The project team estimates the development cost of the system to be $24,650, with a $3,000 per year ongoing management cost. The system can be operational in approximately 90 work days with an appropriate commitment from Horatio personnel and vendors. See Figure 6.2.

Capability	Benefit	Value ($/year)	% of Annual Dept. Budget	Likelihood
Job cost reports	Replace report preparer	18,000	0.7	certain
	Save 1 hour per day of each engineer's time	125,000	4.8	high
Monthly budgets	Eliminate 4% average cost overrun	104,000	4.0	even
Professional development plans	Avoid resignations in the engineering department	10,800 each	0.4	even
Reorganization of vendor base	Decrease cost of materials by 1%	16,000	0.6	uncertain

FIGURE 6.1
Estimated benefits of the cost control system

Participant	Role	Commitment over Next 90 Days
Sam Tilden	Chief user/designer	11 days
Betsy Klein	Chief programmer	20.5 days
Pete Willard	Consultant	8 days
Engineers	Users/designers	4.5 days
Accounting dept. programmer	Programmer	5 days
Data preparation service	Initial data prep	1 day

FIGURE 6.2
Personnel and vendor requirements

The cost control system database will be stored on the department's local area network (LAN) fileserver. Staff members will access the cost control system from microcomputers on their desks, or from shared workstations near their desks if they do not have or want a microcomputer on their desk.

The cost control system database will be integrated with the existing accounting system at Horatio & Co. As part of the cost control system development project, expense data entry programs in the accounting system will be modified to collect the new data required by the cost control system. Data transfer procedures between the accounting system minicomputer and the LAN upon which the cost control system runs will be developed. The initial records for the cost control system database will be gathered from the manual job cost ledger for the engineering department. With the development of the cost control system, the manual maintenance of the job cost ledger was discontinued.

The software for the cost control system will be developed through prototyping. Prototyping is an iterative process that relies upon modern software tools to produce a working system that satisfies the client's basic requirements early in the development process. The client experiments with the working prototype and provides feedback to the developer, who uses this feedback to refine the prototype. This process continues until the client is satisfied with the system. Although it is impossible to predict the number of iterations with certainty, the project team estimates four iterations of the prototyping process for this project.

R.T.C. LIBRARY, LETTERKENNY

Business Objective

Maintain the current level of profit in the engineering department by

    decreasing clerical costs

    identifying cost overruns within 30 days

    decreasing the cost of materials

    decreasing turnover

Business Tactics

1. Eliminate manual preparation of job cost reports
2. Institute a monthly budgeting system by job number and general ledger account, to replace the current annual system by general ledger account only
3. Reorganize the vendor base for higher volumes with fewer vendors
4. Institute professional development plans for engineering personnel

System Objective

Reports and inquiries on demand, including:

    Budget versus Actual Reports by job number and general ledger account on a monthly basis

    Job Cost Summary Reports and Job Cost Detail reports

    Detail inquiry by source of expense or vendor

FIGURE 6.3
Business objectives and tactics for the project

Supporting Detail

This analysis was undertaken to study the merits of an information systems solution to the problem of how to decrease costs in the engineering department by 10 percent. Business tactics to support this objective were uncovered in an earlier phase of this project; the information system proposed here would support those tactics. A statement of business objectives and tactics appears in Figure 6.3.

The choices made by the project analysts for the cost control system are presented in Figure 6.4. Choices marked with an X represent options chosen for the new system; choices marked NOW represent characteristics of the current manual system.

```
                    DESIGNER'S TRADEOFF CHART

                Access
X               Direct access points on desks
X               Shared direct access points near desks
      NOW       One shared direct access point
      NOW       Access through intermediary

                Flexibility of Output
X     NOW       Ad hoc reporting (selection of presentation and data)
X               Several predetermined presentations with selection of data
                One predetermined presentation with selection of data
                Several predetermined presentations with no selection of data
                One predetermined presentation with no selection of data

                Turnaround Time on Output
X               While you wait (seconds)
                While you wait (minutes)
                Come back later (hours)
      NOW       Come back later (days)

                Timeliness of Data
                Up to the minute
X     NOW       One day old
                One week old
      NOW       One month old or more

                System Responsibilities
X               Responsible for hardware and software
                Responsible for hardware
                Responsible for software
      NOW       Responsible for neither hardware nor software

                Data Responsibilities
X               Responsible for initial data conversion
X     NOW       Responsible for source documents
X     NOW       Responsible for data entry
X               Responsible for updating and purging
X               Responsible for backup and restore
X               Responsible for match with other company systems
X     NOW       Responsible for security and confidentiality

                Learning
                Everyone must learn everything
X               Someone must learn everything; everyone must learn something
                No one need learn everything; everyone must learn something
                Someone must learn something; others need learn nothing
      NOW       No one need learn anything significant
```

FIGURE 6.4
**Designer's Tradeoff Chart for the cost control
system**

A detailed schedule of direct costs, consisting of staff time and expenses for materials and services, is shown in Figure 6.5. Staff time expenses are estimated from payroll data. The estimated cost is the daily or hourly cost (including fringe benefits) for each participant, multiplied by the estimated number of days or hours required for the project. Estimated expenses for materials and services are based on quotes or bids from the vendors.

Figure 6.6 shows the assignment of development and implementation tasks to staff members and vendors. The amount of time required to perform the tasks is also listed. These estimates do not take into account the participants' other duties; they represent how long the tasks will take if the participants work on these tasks exclusively.

The development and implementation tasks are presented in Figure 6.7 as a network that is read from left to right. Each solid line represents a development and implementation task. Each circle (node) represents the completion of the task(s) leading into it and the beginning of the task(s) emanating from it.

```
                        DIRECT COSTS

Additional network station                $2,000
Minicomputer to PC line                   negligible
dBASE III PLUS network version            1,500
Software development (Sam and Betsy)      4,000
System manager                            3,000 per year
Minicomputer data entry programming       2,500
Minicomputer to PC communication software   250
Integrate manual and automated procedures   400
Conversion of job cost ledger entries       900
Preparation of monthly budgets              600
Training (menu system)                      500
Training (ad hoc reporting)               5,000
Software development (Pete)               4.000

Total:  New system startup               $24.650

Ongoing                                   $3,000 per year
This analysis                             $4,000
```

FIGURE 6.5

**Direct costs for the development and
implementation of the cost control system**

DEVELOPMENT AND IMPLEMENTATION TASK ASSIGNMENTS

A. Prototype training;   Pete 2 days
   build initial prototype   Betsy 2 days
B. Install network station   Betsy 2 days
   and network dBASE III PLUS
C. Test prototype   Sam 2 days each for
                                 versions 1, 2, 3, 4
                                 Engineers 2 days, version 2
                                 Betsy 2 days, version 4
D. Revise prototype   Pete 2 days, version 1
                                 Betsy 2 days each for
                                 versions 1, 2, 3, 4
E. Develop ad hoc   Pete 2 days
   reporting training
F. Integrate automated and   Sam 1 day
   manual procedures   Betsy 1 day
G. Develop monthly budgets   Sam 2 days
H. Standardize and proof job   Pete 2 days
   cost ledger entries   Betsy 2 days
I. Ad hoc reporting training   Engineers 2.5 days in 5 weeks
                                 Betsy 3.5 days in 5 weeks
                                 (includes preparation)
J. Key job cost ledger   Data prep service 1 day
   entries to diskette
K. Develop accounting system   Accounting programmer, 5 days
   data entry program
L. Test data entry program   Betsy 2 days
M. Build and test file   Betsy 1 day
   transfers

FIGURE 6.6
Development and implementation tasks

The duration of each task is shown in days on the network. These figures represent the actual time required to complete the tasks, taking into account the participants' other duties. It is assumed that each participant will commit no more than one-third of his or her time to any cost control system task.

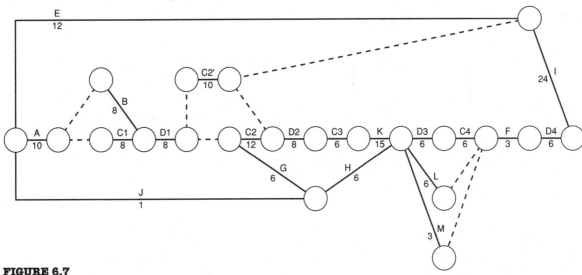

FIGURE 6.7
**Network model for the development and
implementation tasks of the cost control system**

The dashed lines are used for drawing convenience; their duration is always zero. They are used primarily when a task has more than one predecessor.

The network shows, at a glance, the critical role of the prototype development tasks, C1 through C4 and D1 through D4. Eighty-eight days are allocated to these tasks, which must be completed on time or else the entire project is delayed. Training, accounting system programming, and the like will occur around these critical path activities. The progress and quality of the project will be monitored and controlled through weekly review meetings of the project team.

Personnel commitments for the development and implementation tasks are shown in Figure 6.8. Because she has to complete several tasks in the six-day period from day 67 through day 73, Betsy Klein's commitment to the cost control system exceeds the one-third maximum during these six days. This is the only time the one-third maximum is exceeded.

Management's Reaction

Frank Chapin and Dan Klockner both agreed to support the cost control system project through the Design New System Phase. Frank Chapin concentrated on Sam's executive summary. He glanced over the supporting detail

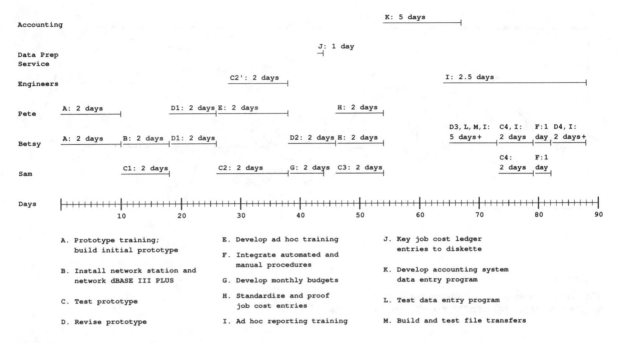

FIGURE 6.8

Gantt chart for development and implementation tasks of cost control system

and said that it looked all right. Dan Klockner examined the supporting detail more closely and was also satisfied. Sam referred to the supporting detail to answer several questions from both Chapin and Klockner.

Mr. Chapin was concerned with how long it would take to achieve the benefits identified in Sam's analysis. After some discussion, the group agreed upon a two-year time frame, with the bulk of the benefits coming in the second year.

Mr. Chapin was especially pleased to note the low risk of the project. Even if the company only achieved the benefit of replacing the report preparer, the system would pay for itself in about a year and a half.

Dan Klockner raised the idea of sharing the benefits of the cost control system with other departments in the firm. He suggested that Mr. Chapin introduce the engineering department's project to the rest of the firm as a pilot project for a company-wide cost control system. If it was successful, then other departments could adopt it.

Mr. Chapin promised to encourage other department managers to follow the progress of the engineering department's system.

THE WHAT, HOW, AND WHY

The deliverables of this chapter are aimed at obtaining management approval for the second go/no go decision of the project, namely, continuing the project into the Design New System Phase of the systems development life cycle. If the continuation is approved, then these deliverables are also used to monitor and control the tasks that follow.

For the second go/no go decision, management is concerned with

1. how much the proposed work will cost
2. how long the proposed work will take
3. what resources are needed to complete the proposed work
4. whether the expected benefits will exceed these costs

Since the commitment for the second go/no go decision is large, the analysis is more detailed and specific than that presented for the first go/no go decision [6].

The project management (planning and control) techniques presented in this chapter are not confined to gaining management approval or to the Design New System Phase of the life cycle. Depending on the size of the project, every phase of the life cycle might be planned and controlled with these techniques. On a very large project, these techniques might be applied to the completion of a single deliverable. In addition, the project as a whole, that is, all phases combined, might also be managed along these lines.

The Project Management Cycle

A project is born when a problem has been recognized and accepted, solution objectives have been set, and resources (people, time, equipment, money) have been committed.

The **project management cycle** begins with the identification of the tasks that must be performed in order to achieve the objectives of the project. Once the tasks have been identified, they must be scheduled and assigned to workers and managers, all within the bounds of the approved budget. In addition, standards for quality and performance must be established.

Once the tasks begin, the managers monitor activities and use the standards, schedule, and budget to control the quality, progress, and cost of the project. Throughout the project, project managers also compare finished

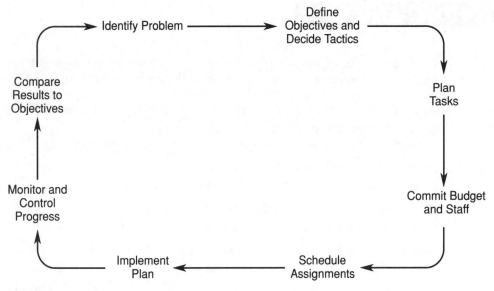

FIGURE 6.9
The project management cycle

products and works-in-process to the original problem identification and solution objectives, which serve as high-level standards for the project.

Figure 6.9 [7] summarizes the project management cycle. Figure 6.9 depicts the cycle as a linear sequence; in actuality, phases of the cycle will often occur simultaneously, along with a fair amount of jumping ahead and looping back, depending upon circumstances and results.

In the early stages of the project management cycle, the project manager is concerned with identifying the tasks required to achieve the objectives of the project and with identifying the resources needed to carry out the tasks. The needed resources usually involve people, equipment, material, and money. The early phase of the project management cycle ends with a commitment of the needed resources from the organization. This commitment usually takes the form of an approved budget.

In the middle stages of the project management cycle, the project manager is concerned with getting the project under way. He or she determines how the committed resources will be used to accomplish the tasks identified earlier. Depending upon the results of this phase, some of the planning and budgeting activities of the early phases may be repeated. The middle phase of the project management cycle ends with a schedule of tasks and personnel assignments.

In the later stages of the project management cycle, the project manager is concerned with controlling the project. Tasks are reviewed as they are performed. Task evaluation usually involves assessing how well the task supports the objectives of the project, whether the task was completed on time, and what resources were used to complete the task. Task evaluation could lead to changes in the project plan, budget, schedule, or staffing.

Unfortunately, many project managers get to the later stages of the project management cycle and discover that the project has moved far away from the original objectives [3]. At this point, the manager must choose one of several difficult options. He or she can

sign off on the project and risk delivering a system that nobody uses

abandon the project and begin again

redo the project keeping a closer eye on the objectives proposed early in the process

The remainder of this section is devoted to the concepts underlying the project management cycle. You will see that the cost control system figures presented in the previous section represent specific implementations of these concepts.

These concepts are viable for all types of projects and organizations. On large projects, it is essential to develop planning and control details into tables and charts like those presented earlier in this chapter. On smaller projects or smaller parts of large projects, these concepts might be applied in a less formal way.

Tasks

Our definition of **task** is a unit of work for which and from which estimates are made, schedules are set, responsibilities are assigned, and performance is measured [7]. Tasks are the building blocks that comprise a systems development project. Tasks also form the foundation of the project management cycle. The project manager plans, organizes, and controls his or her project through its tasks.

In breaking the work of a project down into tasks, the project manager focuses on deliverables. To develop the project tasks, the manager combines the specifications of the Designer's Tradeoff Chart, Figure 6.4, and the direct costs for the project, Figure 6.5, with his or her general knowledge of business and system functions.

The deliverables of the development and implementation tasks of the cost control system project are the hardware, software, data, procedures, and personnel components of the finished, working system. Analyzing the hardware deliverables of the cost control system reveals the need for an additional work station on the local area network upon which the cost control system will run. It also reveals a need to establish a link between the accounting system minicomputer and the network file server.

Analyzing the data deliverables shows the need to convert the manual Job Cost ledger to electronic media compatible with the cost control system hardware and software. It also shows the need to prepare monthly budget figures.

Analyzing software, procedures, and personnel deliverables is done in the same way. The process of developing tasks from deliverables continues until the project manager has a list of work units that accomplish the objectives of the project and that can be estimated, budgeted, staffed, and scheduled. Figure 6.10 shows the complete list of tasks for the development and implementation phases of the cost control system project.

Estimating the personnel, time, materials, equipment, and monetary resources required to complete a set of tasks is similar to the how long–how much analysis for quantifying system benefits. Project managers also rely upon comparisons between current tasks and tasks they have managed in the

---

DEVELOPMENT AND IMPLEMENTATION TASKS

A. Prototype training; build initial prototype

B. Install network station and network dBASE III PLUS

C. Test prototype (4 times)

D. Revise prototype (4 times)

E. Develop ad hoc reporting training

F. Integrate automated and manual procedures

G. Develop monthly budgets

H. Standardize and proof job cost ledger entries

I. Ad hoc reporting training

J. Key job cost ledger entries to diskette

K. Develop accounting system data entry program

L. Test data entry program

M. Build and test file transfers

FIGURE 6.10
Development and implementation tasks

past (analogical reasoning). Of course, emergencies and unforeseen circumstances can never be predicted, so any estimates should be evaluated with the proviso "assuming all goes well."

Scheduling

If management approves the task and resource estimates for a project, then a budget and a staff is usually assigned. At this point in the project management cycle, the project manager turns his or her attention to scheduling the project tasks.

Developing the list presented in Figure 6.10 into a realistic project schedule requires several modifications. Figure 6.11 shows the tasks of Figure 6.10 in more detail. Tasks C, Test prototype, and D, Revise prototype, must be repeated four times throughout the project; they are now shown as tasks C1 through C4 and D1 through D4, respectively. Task C2, Test prototype 2, is further broken down into two tasks, task C2 being the testing done by Sam Tilden and task C2' being the testing done independently by the engineers.

Figure 6.11 also shows time allotments that allow for the fact that the participants cannot work on these tasks exclusively. (In Figure 6.6, Task A calls for 2 days of time from Pete and Betsy. In Figure 6.11, Task A is allotted 10 days, indicating that Pete and Betsy will devote about one-third of their time to Task A over the 10-day period.) The duration figures presented in Figure 6.11 represent a combination of the estimates of time required to complete the tasks and the estimates of the percentage of their time that the participants can devote to them.

The final addition to Figure 6.10 is the column in Figure 6.11 marked "Predecessors." A task's predecessors are the tasks that must be completed before the given task can begin.

Sometimes a task's predecessors are obvious. Task I, Ad hoc reporting training, cannot begin before task E, Develop ad hoc reporting training, is complete. At other times, the determination of predecessors depends upon circumstances; it rests, finally, with the judgment of the project manager. The decision to develop monthly budgets, task G, after the first revision of the prototype, task D1, is an example of such a determination; so is the decision to precede D3 with H and K.

When a project schedule is developed to the point of detailed tasks and predecessors, a graphical presentation is helpful. Figure 6.7 represents the information of Figure 6.11 organized into a network.

The network presented in Figure 6.7 plays an important role in gaining management approval. In combination with the budget presented in Figure 6.5, the network summarizes the details of planning, budgeting and staffing,

DETAILED DEVELOPMENT AND IMPLEMENTATION TASKS WITH PREDECESSORS

Task		Duration	Predecessors
A.	Prototype training; build initial prototype	10	—
B.	Install network station and network dBASE III PLUS	8	A
C1.	Test prototype 1	8	A
D1.	Revise prototype 1	8	C1, B
C2.	Test prototype 2 (Sam)	12	D1
C2'.	Test prototype 2 (Engineers)	10	D1
D2.	Revise prototype 2	8	C2, C2'
C3.	Test prototype 3	6	D2
K.	Develop accounting system data entry program	15	C3
D3.	Revise prototype 3	6	H, K
C4.	Test prototype 4	6	D3
F.	Integrate automated and manual procedures	3	C4, L, M
D4.	Revise prototype 4	6	F
J.	Key Job Cost ledger entries to diskette	1	—
G.	Develop monthly budgets	6	D1
H.	Standardize and proof Job Cost ledger entries	6	G
L.	Test data entry program	6	K
M.	Build and test file transfers	3	K
E.	Develop ad hoc reporting training	12	—
I.	Ad hoc reporting training	24	E

FIGURE 6.11
**Detailed development and implementation
tasks with predecessors**

and scheduling into a simple diagram that answers key management questions.

Critical Path Analysis

The central role of the prototyping process can be seen in Figure 6.7. Sometimes, however, the set of tasks that play this central role is not obvious from the network model of the project. In such cases, the identification of this crucial set of tasks is accomplished through a mathematical analysis of the network.

CRITICAL PATH CALCULATIONS

Path	Total Duration
E-I	36
A-B-D1-C2'-I	60
A-B-D1-C2'-D2-C3-K-D3-C4-F-D4	78
A-B-D1-C2'-G-H-M-F-D4	60
A-B-D1-C2'-G-H-L-F-D4	63
A-B-D1-C2'-G-H-D3-C4-F-D4	69
A-B-D1-C2-D2-C3-K-D3-C4-F-D4	88
A-B-D1-C2-G-H-M-F-D4	62
A-B-D1-C2-G-H-L-F-D4	65
A-B-D1-C2-G-H-D3-C4-F-D4	71
A-C1-D1-C2'-I	60
A-C1-D1-C2'-D2-C3-K-D3-C4-F-D4	86
A-C1-D1-C2'-G-H-M-F-D4	60
A-C1-D1-C2'-G-H-L-F-D4	63
A-C1-D1-C2'-G-H-D3-C4-F-D4	69
A-C1-D1-C2-D2-C3-K-D3-C4-F-D4	88
A-C1-D1-C2-G-H-M-F-D4	62
A-C1-D1-C2-G-H-L-F-D4	65
A-C1-D1-C2-G-H-D3-C4-F-D4	71
J-H-M-F-D4	19
J-H-L-F-D4	22
J-H-D3-C4-F-D4	28

FIGURE 6.12
Critical path calculations

In Figure 6.7, the prototyping tasks lie along the **critical path** of the network. The critical path is the set of tasks that must be completed on time or else the entire project is delayed [8]. The critical path is found by calculating the total duration of each path (that is, each sequence of tasks) through the network. The critical path is the longest one.

Figure 6.12 shows the critical path calculations for the cost control system. Paths A-B-D1-C2-D2-C3-K-D3-C4-F-D4 and A-C1-D1-C2-D2-C3-K-D3-C4-F-D4 are seen to be tied for the critical path, each requiring a total duration of 88 days. The tasks in these paths cannot be delayed without delaying the entire project. This indicates that the development and implementation of the cost control system will require 88 workdays, assuming no delays. Assuming a 5-day work week, the project will take approximately 18 weeks.

After identifying the tasks of the critical path, the analysis can be taken further by calculating the **slack** of each task. Slack is defined as the difference between the latest completion time and the earliest completion time for the task [8].

To calculate the earliest possible completion times, work across the network from left to right, adding the durations. The earliest completion time for A is 10 days; the earliest time for B is $10 + 8 = 18$ days; for C1 it is $10 + 8 = 18$ days; for D1 it is $10 + 8 + 8 = 26$ days, and so on.

To calculate latest completion times, work across the network from right to left, subtracting the durations from the total. (How late can this task be completed without delaying the project?) For D4, the latest completion time is 88 days; for I it is 88 days; for F it is $88 - 6 = 82$ days; for C4 it is $82 - 3 = 79$ days; for L and M it is 79 days, and so on.

The earliest and latest completion times and the slack for each task are shown in Figure 6.13. Tasks J, E, and I have the most slack. Naturally, the tasks on the critical path have zero slack.

Gantt Chart

The data presented in Figures 6.10 through 6.13 provides insight into the relationships among the tasks of the project, and provides a means to control the project schedule and analyze the implications of variations in the schedule. These insights can be combined with the personnel data presented in Figure 6.6 to produce a schedule of assignments, Figure 6.8.

The graphical model presented in Figure 6.8 is called a **Gantt chart.** By drawing a vertical line through any given day on the horizontal time axis, you can see what tasks should be completed and what tasks should be active on that day. For example, a vertical line drawn at day 24 of the cost control system project indicates that Pete and Betsy should be working on task D1, that they should have completed tasks A and B by that date, and that Sam should have completed task C1.

It is common to post a Gantt chart for a project on a wall and to mark the tasks on the chart as they are completed. In this way, the project participants can see at a glance how the project is progressing compared to the predetermined schedule. If a project falls behind schedule or a participant becomes unavailable, an analysis similar to that presented for the critical path is done. This analysis helps to determine the implications of the delay and to decide on alterations to the schedule. These alterations should be reflected in an updated Gantt chart.

	SLACK CALCULATIONS		
Task	Earliest Completion Time (days from start)	Latest Completion Time (days from start)	Slack (days)
A	10	10	0
B	18	18	0
C1	18	18	0
D1	26	26	0
C2	38	38	0
C2'	36	38	2
D2	46	46	0
C3	52	52	0
K	67	67	0
D3	73	73	0
C4	76	76	0
F	77	77	0
D4	80	80	0
J	1	61	60
G	44	61	15
H	50	67	17
L	73	79	6
M	70	79	9
E	12	64	52
I	36	88	52

FIGURE 6.13
Slack calculations for the cost control system

Financial Analysis of the Decision

Sam Tilden decided to support the decision to proceed to the Design New System Phase because the **payback period** was less than 2 years. Even if the system achieved only the $18,000-a-year benefit of reassigning the manual report preparer to other productive work, the benefit would exceed the costs in less than two years.

Some decision makers use other methods of evaluating costs versus benefits. Figure 6.14 shows a **present value analysis** prepared with a spreadsheet program. The analysis assumes a six-year useful life for the system. Assuming a 10 percent annual rate of interest, $68,234.16 would have to be deposited now to generate the stream of $18,000 benefits shown. This is the present value of the benefits. To pay the stream of costs shown in Figure 6.6, $39,022.36 would have to be deposited now. This is the present value of the costs. The difference shows the present value of the system. For a stream of costs worth $39,022.36, we get a system worth $68,234.16, assuming a 10 percent annual rate of interest.

Some decision makers like to use the internal rate of return method of evaluation. This method finds the annual interest rate at which the present values for the benefits stream and the cost stream are identical. There is no formula for calculating it. The rate is usually determined through an interactive computer program that allows the decision maker to hunt for it by entering interest rate values and observing the present values of benefits and costs that result. The spreadsheet template shown in Figure 6.14 can be used to

RETURN ON INVESTMENT/PRESENT VALUE ANALYZER

Enter annual interest rate, yearly benefits and costs
Observe present values of benefits and costs, difference, and direction of internal rate of return

Annual interest rate

10.00

	Year 1	Year 2	Year 3	Year 4	Year 5	Year 6
Present Value			Benefits			
68234.16	0.00	18000.00	18000.00	18000.00	18000.00	18000.00
			Costs			
39022.36	27650.00	3000.00	3000.00	3000.00	3000.00	3000.00
Difference						
29211.80	Internal rate of return is HIGHER than current annual rate					

FIGURE 6.14
Present value analysis

hunt for the internal rate of return. From Figure 6.14 we know that the internal rate of return is higher than 10 percent, the annual interest rate that we assumed. By entering higher and higher values for the annual interest rate, we arrive at Figure 6.15, which shows that the present values of costs and benefits will balance at an annual interest rate of 46.10 percent. In other words, the cost control system's costs will bring a 46.10 percent return on investment if the assumed stream of $18,000 benefits is achieved. Note that it is usually not possible to manipulate the "Difference" figure down to exactly zero.

The spreadsheet template used for these figures is included on the Horatio & Co. Cost Control System diskette that accompanies this book. The file name is FIG6_14.WK1.

Reporting and Control

Once the work of the project gets under way, the project manager is concerned with monitoring and controlling progress (see Figure 6.9). The man-

---

RETURN ON INVESTMENT/PRESENT VALUE ANALYZER

Enter annual interest rate, yearly benefits and costs

Observe present values of benefits and costs, difference, and direction of internal rate of return

Annual interest rate

46.10

	Year 1	Year 2	Year 3	Year 4	Year 5	Year 6
Present Value			**Benefits**			
33179.84	0.00	18000.00	18000.00	18000.00	18000.00	18000.00
			Costs			
33179.97	27650.00	3000.00	3000.00	3000.00	3000.00	3000.00

Difference

−0.13 Internal rate of return is LOWER than current annual rate

FIGURE 6.15
Internal rate of return analysis

ager is concerned with identifying problems and deviations from the project plan before they cause irreparable damage (monitoring). If these problems and deviations occur, the project plan or its implementation must be revised (controlling).

The primary means of monitoring the project is through feedback from the project team. Each manager acquires feedback in a way that suits his or her management style and the circumstances of the project. Some feedback options [9,4] are:

1. Detailed logs of time spent and tasks accomplished by each member of the project team (management analysis of the logs is usually done by computer)
2. Regular written reports on the project's status (highlight progress, cite problems, suggest solutions)
3. Regular project team reviews
4. The "grapevine" and other informal feedback mechanisms

Option 1 and, to a lesser extent, option 2 are concerned primarily with the fulfillment of the project budget and schedule—an important project management concern. Regular Budget versus Actual Reports and Cost Estimate to Complete Reports advise the manager of what resources were committed and spent to date, and predict whether or not the deliverables will be completed on time and within budget [1].

Option 3 is concerned with the quality of the project deliverables. The **team review** is a "major and formal checkpoint in a project at which you take stock of the work done to date, evaluate its quality and relevance to the project objectives, and set an appropriate strategy for the next stage of the project" [9].

No matter how sophisticated the network diagrams and computer analysis of time logs, there is no substitute for regular project team review meetings. At these meetings, the clients and the developers come face-to-face to review the project. This is their best opportunity to discuss problems, concerns, and differences.

YOU DO IT

Use the cost control system material, the What, How, and Why section material, and the action documents of this section to guide your efforts in developing the materials to support your second go/no go decision.

If your project involves a "live client," you will evaluate alternatives with your client. If you are using the accompanying written case project

(Chapter 10), you will evaluate alternatives according to the directions provided by your instructor.

Action Documents for Project Planning and Control and Gaining Management Approval

The deliverables for the second go/no go decision are summarized in Action Document 6.1. An Action Document for planning and scheduling these tasks and identifying the necessary inputs and outputs appears at the end of this section.

Obtaining Management Approval

Action Document 6.2 will help you prepare for the formal presentation to management regarding the second go/no go decision. Before you use it, reread Chapter 3 to refresh your memory of effective communication and creative problem-solving concepts.

Team Reviews

The content of a project team review meeting will vary depending upon the project and the stage of progress. Meetings early in the project management cycle will be formative; objectives and solutions will still be evolving, and some budgeting, staffing, and scheduling uncertainties will be unavoidable. Meetings later in the project management cycle will be better able to review progress in the strict sense of the word. An agenda for a successful project team review meeting is presented in Action Document 6.3.

Use Action Document 6.4 to plan and control your project planning and control and gaining management approval activities. At the end of this work, collect all relevant documents and other materials, and use the cover sheet, Action Document 6.5, to submit your work as a progress report to your instructor.

References

1. Adams, J., S. Barndt, and M. Martin. *Managing by Project Management.* Dayton, Ohio: Universal Technology Corp., 1979.

2. Amadio, W. *Systems Development: A Practical Approach.* Watsonville, Calif.: Mitchell Publishing, 1989.

3. DeMarco, T. *Controlling Software Projects*. New York: Yourdon Press, 1982.

4. Hetzel, W. and D. Adams. *Computer Information Systems Development: Principles and Case Study*. Cincinnati: South-Western Publishing Co., 1985.

5. Jenkins, A. M. "Prototyping: A Methodology for the Design and Development of Application Systems." *Spectrum* Volume 2, Number 2 (April 1985): pp. 1–8.

6. Keen, P. "Value Analysis: Justifying Decision Support Systems" *MIS Quarterly* Volume 5, Number 1 (March 1981): pp. 1–15.

7. Madden, Madden, and Associates. *Project Management*. Washington, D.C.: U.S. Office of Personnel Management, Management Sciences Training Center, 1982.

8. McClain, J. and L. Thomas. *Operations Management*. Englewood Cliffs, N.J.: Prentice-Hall, 1985.

9. Page-Jones, M. *Practical Project Management*. New York: Dorset House Publishing Co., 1985.

SECOND GO/NO GO DECISION DELIVERABLES

1.   Assignment of tasks to personnel and estimation of raw time requirements
2.   Budget of direct costs
3.   Financial analysis of costs and benefits
4.   List of detailed tasks with predecessors and actual time to complete
5.   Network diagram of detailed tasks
6.   Critical path and slack calculations
7.   Gantt chart
8.   Feedback mechanisms
9.   Presentation to management, consisting of an executive summary and supporting detail

ACTION DOCUMENT 6.1
**Deliverables for the second go/no go
decision**

PRESENTATION TO MANAGEMENT CHECKLIST

1. The nine Ws.
2. Collect background information.
3. Prepare an executive summary, cover letter, and agenda for presentation.
4. Decide how to record and address audience response.
5. Prepare spreadsheets and any other necessary visual aids.
6. Choose a date, time, and place.
7. Notify participants.
8. Distribute the executive summary, cover letter, and agenda to participants.

ACTION DOCUMENT 6.2
**Preparing for the presentation to
management**

AGENDA

1. Review the project objectives.
2. Judge the suitability of the chosen solutions.
3. Judge the success of the project, to date, in implementing the chosen solutions.
4. Evaluate expenditures, to date, in terms of budget and schedule.
5. Agree upon corrective actions, if necessary.
6. Reaffirm commitment to the project.

ACTION DOCUMENT 6.3
**Agenda for a successful project team
review meeting**

Deliverable 1: Task assignments and raw time requirements

Task	User/Mgt People	IS People	Documents Needed	Documents Produced	Estimated Duration

Deliverable 2: Budget of direct costs

Task	User/Mgt People	IS People	Documents Needed	Documents Produced	Estimated Duration

Deliverable 3: Financial analysis of benefits and costs

Task	User/Mgt People	IS People	Documents Needed	Documents Produced	Estimated Duration

ACTION DOCUMENT 6.4
Tasks for each deliverable (page 1 of 3)

Deliverable 4: Detailed tasks with predecessors and actual times

Task	User/Mgt People	IS People	Documents Needed	Documents Produced	Estimated Duration

Deliverable 5: Network diagram

Task	User/Mgt People	IS People	Documents Needed	Documents Produced	Estimated Duration

Deliverable 6: Critical path and slack calculations

Task	User/Mgt People	IS People	Documents Needed	Documents Produced	Estimated Duration

**ACTION DOCUMENT 6.4
Tasks for each deliverable (page 2 of 3)**

Deliverable 7: Gantt chart

Task	User/Mgt People	IS People	Documents Needed	Documents Produced	Estimated Duration

Deliverable 8: Feedback mechanisms

Task	User/Mgt People	IS People	Documents Needed	Documents Produced	Estimated Duration

Deliverable 9: Presentation to management

Task	User/Mgt People	IS People	Documents Needed	Documents Produced	Estimated Duration

**ACTION DOCUMENT 6.4
Tasks for each deliverable (page 3 of 3)**

Date _____

To _____

From _____

Re: Second go/no go decision

The following documents are included in this analysis:

☐   Task assignments and raw time requirements

☐   Budget of direct costs

☐   Financial analysis of benefits and costs

☐   Detailed tasks with predecessors and actual times

☐   Network diagram

☐   Critical path and slack calculations

☐   Gantt chart

☐   Feedback mechanisms

☐   Presentation to management

☐   Other _____

_____

☐   Other _____

_____

☐   Other _____

_____

The following activities were carried out during this analysis:

☐   Interviews with _____

_____

☐   Written exercises with _____

_____

☐   Other _____

_____

☐   Other _____

_____

☐   Other _____

_____

**ACTION DOCUMENT 6.5
Cover sheet for second go/no go decision**

CHAPTER 7

The Design New System Phase

If the second go/no go decision of a systems development project is positive, the project proceeds to the Design New System Phase of the life cycle. This chapter concerns the tools and techniques of new system design that are applied in that phase.

New system design involves all five components of a computer-based information system: hardware, software, data, procedures, and personnel. Early decisions, made during the Evaluation of Alternatives Phase of the life cycle, provide the framework within which the design is carried out.

The Horatio & Co. section of this chapter discusses Sam, Betsy, and Pete's design of the first prototype of the cost control system. Because the project team chose to develop software instead of buy it, their design environment for all five components of the new system is more flexible. Because they chose prototyping instead of the detailed design method of development, they can afford to let the details of the entire design evolve throughout the software development process.

The What, How, and Why section of this chapter provides detailed explanations of how to develop the deliverables presented in the previous section. The concepts of hardware, procedures, and personnel design apply to all projects, regardless of the software development method. The concepts of database and software design apply in varying degrees of detail, depending upon the software development method.

If software is purchased, very little database and software design is done. If prototyping is used to develop software, a rough design is implemented quickly and refined through hands-on testing. If the detailed design method of software development is chosen, then all design details are confirmed and frozen before any programming begins.

The final section, You Do It, provides guidelines, exercises, and action documents to help you design a new system for your project.

After completing this chapter you will have

1. understood the tools and techniques used in designing the hardware, software, data, procedures, and personnel components of a new system

2. applied these tools and techniques to the design of a new system for your project

HORATIO & CO. COST CONTROL SYSTEM

Although many other people were involved, Sam Tilden was the primary designer of the cost control system. Betsy Klein was the system builder, and Pete Willard acted as consultant. As the project progressed, Pete's role diminished as planned.

Another important player in the design and development of the new cost control system was the manager of the accounting department, Ed Henderson. The project team kept in touch with Ed from the very beginning of their work because much of the data for the cost control system was already being maintained by the central accounting system. Working closely with Ed would help avoid duplication of effort and guarantee a smooth interface between the two systems.

Designing Hardware, Procedures, and Personnel

Sam and Pete considered a computer-based information system to be made up of five components: hardware, software, data, procedures, and personnel [3]. Once they had approval to proceed to the Design New System Phase of the life cycle, Sam and Pete turned their attention to hardware, procedures, and personnel. The final Designer's Tradeoff Chart, Figure 5.6, served as a guide to the design of these three components.

For hardware, Sam and Pete considered the specifications of the Access, Flexibility of Output, Turnaround Time on Output, and Timeliness of Data sections of the Tradeoff Chart. The Flexibility of Output and Timeliness of Data specifications dictated a hardware configuration of workstations with free access by engineering department personnel. The Access section of the chart told Sam and Pete how many individual and group stations were needed. The Turnaround Time on Output also told how many stations would be needed, because turnaround time is naturally affected by time spent waiting for a station. Turnaround Time on Output also dictated the speed of processing on the local area network.

Personnel design choices are made by reviewing System Responsibilities through Learning and then looping back through the Output sections of the Tradeoff Chart. Most of the responsibilities for system operation and management were assigned to Betsy Klein, Sam's administrative assistant. Betsy agreed to undertake these new responsibilities after negotiating a reduction of her current responsibilities.

Design choices about procedures were made by reviewing the Timeliness of Data and Data Responsibilities specifications of the final Tradeoff Chart. The specification of one-day-old data dictates daily data entry procedures. Other procedures were specified for updating and purging, backup and restore, match with other company systems, and security and confidentiality.

Database Design

The Design DFD, Figure 5.3, that Pete developed for the automated portion of the new system contained three data stores: EXPENSES, BUDGETS, and PLANS. Pete and Sam developed one file to represent EXPENSES in the database and two files to represent BUDGETS. They decided to maintain PLANS manually, so no files were included in the data base to represent that data store.

Pete called the file representing the EXPENSES data store by the name EXPENSES. He called the files representing the BUDGETS data store by the names ID and BUDGET. The contents of EXPENSES, ID, and BUDGET are shown in Figures 7.1, 7.2, and 7.3.

Database Access Paths

Access paths represent the ways in which a system's programs access the data in the system's files. The **unique identification key** is the component or combination of components that identifies each record in a file uniquely. The unique identification key is always listed as an access path for each file in the database.

Report and inquiry sequences also dictate access paths. A review of the outputs of the cost control system listed in the Design DFD, Figure 5.3, showed that EXPENSES was the primary source of all reports and inquiries. Pete's analysis showed that data from EXPENSES would have to be printed

File: EXPENSES

Component	Comments
Date	key
Account Number	key
Job Number	key
Source	key
Description	key
Amount	
Hours	

FIGURE 7.1
The EXPENSES file

File: ID

Component	Comments
Account Number	key
Account Name	

FIGURE 7.2
The ID file

File: BUDGET

Component	Comments
Account Number	key
Job Number	key
Month Ending Date	key
Budget Amount	

FIGURE 7.3
The BUDGET File

Data File	Required Access Paths
ID	Account Number
BUDGET	Account Number + Job Number + Month
EXPENSES	Date + Account Number + Job Number + Source + Description
	Account Number + Date
	Job Number + Date

FIGURE 7.4
Cost control system access paths

in Account Number + Date sequence for the Budget versus Actual Report and in Job Number + Date sequence for the Job Cost Reports. Since ID and BUDGET did not drive any reports and inquiries, no additional access paths were required for these files.

Figure 7.4 shows a list of all required access paths—the unique identification keys and the access paths required for reports and inquiries—for the cost control system's database.

Data Structure Diagram

In order to show the relationships among the files in the cost control system database, Pete constructed the diagram shown in Figure 7.5. He called it a **data structure diagram**.

Pete constructed the data structure diagram by examining the unique identification key component(s) of each file. If many records exist in another file for each value of the key, then the files are connected on the data structure diagram with an arrow in the direction of the relationship. Thus, ID is connected to BUDGET (ID *owns* BUDGET, or BUDGET is *subordinate* to ID) because there are many records in BUDGET for each value of Account Number, the unique identification key for ID.

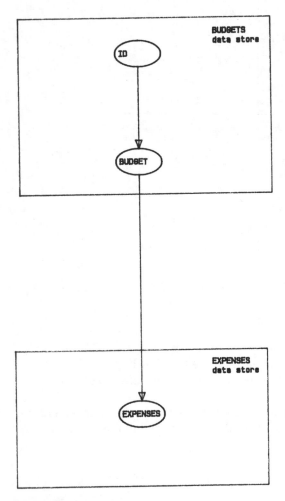

FIGURE 7.5
Data structure diagram for the
design DFD database (produced
on a pen plotter using
EXCELERATOR)

Figure 7.5 can be expanded into Figure 7.6 by examining the system E-R model, Figure 5.5, for additional relationships. Observe that JOB owns BUDGET through the Job Number field, in the same way that ID owns BUDGET through the Account Number field. ACTIVITY and SOURCE also own EXPENSES through the Description and Source fields, respectively.

The data structure diagram provides information for the design of **validation** procedures for the data entry programs of a system. Each value

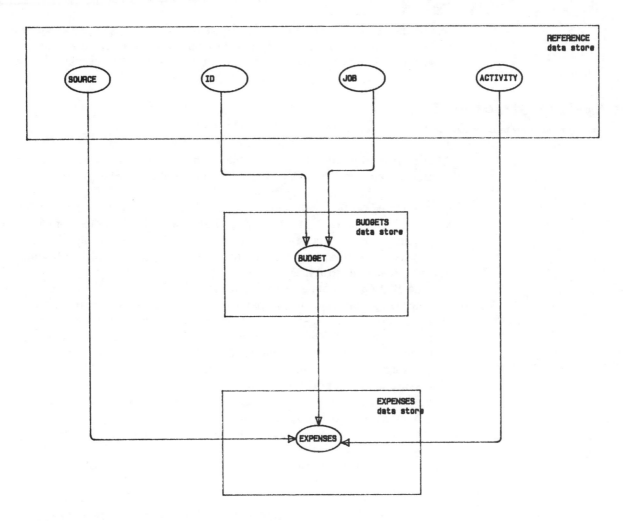

FIGURE 7.6
Data structure diagram expanded through
analysis of system E-R model (produced on
a pen plotter using EXCELERATOR)

entered for a field that corresponds to an owner file should be checked against the owner for validity. If an existing owner record is not found, the entry is rejected.

In the first prototype of the cost control system, Pete and Betsy implemented only the files of Figure 7.5. They supplied validation procedures for the Account Number field of BUDGET and for the Account Number + Job + Month Ending Date combination of EXPENSES. As a result, a BUDGET record in the first prototype cannot be created for a nonexistent general ledger account, and an EXPENSES record cannot be charged to a general ledger–job–month combination for which no BUDGET record exists.

System Structure Chart

After their work on the database of the automated portion of the new cost control system, Pete and Sam turned their attention to the processes or functions that the new system must provide. The Design DFD, Figure 5.3, for the automated portion of the new cost control system shows three processes: MAINTAIN BUDGETS, MAINTAIN EXPENSES, and REPORTS. Pete and Sam identified other processes required for the new system by examining the system data structure diagram, Figure 7.5, for the purposes of identifying **master/transaction structures.**

The BUDGETS data store files, ID and BUDGET, can be viewed as holding background data like the names of the general ledger accounts, and/or status information like the amount budgeted for a particular account and job in a certain month. The EXPENSES file can be viewed as holding data that represents the activity of the system against the background and status data.

A system like the one described above is often called a **transaction processing and/or reporting system.** Data stores holding background and status information are called **master** data stores, and data stores holding activity information are called **transaction** data stores.

Several processes not shown in the Design DFD, Figure 5.3, are required to support a transaction processing and/or reporting system properly. Once Pete identified the new cost control system as a transaction processing and/or reporting system, he knew these processes would have to be addressed in the Design New System Phase.

The additional processes required for transaction processing and/or reporting systems are updating, purging, and reorganization. **Updating** refers to summarizing activity or transaction data and storing it in a status field of the corresponding master data stores. **Purging** refers to the removal of obsolete master and transaction records, and **reorganization** refers to the process of physically rearranging the records of the database for optimal processing efficiency.

While updating, purging, and reorganization must be addressed in the design of a transaction processing and/or reporting system, they do not have to be included in every system. For the first prototype of the cost control system, Pete decided to include purging budget and expense records by job number and reorganizing all files. He decided not to include updating in the first prototype of the cost control system. Experience had taught him to wait

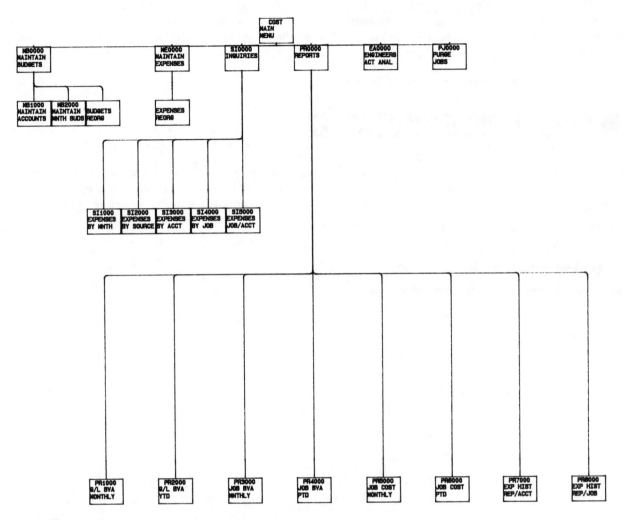

FIGURE 7.7
System structure chart for the cost control system (produced on a pen plotter using EXCELERATOR)

for user feedback from the early hands-on tests to make final design decisions regarding updating.

Pete and Sam organized their processing choices for the first prototype of the cost control system into the **system structure chart** shown in Figure 7.7. The chart shows the cost control system's processes organized into a hierarchy. Each box or node of the hierarchy represents a program in the final system. Pete named the programs using a two-letter abbreviation of the process and a four-digit code to represent the level of the program in the hierarchy.

THE WHAT, HOW, AND WHY

The concepts of new system design presented in this section were used to develop the cost control system deliverables discussed in the previous section. The action documents presented in the You Do It section will help you apply these concepts to your project.

Database Design

The database design method proposed in this book [1] begins with the outputs shown in the Design DFD, Figure 5.3. Once fields that support the outputs are specified, the designer carries out a process called **normalization** that trims the database down to a form that can be maintained most effectively.

Supporting Outputs

Preliminary database design activities revolve around defining data stores that will support the outputs specified in the Requirements Model. For example, Figure 7.8 shows a page of the manual job cost ledger that would be replaced by the automated cost control system. Sam and Pete's initial design of the EXPENSES file was based upon supporting this output. The initial contents form for EXPENSES is shown in Figure 7.9.

Later on, when their discussion turned to the engineers' activity analysis, Sam and Pete realized that they needed to store information about the activities associated with each expense and the staff hours, if any, associated with the expense. As a result they expanded the contents form for EXPENSES to the one shown in Figure 7.10.

Normalizing the Database

Normalization is carried out to produce a database that can be maintained effectively. Experience has shown that effective maintenance can be achieved when each nonkey field in each file depends upon the whole unique

JOB COST LEDGER

Job: C722

Date	Source	Account	Amount	Cum. Balance
	Balance Forward			75685.20
4/1/88	Marjam Supply	200-Materials	3672.00	79357.20
4/8/88	Dial-a-Temp	400-Subcontractors	200.00	79557.20
4/11/88	Allison Motor	300-Equipment	867.49	80424.69
4/29/88	Bob Jones	100-Engineering	4000.00	84424.69
4/29/88	John Chen	100-Engineering	3750.00	88174.69

Figure 7.8
Manual job cost ledger

DATA STORE CONTENTS

Data Store Name: EXPENSES

Repetitions	*Component*	*Comments*
	Date	
	Account Number	
	Account Name	
	Job Number	
	Source	
	Amount	

FIGURE 7.9
Initial contents of the EXPENSES data store

DATA STORE CONTENTS

Data Store Name: EXPENSES

Repetitions	*Component*	*Comments*
	Date	
	Account Number	
	Account Name	
	Job Number	
	Source	
	Description	
	Amount	
	Hours	

FIGURE 7.10
Revised contents of the EXPENSES data store

identification key for the file and nothing but the key. Some authors call this state third normal form.

Normalization is achieved by reviewing the contents of each file in the database and correcting conditions that violate the rule of dependence on the whole key and nothing but the key. The violations are often called **anomalies**. A comparison of Figures 7.9 and 7.1 illustrates the effect of the review process.

Figure 7.9 lists Account Name in the contents of the EXPENSES data store, because the account name was included in manual entries in the Job Cost ledger (Figure 7.8). But Account Name depends upon Account Number, which is only one part of the unique identification key for the EXPENSES file; so Account Name was removed from the EXPENSES file during the normalization review process—see Figure 7.1. Account Name is, of course, still maintained in the database, but it is maintained in the ID file, (see Figure 7.2), where it depends upon the whole unique identification key of that file and nothing but the key.

The anomaly described above is called a **partial dependency** because a nonkey field depends upon only part of the unique identification key. Other anomalies eliminated by normalization are:

Redundant nonkey components: Components that appear in more than one file and that are not part of the key of any file

Repeating components: Components that depend upon position in a sequence, for example, 12 numeric fields that represent budget allocations for January, February, and so on.

Transitive dependencies: Components that depend upon nonkey components

The You Do It section of this chapter presents action documents and specific guidelines for carrying out the normalization process.

Data Structure Chart

The data structure diagram identifies the **one-to-many relationships** in a database. A one-to-many relationship exists when many records can exist in the subordinate file (the many side) for each record in the owner file (the one side).

The data structure diagram should be used carefully to construct data entry validation procedures. Many times these procedures are designed and implemented at random, leading to too few, too many, or completely inappropriate error checks.

For instance, without the data structure diagram, one might be tempted to check a new expense record for a valid general ledger account number, but this control is trivial compared to checking the expense against a file of valid budget records. The check against the budgets guarantees a valid general ledger account number for the expense, and in addition it guarantees that plans were actually made to spend money in the current month for the account and for the job as well.

Of course, the development team must weigh the benefits of this type of control against the costs. In certain situations, legitimate expenses may occur without matching budget records. In this case, validation against budget records could bring data entry activities to a halt, and the development team may decide to control accuracy at some point other than data entry; for example, a formal review from a printed list after a batch of expenses has been entered.

System Structure Chart

The system structure chart is a graphical model of the organization of a system's programs. In a menu-driven system, each node of the chart would represent an option on one of the system's menus.

The development team can organize a system's programs along several lines. Pete and Sam chose **organization by function** (see Figure 7.7). Each option of the main menu represented a different function: maintenance, reports, purging, and so on. Inquiries were separated from reports, to distinguish between functions that select and display specified records and functions that use all records in a display.

Another choice for organizing programs is **organization by entity.** If this method were used for the cost control system, an organization chart similar to the one shown in Figure 7.11 might have evolved.

The development team should choose an organization method on the basis of user feedback. The prototyping process is ideal for collecting this feedback, because the users work hands-on with a real system. For this reason, some authors identify the user as the designer in the prototyping process and the information systems professional as the builder of the system [2]. The builder (information system professional) responds to the features specified by the designer (user).

With the detailed design method, users provide feedback for such choices in review meetings or **walkthroughs**, based upon paper and pencil mockups or automated slide shows of the system organization. Although much effort has gone into developing walkthrough techniques and automating the process, there is really no substitute for working hands-on with a real system for stimulating and collecting user feedback.

No matter what software development method is chosen, menus should be designed to strike the optimal balance between keeping the number of choices on each menu small and keeping the number of levels in the structure chart small. If the number of choices on a menu is large, the screen looks cluttered, and it is difficult to find the desired option. If the number of levels in the structure chart is large, finding one's choice means passing through many screens before the screen containing the desired option is reached.

Consistency is also important in menu design. If the name of the main menu appears in the upper right-hand corner of the first screen, then the name of each subsequent menu should appear in the upper right-hand corner of subsequent screens. Attention to such details can greatly improve the human operating efficiency of the system.

YOU DO IT

Use the cost control system material, the What, How, and Why section material, and the action documents of this section to guide your efforts in designing the new system for your project.

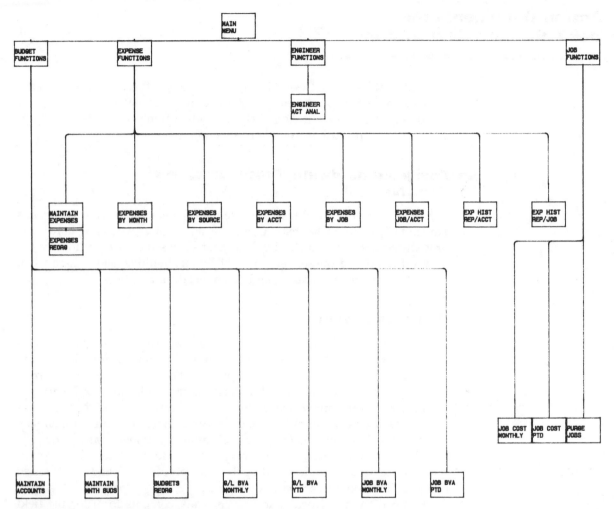

FIGURE 7.11
System structure chart organized by entity
(produced on a pen plotter using
EXCELERATOR)

If your project involves a "live client," you will work with your client on the design, collecting feedback and refining the design until he or she is satisfied. If you are using the accompanying written case project (Chapter 10), you will develop your design according to the directions provided by your instructor.

Action Documents for Designing the New System

The deliverables of the Design New System Phase of the life cycle are summarized in Action Document 7.1. An action document for planning and scheduling design new system tasks, and identifying the necessary inputs and outputs appears at the end of this section.

Designing Hardware, Procedures, and Personnel

Action Document 7.2 will help you use the final version of your Designer's Tradeoff Chart from Chapter 5 to make design choices regarding hardware, procedures, and personnel. The document shows the specifications of the Tradeoff Chart and the sequence in which you should consider them when making hardware, procedures, and personnel design choices.

Database Design

Action Document 7.3 will help you with database design. In parts 1 through 4 of Action Document 7.3, the left-hand column shows an example of one of the anomalies you should look for in the normalization review process. A correction for the anomaly is suggested in the right-hand column of each part.

In carrying out your normalization process, find and correct the anomalies in the order used in Figure 7.14; that is, find and correct all redundant nonkey components, then find and correct all repeating components, and so on.

The files used in the examples are typical files found in common applications. Concentrate on understanding the concepts of review and correction so that you can apply these to your own project.

Part 5 of Action Document 7.3 is a blank contents form for the field specifications of your project database.

System Structure Chart

Action Document 7.4 lists the points to consider in developing the system structure chart. Use them as you see fit: as a checklist to review a system structure chart, as a guide to developing the chart, or as a guide to developing questions to ask during an interview.

Use Action Document 7.5 to plan and control your design activities. At the end of this phase, collect all the relevant models, documents, and other materials, and use the cover sheet, Action Document 7.6, to submit your work as a progress report to your instructor.

References

1. Amadio, W. *Systems Development: A Practical Approach.* Watsonville, Calif.: Mitchell Publishing, 1989.

2. Jenkins, M. "Prototyping: A Methodology for the Design and Development of Application Systems." *Spectrum* Volume 2, Number 2 (April 1985): pp. 1–8.

3. Kroenke, D. , and K. Dolan. *Business Computer Systems.* Watsonville, Calif.: Mitchell Publishing, 1990.

DESIGN NEW SYSTEM DELIVERABLES

1. Hardware, procedures, and personnel design
2. Database design
3. Database access paths
4. A data structure diagram
5. A system structure chart

ACTION DOCUMENT 7.1
Design new system deliverables

Design Choice	Tradeoff Chart Specifications
Hardware	Access
	Flexibility of Output
	Turnaround Time on Output
	Timeliness of Data
Procedures	Data Responsibilities
	Timeliness of Data
Personnel	System Responsibilities
	Data Responsibilities
	Learning
	Flexibility of Output
	Turnaround Time on Output

ACTION DOCUMENT 7.2
Making hardware, procedures, and personnel design choices

ANOMALY: REDUNDANT NONKEY COMPONENT

File: CUSTOMER

Component

Customer Number

Customer Name

Customer Address

Total Sales YTD

Outstanding Balance

File: YTD PRODUCT SALES

Component

Product Number

Customer Number

Customer Name

YTD Sales

Customer Name appears
in two files.

File: CUSTOMER

Component

Customer Number

Customer Name

Customer Address

Total Sales YTD

Outstanding Balance

File: YTD PRODUCT SALES

Component

Product Number

Customer Number

YTD Sales

Leave Customer
Name in CUSTOMER
file, where it
depends upon the
whole key and
nothing but the key.

Remove Customer
Name from YTD
PRODUCT SALES file.

ACTION DOCUMENT 7.3 (part 1)
Removing redundant nonkey components

ANOMALY: REPEATING COMPONENT

File: GRADES

Component

- Student Number
- Course Number 1
- Grade 1
- Course Number 2
- Grade 2
- Course Number 3
- Grade 3
- Course Number 4
- Grade 4
- Course Number 5
- Grade 5

File: GRADES

Component

- Student Number
- Course Number
- Grade

Redesign GRADES file with a new key that uniquely determines a grade.

Five grades are stored in a single record for each student; records represent students, not grades.

ACTION DOCUMENT 7.3 (part 2)
Removing repeating components

ANOMALY: PARTIAL DEPENDENCY

File: BUDGET

Component

Account Number
Month
Account Name
Budget Amount

Account Name
depends on
Account Number
only.

File: BUDGET

Component

Account Number
Month
Budget

File: ACCOUNT

Component

Account Number
Account Name

Remove Account
Name from
BUDGET file.

Store Account Name
in a file whose unique
identification key is
Account Number.

ACTION DOCUMENT 7.3 (part 3)
Removing partial dependencies

ANOMALY: TRANSITIVE DEPENDENCY

File: EMPLOYEE

Component

Social Security Number

Employee name

Department Number ⌐

Department Name ↙

Department Name
depends upon
Department Number,
a nonkey component.

File: EMPLOYEE

Component

Social Security Number

Employee Name

Department Number

File: DEPARTMENT

Component

Department Number

Department Name

Remove Department
Name from
EMPLOYEE file.

Store Department
Name in a file
whose unique
identification key is
Department Number.

ACTION DOCUMENT 7.3 (part 4)
Removing transitive dependencies

DATA STORE CONTENTS

Data Store Name:

Repetitions	Component	Comments

ACTION DOCUMENT 7.3 (part 5)
A blank contents form

Process	Choice
Transaction maintenance	add, change, inquire, delete, list
Master maintenance	add, change, inquire, delete, list
Updating	yes/no If yes: how often 　　　　　automatic vs. user initiated
Purging	how often automatic vs. user initiated
Reorganization	how often automatic vs. user initiated

ACTION DOCUMENT 7.4
System structure chart considerations

Deliverable 1: Hardware, procedures, and personnel design

Task	User/Mgt People	IS People	Documents Needed	Documents Produced	Estimated Duration

Deliverable 2: Database design

Task	User/Mgt People	IS People	Documents Needed	Documents Produced	Estimated Duration

Deliverable 3: Database access paths

Task	User/Mgt People	IS People	Documents Needed	Documents Produced	Estimated Duration

ACTION DOCUMENT 7.5
Tasks for each deliverable (page 1 of 2)

Deliverable 4: Data structure diagram

Task	User/Mgt People	IS People	Documents Needed	Documents Produced	Estimated Duration

Deliverable 5: System structure chart

Task	User/Mgt People	IS People	Documents Needed	Documents Produced	Estimated Duration

ACTION DOCUMENT 7.5
Tasks for each deliverable (page 2 of 2)

Date _____

To _____

From _____

Re: Systems analysis models

The following documents are included in this analysis:

☐   Hardware, procedures, and personnel design

☐   Database design

☐   Database access paths

☐   Data structure diagram

☐   System structure chart

☐   Other _____

_____

☐   Other _____

_____

☐   Other _____

_____

☐   Other _____

_____

The following activities were carried out during this analysis:

☐   Interviews with _____

_____

☐   Written exercises with _____

_____

☐   Other _____

_____

☐   Other _____

_____

☐   Other _____

_____

ACTION DOCUMENT 7.6
Cover sheet for systems analysis models

CHAPTER 8

Design New System II: Approaching the Final Go/No Go Decision

This chapter concerns the development/design work that follows the completion of the system structure chart (Chapter 7) and that leads to the final go/no go decision of the systems development life cycle, Figure 1.4. Depending upon the software acquisition/development method chosen for the project, this work involves either

1. building the initial prototype of the software component, or
2. developing detailed program specifications for the software component and choosing a prewritten package for testing, or
3. developing detailed program specifications for the software component and providing a final estimate of required programming resources

The system structure chart represents the first step in the design of the software component of a new system. If the software component is being developed through prototyping, this is usually enough design work to start building the initial prototype. If the software component is being developed through the detailed design method, or if the software component is being purchased, then further specifications must be made before programming the detailed design or shopping for the right software package can begin.

The Horatio & Co. section of this chapter examines the software of the cost control system as a particular example of a transaction processing and/or reporting system. Seven fundamental functions, common to all transaction processing and/or reporting systems, are identified. In reading this first section, simply try to observe the functions and their effect on the cost control system database.

The software component of the Horatio & Co. Cost Control System was developed through prototyping with dBASE III PLUS supplemented by GENIFER, a CASE tool supporting the later phases of the life cycle (see the chapter entitled Before You Begin). The second section of this chapter, the

What, How, and Why, presents a general analysis of the seven fundamental transaction processing and/or reporting functions, along with details of how to implement these functions in the GENIFER/dBASE environment.

(GENIFER and dBASE III PLUS are available free to users of this book. References for implementing the seven fundamental transaction processing and/or reporting functions in the RBASE environment or with the dBASE IV Applications Generator are presented in an appendix at the end of this book.)

The final section of this chapter, You Do It, begins with a tutorial for understanding any software development environment. The section concludes with guidelines, exercises, and action documents to apply to the development of the initial prototype or the detailed program specifications for your project.

After completing this chapter you will

1. understand the seven fundamental transaction processing and/or reporting functions and how they work together in a finished system

2. understand how to implement these functions in the software development environment for your project system

3. apply the above to the development of either the initial prototype or the detailed program specifications for your project

HORATIO & CO. COST CONTROL SYSTEM

Figure 8.1 shows the main menu of the initial prototype of the Horatio & Co. Cost Control System software. This software is supplied on diskette with this book. Refer to the chapter entitled Before You Begin for instructions on how to install and run this software.

Maintaining Data

Users maintain the data of the cost control system database through menu options 1 and 2. For practice, enter the expenses shown in Figure 8.2 through option 2, MAINTAIN EXPENSES, of the main menu. Choose Add from the maintenance option menu along the bottom of the screen, and enter the records. Terminate the Add session by pressing Esc while the system is waiting to accept a new record. If you are running the cost control system

HORATIO & CO.
COST CONTROL SYSTEM
MAIN MENU

      1. MAINTAIN BUDGETS
      2. MAINTAIN EXPENSES
      3. INQUIRIES
      4. REPORTS
      5. ENGINEERS' ACTIVITY ANALYSIS
      6. PURGE JOBS
      Q. QUIT

FIGURE 8.1
**Main menu of the Horatio & Co. Cost
Control System**

Data	Acct	Job	Source	Description	Amount	Hours
03/01/90	4400	B107	ASPEN ENGINEERING	CLEAN AIR DESIGN	5000.00	0
03/01/90	4200	B107	ADAMS SUPPLY	PROTOTYPE MATERIALS	4000.00	0
03/10/90	4200	A141	NAL-TECH	TEST MATERIALS	1500.00	0
03/15/90	4200	B762	ADAMS SUPPLY	FOUNDATION BLOCKS	2000.00	0
03/25/90	4100	A141	BOB JONES	DESIGN	4950.00	55
03/25/90	4100	B762	BOB JONES	DESIGN	990.00	11
03/25/90	4100	B107	SAM TILDEN	CONSULTATION	2400.00	40
03/25/90	4100	A141	SARAH LUDWIG	STRUCTURAL TESTING	1200.00	30
03/25/90	4100	B762	SARAH LUDWIG	DESIGN	2400.00	60

FIGURE 8.2
**Expenses to be entered in the cost control
system database**

under the student edition of dBASE III PLUS, remember there is a 30-record maximum for any file.

The MAINTAIN EXPENSES program checks each new entry for accuracy. For example, the program does not allow the user to enter an expense for which no matching budget record exists. Budget records are entered monthly for each account number/job number combination. Users use option 1, MAINTAIN BUDGETS, of the cost control system main menu for this purpose.

In addition to checking the accuracy of the entries, the MAINTAIN EXPENSES program displays descriptive information to help the user evaluate the entry. When an account number for an expense is entered, the program displays the name of the account so that the user can determine that the proper account is charged with the expense.

Reorganizing the Database

Run the MAINTAIN EXPENSES program, delete one or two records, and choose Quit to return to the cost control system main menu. Notice the prompt to "remove deleted records from EXPENSE TRANSACTIONS." Answer yes by typing Y.

Removing deleted records permanently from the database is one of several housekeeping functions that are collectively called reorganization. Purging records, option 6 on the cost control system main menu, is another. Purging usually refers to deleting obsolete records from the active database after copying them to some kind of archive storage.

Selecting and Sequencing Data

The inquiries of option 3 of the cost control system main menu, and the engineers' activity analysis of option 5, allow the user to select data from the database. Refer to the chapter entitled Before You Begin for instructions on running these options.

For practice, choose option 3, INQUIRIES, from the cost control system main menu and then run an inquiry for ASPEN ENGINEERING and a second inquiry for NAL-TECH.

For practice with the ENGINEERS' ACTIVITY ANALYSIS, choose option 5 from the cost control system main menu and enter LUDWIG as the engineer's name.

When you run these inquiries and analyses, notice that in addition to selecting only the few records you specify, the cost control system displays the records in two different sequences. In the inquiries, the records are displayed in date sequence, so that January's records are printed and subtotaled first, followed by February's records. In the activity analysis, Sarah Ludwig's design records precede her structural testing records in the presentation.

Displaying Inquiries and Reports

All of the cost control system inquiries and reports share a common display format. The display is made up of columns of data that are listed in a specific sequence, with various totals and subtotals displayed as needed. While the details vary from one inquiry or report to another, the basic format of the display is the same.

For practice, compare the inquiries and analyses you ran in the previous section to the Expense History Report by Job, shown in Figure 8.3. Choose the default starting and ending dates when you run the Expense History Report by Job and observe the differences among the details of the displays along with the similarities in the basic display format.

THE WHAT, HOW, AND WHY

Many projects fall into the category of transaction processing and/or management reporting systems. The deliverables of the current phase of a transaction processing and/or reporting project can be organized according to the following framework of seven fundamental transaction processing and/or reporting functions:

1. Maintaining data
2. Validating entries
3. Updating from transactions
4. Reorganizing the database
5. Selecting data
6. Sequencing data
7. Displaying inquiries and reports

```
DATE:  XX/XX/XX
TIME:  XX:XX                                                          PAGE: 1

                       EXPENSE HISTORY REPORT BY JOB

       DATE         SOURCE              DESCRIPTION              ACCT       AMOUNT
 **  Job A141
 *** January, 1990
       01/13/90     NAL-TECH            TEST MATERIALS           4200       3500.00
       01/25/90     BOB JONES           DESIGN                   4100       3600.00
       01/25/90     SARAH LUDWIG        STRUCTURAL TESTING       4100       3000.00
 *** Subtotal for month                                                    10100.00

 *** February, 1990
       02/10/90     NAL-TECH            TEST MATERIALS           4200       2500.00
       02/25/90     BOB JONES           DESIGN                   4100       4500.00
       02/25/90     SARAH LUDWIG        STRUCTURAL TESTING       4100       2000.00
 *** Subtotal for month                                                     9000.00

 **  Subtotal for job                                                      19100.00

 **  Job B107

 *** January, 1990
       01/01/90     ETW LEASING         CAD COMPUTER SYSTEM      4300       4500.00
       01/01/90     ASPEN ENGINEERING   CLEAN AIR DESIGN         4400       5000.00
       01/25/90     SAM TILDEN          CONSULTATION             4100       2400.00
 *** Subtotal for month                                                    11900.00

 *** February, 1990
       02/01/90     ETW LEASING         CAD COMPUTER SYSTEM      4300       4500.00
       02/01/90     ASPEN ENGINEERING   CLEAN AIR DESIGN         4400       5000.00
       02/01/90     ASPEN ENGINEERING   CAD PROGRAMMING          4400       2500.00
       02/01/90     ADAMS SUPPLY        PROTOTYPE MATERIALS      4200       1500.00
       02/25/90     SAM TILDEN          CONSULTATION             4100       2400.00
 *** Subtotal for month                                                    15900.00

 **  Subtotal for job                                                      27800.00

 **  Job B762

 *** January, 1990
       01/25/90     BOB JONES           DESIGN                   4100       3600.00
       01/25/90     SARAH LUDWIG        DESIGN                   4100        600.00
 *** Subtotal for month                                                     4200.00

 *** February, 1990
       02/25/90     BOB JONES           DESIGN                   4100       1800.00
       02/25/90     SARAH LUDWIG        DESIGN                   4100       1600.00
 *** Subtotal for month                                                     3400.00

 **  Subtotal for job                                                       7600.00

 *   Grand total                                                           54500.00
```

FIGURE 8.3
The Expense History Report by Job

This section presents the details of implementing the seven fundamental transaction processing and/or reporting functions in the GENIFER/dBASE environment. GENIFER and dBASE III PLUS are available free to users of this book. If you are using RBASE or the dBASE IV Applications Generator, references for implementing these functions are presented in an appendix at the end of this book. If you are using any other software development environment, use the seven fundamental functions framework as a guide to learning and using that environment.

GENIFER

GENIFER is an applications generator for the dBASE environment. Using GENIFER involves making design specifications for the application's data files, indexes, screens, and reports and generating dBASE files and programs that implement the design. In production, the application runs under dBASE, independently of GENIFER. GENIFER users can generate applications targeted to dBASE III PLUS, dBASE IV, and several dBASE compilers and "workalikes."

GENIFER generates programs through the use of templates. The template provides a skeleton outline of a particular type of program which the code generator "fills in" using the specifications supplied by the human developer.

The original GENIFER package contains templates for menu programs, file maintenance programs, and inquiry and report programs. The supporting Horatio & Co. Cost Control System diskettes supplied to your instructor provide several additional templates for generating programs beyond the scope of the original set of GENIFER templates. Your instructor will provide details for using these templates as they are needed.

GENIFER is a menu-driven system. Like the Horatio & Co. Cost Control System, GENIFER menus present options along the bottom of the screen. Anytime you are unsure of what to do, press the F1 key to use GENIFER's on-line help.

The You Do It section of this chapter asks you to implement the seven fundamental functions for a simple practice system. If you are using GENIFER/dBASE for your project, then use it for the practice exercises of the next section. If you are using a software development environment other than GENIFER/dBASE for your project, then read this section to learn how to analyze a software development environment. When you understand how to organize the analysis, analyze your own environment and then apply the results of your analysis to the implementation of the practice system.

Maintaining Data

Maintenance refers to the operations performed to collect and store data accurately. Typical maintenance operations are add, modify, delete, retrieve, and list.

Early computer-based systems focused on transaction processing applications such as accounting. Accurate data maintenance is an important part of any transaction processing system.

It is possible, however, that your project might not involve data maintenance. Many reporting and analysis applications rely upon data that is collected and maintained by other systems. In these systems, the focus is on accessing, organizing, and presenting the data rather than maintaining it.

Maintaining Data with GENIFER/dBASE

Data maintenance programs are one of the most important outputs of the GENIFER/dBASE environment. Usually, the developer specifies and generates one maintenance program for each file in the database.

Data maintenance program development begins with the GENIFER Data Dictionary. This component of GENIFER stores information about the files of a system's database along with information about general nonfile variables such as the current date or the name of the company. No file can be used by GENIFER unless a data dictionary entry for the file has been made.

The information on each file represented in the GENIFER Data Dictionary is accessed through an identification screen that shows the name of the database file and a brief description. The List option shows the names of all files represented in the dictionary. The identification screen for any individual file can be accessed by using the Retrieve option if the file name is known, or the Begin, End, Next, or Prev options if one needs to search for a given screen.

Once the appropriate identification screen is retrieved, detailed information about the file is accessed through the Zoom option. Information on file fields is kept separate from information about the various indexes associated with the file. The developer establishes an index for a file when the file data is accessed or presented in a sequence other than the order of original entry.

Figure 8.4 illustrates the organization of the GENIFER Data Dictionary information. Each field or variable has its own screen. The developer navigates through the field and variable screens by using the Retrieve, Begin, End, Next, and Prev options. In Figure 8.4, the ACCOUNT field and the variable GR_TOT1 are displayed.

Once information about a file has been entered into the GENIFER Data Dictionary, the developer creates the actual dBASE data file by choosing the

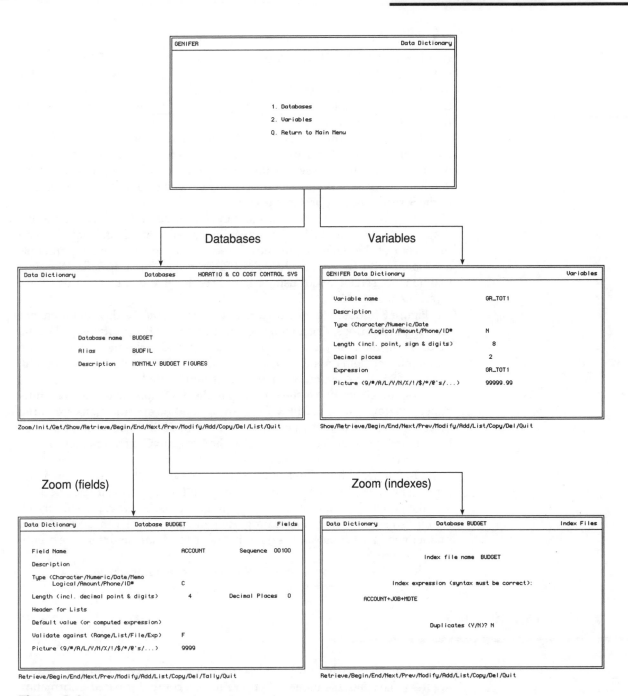

Figure 8.4
The GENIFER Data Dictionary screens

Init option from the identification screen in question. If the developer is creating a GENIFER Data Dictionary entry for an existing dBASE data file, then he or she can avoid entering the field specifications by creating the identification screen for the file and choosing the Get option. The Get option creates the data dictionary entries automatically. These entries can be modified, if necessary, by the developer.

Once information about a file has been entered into the GENIFER Data Dictionary, the developer turns his or her attention to the specifications for maintaining the file. These specifications are found under option 2, Screens and Reports, of the GENIFER Main Menu, followed by option 3, Data Screens, of the Screens and Reports menu.

Data maintenance screens are organized the same way as the data dictionary entries. An identification screen precedes detailed information about the layout of the data maintenance screens and the data field assignments associated with the layout. In GENIFER, the developer specifies the data maintenance screen layout using a simple editor that is called, in this case, a screen painter.

Figure 8.5 illustrates the organization of GENIFER's data maintenance screen specifications. The layout specification shows the positions of the data fields on the data maintenance screen, and the field assignment specification highlights one field on the layout and displays detailed information about it. In Figure 8.5, the Account Number field is highlighted.

Program generation is the final step in the development of a data maintenance program with GENIFER. Program generation specifications are found under option 3, Program Generators, of the GENIFER Main Menu, followed by option 3, Maintenance Programs, of the Program Generators menu.

GENIFER maintenance program specifications consist of, in essence, the program name, a short description, the name used to store the maintenance screen specifications, the name used to store the help screen specification, and the name of the template file used to generate the program—all organized into a single screen. These program generator screens are accessed and maintained in the same way as data dictionary and data maintenance identification screens.

Figure 8.6 illustrates a GENIFER program generator screen.

Validating Entries

Validation refers to the automated examination of keyboard entries to ensure accuracy. The data maintenance programs of a computer-based information system are the most likely places to find validation features. For example, the Maintain Expenses option of the Horatio & Co. Cost Control System checks

```
Screens and Reports                                    Data Screens




                    Screen Set        MB2000

                    Page Number       1

                    Description       MAINTAIN BUDGET FIGURES

                    Primary database  BUDGET




Zoom/Show/Retrieve/Begin/End/Next/Prev/Modi/Add/Copy/Del/List/Quit
```

                    Zoom (layout)   Zoom (fields)

```
                                          HORATIO & CO COST CONTROL SYS            MAINTAIN BUDGET FIGURES

Account                  Account          Account                    Account
Number  ____             Name _____ Number   ██                Name _____

Job     ____                              Job      ____

Month                                     Month
Ending Date _____                      Ending Date _____

Budget                                    Budget
Amount      _____                      Amount      _____


                                          Database BUDGET   Lookup N Link        Field ACCOUNT      Key Y Get Y Compute N
                                          Begin/End/Next/Prev/Modify/Insert/Del/Quit
```

FIGURE 8.5
The GENIFER data maintenance screens

```
Program Generators                                    Maintenance

            Program Name     MB2000

            Procedure Name   MB2000

            Description      MAINTAIN BUDGET FIGURES

            Data screen set  MB2000

            Help screen

            Identifier

            Template File    GENMNT

            Overlay code


Index/Generate/Retrieve/Begin/End/Next/Prev/Modify/Add/Copy/Del/List/Quit
```

FIGURE 8.6
A GENIFER program generator screen

each entry and displays diagnostic and descriptive information to help the user evaluate data entry accuracy.

If your project system provides data maintenance capabilities, then you must consider the validation of keyboard entries. There are two basic methods:

1. Checking the entry against a file or range of valid values
2. Displaying descriptive information about the entry to assist the operator in deciding upon the accuracy of the entry

Validation in GENIFER/dBASE

In the GENIFER/dBASE environment, checking an entry against a file or range is called validation, and displaying descriptive information is accomplished through a device called a lookup. Validation specifications are made through the GENIFER Data Dictionary, and lookup specifications are made in the Layout and Fields specifications of the data maintenance screen. See Figures 8.7 and 8.8.

Updating from Transactions

Many computer-based information systems maintain status information about the entities represented by the system. For instance, a basic entity represented by the cost control system is a G/L (general ledger) account. As expenses are incurred, the money is charged to the appropriate G/L accounts. The amount of money charged to an account represents status information about the account, and the expenses represent day-to-day activities called transactions. The process of increasing the amount of money charged to a G/L account every time an expense is incurred for the account is called updating the amount charged status from the expense transactions.

Updating in GENIFER/dBASE

It is not possible to enter updating specifications directly into GENIFER. If updating from transactions is required, then the developer must write a special update program in the dBASE programming language. GENIFER provides the capability to maintain the names of specially written programs under option 5, Special Programs, of the Program Generators menu.

The Horatio & Co. Cost Control System does not employ updating from transactions anywhere. In case your project requires this function, one of the custom templates supplied with this book is designed to generate a file maintenance program that executes a developer-written batch update program immediately upon exit. Your instructor will provide the details of using this template if you require it.

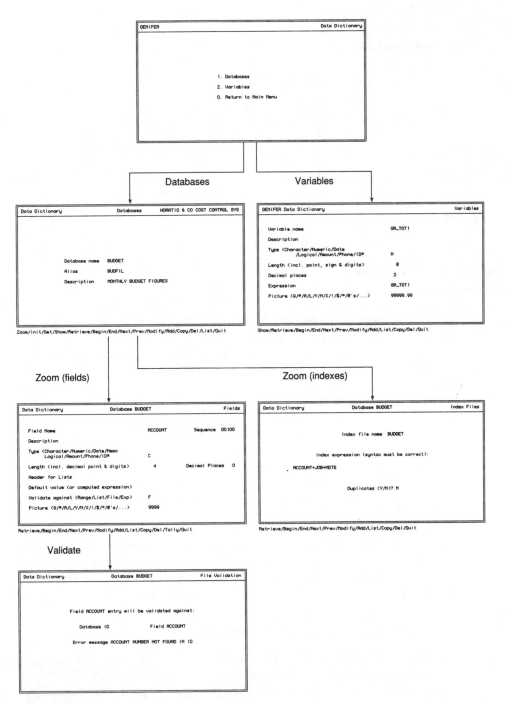

**FIGURE 8.7
Data dictionary entries through validation**

```
 HORATIO & CO COST CONTROL SYS              MAINTAIN BUDGET FIGURES

  Account                      Account
  Number       ____            Name      ██████████████████

  Job          ____

  Month
  Ending Date  _____

  Budget
  Amount       _____



 Database ID     Lookup Y Link BUDGET   Field DESCRIPT      Key N Get N Compute N
```

FIGURE 8.8
A GENIFER lookup specification

Reorganizing the Database

Reorganization refers to certain housekeeping functions that are applied periodically to maintain the efficient running of the database.

A typical reorganization function is purging. **Purging** is a term used to describe the deletion of obsolete records from the database. This process keeps the number of records in the database at a reasonable level. Important purging decisions are how to select records to purge and whether or not to make archive copies of the obsolete records before purging.

Packing the database and rebuilding the indexes are also common reorganization functions. Sometimes a database management system does not remove a record from the database when it is deleted through a program; it merely marks it as deleted, which renders it invisible to future program accesses. **Packing** refers to the physical removal of these records marked for deletion from the database.

Rebuilding the indexes is necessary with the same kind of database management systems. When a record is marked for deletion, its entry in the index is not removed but merely marked as unavailable. Rebuilding the indexes after the database has been packed leaves only those entries for which an active matching data record exists in the index.

Reorganizing in GENIFER/dBASE

Instructions to pack the database and rebuild the indexes are automatically included in all data maintenance programs generated by GENIFER. Whenever a record is deleted, the user is given the option to pack and rebuild upon exit from the data maintenance program.

R.T.C. LIBRARY, LETTERKENNY

It is not possible, however, to enter purging specifications directly into GENIFER. Another special program, written in the dBASE programming language, is needed.

In the cost control system, purging was listed as a main menu option. The file on the cost control system diskette named PJ0000.PRG contains the special program; it can be viewed with any word processor. The powerful set-oriented statements of the dBASE programming language make the program easy to read and understand.

Although PJ0000.PRG was not generated through one of the GENIFER program generator options, a Special Programs screen was set up for it to keep the GENIFER documentation of the cost control system complete. Your instructor can provide more details about the PJ0000 program.

Selecting Data

Selection refers to the process of specifying and applying criteria to include a group of records and exclude others from a system action such as a report. Selection is one of the most important capabilities provided by computer-based information systems.

Selection is used most often in reports and inquiries. Unless he or she is performing an audit of the system, the CBIS user rarely needs to see all of the records in a file or database. More likely the user needs to see the expenses for job C345, or the past due invoices for a certain customer.

The range of selection criteria and the means to specify the criteria are important design considerations that could affect the final success or failure of the entire systems development project.

Selecting Data in GENIFER/dBASE

Report programs generated by GENIFER automatically contain a preliminary section to accept and apply selection criteria. When the report program is run, the user first sees a screen layout for the file providing data to the report. The user fills in selection specifications (called a filter by the program), and the program uses only those records satisfying the specifications for the report (see also the chapter entitled Before You Begin).

For example, if the user needs to see the records for job C345 in the Inquiries option of the cost control system, then the user chooses Filter, followed by Set, and enters C345 in the JOB field of the layout before issuing the Go command for the inquiry.

Sometimes the Filter option is not suitable for the problem at hand. For instance, the fields MNTH and YR were added to the EXPENSES file of the cost control system so that all expenses for a single month could be selected for an inquiry. Filtering on the DATE field provides selection of a single date only.

If the data needed for a selection forms a continuous sequence of records, then the user can employ the < and > options from the data selection screen for the report or inquiry. Using List, Begin, End, Skip, Next, and Prev, the user brings the first record of the sequence onto the screen. Pressing < marks the record as the first to be included in the report. A similar search for the last record of the sequence and a mark with the > option sets up the final record, and the Go option displays the report or inquiry.

Sequencing Data

The **sequence** of a series of data records refers to the order in which they are presented. Sequencing is one of the most powerful organizing features of computer-based information systems.

When a user needs to look up an employee's phone extension, he or she might consult a listing printed in alphabetical order by the employees' names. If another user needs to identify the employees who work for the accounting department, then he or she might consult a listing of employees printed in department name sequence. Both users could answer their respective questions with either listing; however, the accuracy of the answer and the time spent compiling it are clearly affected by the sequence of the listing used.

Sequencing Data in GENIFER/dBASE

Sequencing data in the GENIFER/dBASE environment is accomplished through index files.

All indexes corresponding to a given data file must be specified in the GENIFER Data Dictionary entries for the file (see Figure 8.4). This should be done when the data dictionary entries are first made and before the generation of the data maintenance program for the file.

Before generating a data maintenance or report program, the developer specifies the indexes to be used by the program through the Index option of the first program generator screen for the program (see Figure 8.6).

By choosing the Autoindex option of the indexing specification screen, Figure 8.8, the developer lets GENIFER scan the program specifications to determine the indexing need. The Autoindex option should be run before an original or revised version of a data maintenance or report program is generated.

```
┌─────────────────────────────────────────────────────────────────┐
│ Screen Definition        Screen set: MB2000               Indexing │
│ Database   Type  Link to  Index    Dupl?  Index Expression  (Link + Keys) │
│                                                                   │
│ BUDGET     P              BUDGET   N      ACCOUNT+JOB+MDTE       │
│ ID         L     BUDGET   ID       N      ACCOUNT               │
│                                                                   │
│                                                                   │
│                                                                   │
│                                                                   │
│         Index BUDIN1       Dupl? N      Link                      │
│                                         Keys   ACCOUNT+JOB+MDTE   │
│                                                                   │
└─────────────────────────────────────────────────────────────────┘
```
Autoindex/Begin/End/Next/Prev/Modify/Quit

FIGURE 8.9
A GENIFER Indexing Specification screen

In Figure 8.9, the Type column is important. A P-type database is the principal database for the program; and an L-type database is used to look up related information. Two other types, not shown in Figure 8.9, are: a V-type database, used for validation of entries; and a Z-type database, used to implement the zoom hierarchical relationship between files.

The index chosen for the P-type database must match the desired sequence for the program. If the Autoindex option has not chosen the correct index for the P-type database, the developer can change the specification to the correct index name through the Modify option of the indexing screen.

Upon exit from the indexing specification screen, the developer chooses the Generate option to generate the program from the specifications.

Displaying Inquiries and Reports

This function is probably the most important to computer-based information system users. From the point of view of many users, the inquiries and reports *are* the system.

A popular method of organizing selected and sequenced data into a meaningful presentation of information involves the use of control breaks. All of the inquiries and reports of the cost control system use control breaks.

A **control-break report** is a columnar report which usually prints one line for every input record. The Expense History Report by Job, Figure 8.3, is an example of a control-break report. The input file for this report is EXPENSES. Notice that the lines of the report are grouped by job and within each job by the month and year, represented in EXPENSES by the field YEAR-MONTH. JOB and YEAR-MONTH are called the control fields.

Subtotaling represents the distinguishing characteristic of a control-break report. Examine Figure 8.3; notice that it contains subtotals of $19,100 for Job A141, $27,800 for Job B107, and $7,600 for Job B762. These subtotals sum to $54,500, the total shown at the end of the report. The Expense History Report by Job shows a subtotal every time the control field, JOB, changes or breaks; hence the name control-break report.

A control-break report may have more than one level of subtotal. In the Expense History Report by Job, there are two levels. Within Job A141, notice a subtotal for January of $10,100 and a subtotal for February of $9,000. These subtotals sum to $19,100, the subtotal for Job A141. The Expense History Report by Job produces a subtotal for every break in the control field YEAR-MONTH. At this point, you should verify that the subtotals for Jobs B107 and B762 equal the sum of the subtotals for January and February within each job.

Control-Break Reports in GENIFER/dBASE

Figure 8.10 shows the specifications for the Expense History Report by Job. The figure looks overwhelming at first sight, but it can be mastered with a little knowledge of how it is organized.

GENIFER reports are specified in three components: Layout, Printlines, and Fields. Figure 8.10a shows the Layout and the Printlines specifications.

The Layout specifications are entered through the GENIFER editor, which works like a simple word processor. The underline character (_) is used to mark locations for the variables of the report. Entering Layout specifications in this manner is sometimes called "painting the screen."

When the Layout specifications are complete, GENIFER prompts the developer to identify the function of each line in the layout. These functions are maintained by GENIFER as the Printlines specifications. Report header, page header, break header, detail line, break footer, page footer, and report footer are available in GENIFER.

A header is a set of lines that appears at the start of the report, page, or break section. A footer is a set of lines that appears at the end of the report, page, or break section. Detail lines make up the body of a control break report.

Figure 8.10a also shows two break levels in the Expense History Report by Job: the first by the JOB field and the second by the YEAR_MONTH field. Compare these specifications to the sample of the actual report, Figure 8.3, to determine the effect of specifying a break level in a control-break report.

Figure 8.10b shows the Fields specifications. Notice there are 16 field specifications in the Expense History Report by Job. These fields come from

```
Report: PR8000 (EXPENSE HISTORY BY JOB)                    20:51  01/22/89


RH
PH  DATE: DDDDDDD                                                       -
PH  TIME: TTTTT
PH                                                             PAGE: PPP
PH                     EXPENSE HISTORY REPORT BY JOB
PH
PH       DATE      SOURCE          DESCRIPTION        ACCT   AMOUNT
PH
BH1
BH1 ** Job ____                                                        -
BH2
BH2 *** _____                                                    -
BH2
D     _____   _____   _____   ___  _____  _ _ _
BF2
BF2 *** Subtotal for month                                   _____
BF1
BF1 ** Subtotal for job                                      _____
BF1
RF
RF  * Grand total                                            _____




Break Level  Database  Field      New Page  New Line
-----------  --------  ---------  --------  --------
     1       EXPENSES  JOB           N         Y
     2       EXPENSES  YEAR_MONTH    N         Y
```

**FIGURE 8.10a
GENIFER Layout and Printline
specifications for the Expense History
Report by Job**

the files of the cost control system like EXPENSES and ID, or they come from a database called VARIABLE, which is a file maintained by GENIFER to hold memory variables used for calculations such as subtotals and grand totals.

Field specifications in GENIFER are made in the same way as Printline specifications. When the Fields specification option is chosen, GENIFER moves to each field identified by the underline character and prompts the developer to provide the information shown in Figure 8.10b.

Figure 8.10c shows the sequencing specifications for the Expense History Report by Job. As described in the previous section, the developer asks GENIFER to scan a set of program specifications to determine indexing requirements before the program is generated. In the Expense History Report by Job, the EXPENSES file is sequenced by JOB + DATE in order to implement the break levels by JOB and YEAR_MONTH specified earlier.

```
Report: PR8000 (EXPENSE HISTORY BY JOB)                    20:51  01/22/89


Seq   Database   Field name   Line type  Column   Print?
---   --------   ----------   ---------  ------   ------
  1   VARIABLE   GRTOT1         RH         70        N
      PICTURE: 99999.99
      EXPRESSION: 0
  2   EXPENSES   JOB            BH          7        Y
  3   VARIABLE   SUBTOT1_1      BH         70        N
      PICTURE: 99999.99
      EXPRESSION: 0
  4   VARIABLE   MONTH_HEAD     BH          4        Y
      EXPRESSION: cmonth(date)+', '+str(year(date),4)
  5   VARIABLE   SUBTOT1_2      BH         70        N
      PICTURE: 99999.99
      EXPRESSION: 0
  6   EXPENSES   DATE           D           6        Y
  7   EXPENSES   SOURCE         D          16        Y
  8   EXPENSES   DESCRIPTN      D          35        Y
  9   EXPENSES   ACCOUNT        D          57        Y
 10   EXPENSES   AMOUNT         D          63        Y
 11   VARIABLE   GRTOT1         D          72        N
      PICTURE: 99999.99
      EXPRESSION: GRTOT1 + AMOUNT
 12   VARIABLE   SUBTOT1_1      D          74        N
      PICTURE: 99999.99
      EXPRESSION: SUBTOT1_1 + AMOUNT
 13   VARIABLE   SUBTOT1_2      D          76        N
      PICTURE: 99999.99
      EXPRESSION: SUBTOT1_2 + AMOUNT
 14   VARIABLE   SUBTOT1_2      BF         63        Y
      PICTURE: 99999.99
      EXPRESSION: SUBTOT1_2
 15   VARIABLE   SUBTOT1_1      BF         63        Y
      PICTURE: 99999.99
      EXPRESSION: SUBTOT1_1
 16   VARIABLE   GRTOT1         RF         63        Y
      PICTURE: 99999.99
      EXPRESSION: GRTOT1
```

FIGURE 8.10b
GENIFER fields specifications for the
Expense History Report by Job

```
Report: PR8000 (EXPENSE HISTORY BY JOB)                    20:51  01/22/89


Database  Lookup?  Link to   Index     Dup!?  Index Expression
--------  -------  --------  --------   -----  --------------------------------

EXPENSES     N                EXPIN2      N    JOB+DATE
```

FIGURE 8.10c
GENIFER sequencing specifications for the
Expense History Report by Job

YOU DO IT

Use the cost control system material, the What, How, and Why section material, and the action documents of this section to guide your efforts in developing the initial prototype or detailed program specifications for your project. As always, make the final product and the process by which it is developed uniquely your own.

If your project involves a "live client," you will develop the prototype or the specs for your client. If you are using the accompanying written case project (Chapter 10), you will develop the prototype or the specs according to the directions provided by your instructor.

Tutorial Exercises

These exercises involve a practice system. They are designed to be done before you attempt to develop the initial prototype or detailed program specifications for your project. They will help you to learn the software development environment for your project; practice as many as you need and as many as time permits.

If you are using GENIFER/dBASE for these exercises, enter your specifications and generate the programs of the practice system. If you are using RBASE or the dBASE IV Applications Generator, enter your specifications according to the documentation identified in the appendix of this book. If you are purchasing software or using the detailed design method, use the GENIFER screens presented in the What, How, and Why section of this chapter as models for your specifications.

1. Maintaining Data and Validating Entries

The practice system involves a file called MASTER and a file called TRANS. MASTER holds background and status information about account holders. TRANS holds information on the day-to-day activities of the account holders. Choose whatever interpretation for the context of MASTER and TRANS you wish. Savings accounts, checking accounts, and credit cards are all possibilities.

Your first task is to set up a file or table called MASTER with three fields: ACCOUNT, NAME, and BALANCE. ACCOUNT holds the unique three-digit identification number for the account; NAME holds the name of the account holder (20 characters maximum, all uppercase); and BALANCE holds the current balance for the account.

Next you should set up a file or table called TRANS with four fields: TRANS, DATE, ACCOUNT, and AMOUNT. The TRANS field holds the unique identification number for the transaction; DATE holds the date of the transaction; ACCOUNT holds the account number of the account receiving the transaction; and AMOUNT holds the amount of the transaction.

Once the files are set up, you should develop or specify programs to maintain them. The programs should allow a user to add, change, delete, inquire, and list the records or rows of both MASTER and TRANS. The ACCOUNT field of TRANS should be validated against MASTER, and the name of the account holder should be displayed for verification.

2. Updating from Transactions

Once the maintenance functions are implemented, you should turn your attention toward updating the BALANCE field in MASTER from the AMOUNT field of TRANS. Additions, deletions, and changes to TRANS all affect MASTER. Your instructor will provide the details of writing the special dBASE update program and using the customized file maintenance program template provided with this book.

3. Reorganizing the Database

In this practice system, purging is done at the end of each month. All transactions should be removed from TRANS at that time and copied to some kind of archive file. Your instructor will provide the details of writing the special dBASE purging program.

Recall that the program code for packing and rebuilding the index files is automatically included in every GENIFER-generated file maintenance program.

4. Selecting, Sequencing, and Displaying

Selecting and sequencing data along with displaying a report will be accomplished in one exercise. This exercise requires a control-break report from the TRANS file with one break field on ACCOUNT.

The sequence of the report is ACCOUNT + TRANS. The detail lines should display the transaction number, the date, and the amount of each TRANS record. The break header should display the account number and the name of the account holder, and the break footer should display the total of the amount values for the account. A grand total of all amounts should appear at the end of the report.

Prior to running the report, the user should be able to specify either a single account number or all account numbers for inclusion in the report. The same selection options for the DATE field should be provided. Prior to running the report, the user should also be able to specify the output device for the report, either the screen or the printer.

Action Documents

The deliverables of this chapter are summarized in Action Document 8.1. They are based upon the framework of seven fundamental transaction processing and/or reporting functions.

An action document for planning and scheduling your tasks for this phase of the project appears at the end of this chapter.

GENIFER Dos and Don'ts

Use the list presented in Action Document 8.2 when you are preparing your GENIFER specifications and generating programs. The hints on the list were compiled to make working with GENIFER easier. Some are mandatory; others are just more convenient.

You should read the list before beginning any GENIFER session and keep it handy while working. You can also use the list to troubleshoot problems that surface during GENIFER sessions.

Purchasing Software

The seven fundamental transaction processing and/or reporting system functions are organized in Action Document 8.3 to guide your search for an appropriate software package. In addition to the functions, several other areas need evaluation when purchasing software. These items are also included in Action Document 8.3.

Use Action Document 8.4 to plan and control your design activities. At the end of this phase, collect all relevant models, documents, and other materials, and use the cover sheet, Action Document 8.5, to submit your work as a progress report to your instructor.

DESIGN NEW SYSTEM II DELIVERABLES

1. Data dictionary entries
2. Screen layout and processing specifications for maintaining data
3. Specifications for validating entries
4. Specifications for updating
5. Specifications for reorganizing the database: purging, packing, and rebuilding indexes
6. Specifications for selecting data
7. Specifications for sequencing data
8. Layout and processing specifications for inquiries and reports
9. Initial prototype, prewritten package selection, or final programming estimate

ACTION DOCUMENT 8.1
Chapter deliverables

If dBASE is run immediately after running GENIFER, the performance is very slow. To avoid this, reboot your system after exiting GENIFER and before testing the generated programs.

Always name a validated field with the same name as the field providing the validation, for example, ACCOUNT in TRANS is validated against ACCOUNT in MASTER.

Validations and control breaks may be specified for single database fields only. If you must validate the concatenation of two or more fields, the concatenation must be defined as a single field in both database files. The same holds true for computations derived from database fields in validations and control breaks. Example: The common field named BUDGET in EXPENSES and BUDGET is used to check a new expense for a matching budget record in the cost control system. See the GENIFER Data Dictionary entries for BUDGET and EXPENSES, along with the screen layout and processing specifications for the Maintain Expenses program.

You will mess things up more than once, so backup often and stick with it.

Whenever you change a data dictionary entry, you must regenerate every program that uses the database file in question.

Every time you regenerate a maintenance or report program, you must run the Autoindex option first.

If the Autoindex option cannot determine a required index, the entry in the Index column of the Autoindex screen is left blank. You should highlight the line(s) with the missing entry, choose Modify, and supply a name and key for the new index. GENIFER updates the data dictionary automatically. If you have to regenerate the program, you will be required to make these entries again when you run Autoindex before the regeneration.

When in doubt, Autoindex.

Before any test run of the generated programs, you should delete all dBASE index (.NDX) files from the directory containing the data files. GENIFER-generated maintenance and report programs all contain code to create any required dBASE index files that are missing from the data directory at run time.

In the Customizer, specify the same directory for the Output directory, Data directory, and Template directory. Before beginning work on a project, copy the template files (.GTL) supplied with this book into this directory.

When specifying string constants in computed expressions, use double quotation marks.

When specifying an alias filename in the data dictionary, use something different from the original file name. Using the same name sometimes generates an "Alias already in use" error at run time.

Formulae for computed expressions cannot exceed 60 characters in length. This may cause you to shorten field names in order to use a lengthy formula.

Do a "Show all from the data dictionary" under the Documentation option of the GENIFER main menu before beginning and several times during a GENIFER work session. Check for corrupted entries and correct if necessary. Regenerate any programs that might have used the corrupted entries.

**ACTION DOCUMENT 8.2
GENIFER dos and don'ts**

Maintaining Data

1. Does the package allow data to be added, modified, deleted, retrieved, and listed?
2. Does the package provide security to control access to functions such as modify or delete?

Validating Entries

1. Does the software provide built-in error checking during data entry?
2. How is this accomplished?
   a. Does it check entered data against a valid range of values?
   b. Does it display descriptive information that assists the data entry operator?

Updating from Transactions

Is an update feature provided?
   a. Is it batch?
   b. Is it immediate?

Reorganizing the Database

1. Is a purging feature included?
   a. Can the purging time frame be set?
   b. Can records be selected for purging according to our specifications?
   c. Is an archive feature for purged records included?
2. How is the database packed?
3. How are indexes rebuilt?
4. Are backup and restore options included?

Selecting, Sequencing, and Displaying Data

1. What is involved in accessing, organizing, and presenting data according to specified criteria?
2. Is there a standard set of reports?
3. Are screen inquiries provided?
4. Can the user select the sequence of records in reports and/or inquires?

Vendor Evaluation

1. Is the vendor well known?
2. Can the vendor supply a reference list of current users?
3. Does the vendor supply updates to the package? At what cost?

**ACTION DOCUMENT 8.3
Guidelines for purchasing software (page 1 of 2)**

4. Is any training provided by the vendor?

    a. Is it on-site or off-site?

    b. Is there a tutorial and on-line help?

5. Does the vendor provide ongoing support?

6. Will the vendor guarantee performance quality and efficient response time?

7. Is there a trial period with little or no obligation?

8. Will the vendor customize the software to meet individual needs?

9. Will the vendor allow the user to customize the software to meet individual needs?

10. Does the vendor install the software? If not, is any special training involved?

11. Does the vendor supply a comprehensive, organized manual of operations?

ACTION DOCUMENT 8.3
Guidelines for purchasing software (page 2 of 2)

Deliverable 1: Data dictionary entries

Task	User/Mgt People	IS People	Documents Needed	Documents Produced	Estimated Duration

Deliverable 2: Data maintenance specifications

Task	User/Mgt People	IS People	Documents Needed	Documents Produced	Estimated Duration

Deliverable 3: Validation specifications

Task	User/Mgt People	IS People	Documents Needed	Documents Produced	Estimated Duration

**ACTION DOCUMENT 8.4
Tasks for each deliverable (page 1 of 3)**

Deliverable 4: Updating specifications

Task	User/Mgt People	IS People	Documents Needed	Documents Produced	Estimated Duration

Deliverable 5: Reorganization specifications

Task	User/Mgt People	IS People	Documents Needed	Documents Produced	Estimated Duration

Deliverable 6: Data selection specifications

Task	User/Mgt People	IS People	Documents Needed	Documents Produced	Estimated Duration

ACTION DOCUMENT 8.4
Tasks for each deliverable (page 2 of 3)

Date _____

To _____

From _____

Re: Transition analysis

The following documents are included in this analysis:

☐   Data dictionary entries
☐   Data maintenance specifications
☐   Validation specifications
☐   Updating specifications
☐   Reorganization specifications
☐   Data selection specifications
☐   Data sequencing specifications
☐   Inquiry and report specifications
☐   Initial prototype, package selection, or final programming estimate
☐   Other _____

_____

☐   Other _____

_____

☐   Other _____

_____

☐   Other _____

_____

The following activities were carried out during this analysis:

☐   Interviews with _____

_____

☐   Written exercises with _____

_____

☐   Other _____

_____

☐   Other _____

_____

ACTION DOCUMENT 8.5
Cover sheet for transition analysis

CHAPTER 9

The Buy/Build Software and Implementation Phases

This chapter concerns the work of the Buy/Build Software Phase and beyond. Throughout this book we have tried to stress the inadequacy of the phased, linear model of the systems development life cycle presented in Figure 1.4. In real-life projects, the boundaries of the phases are fuzzy, and the sequence of steps can vary depending upon circumstances.

This variation is no more apparent than in the work of the previous two chapters. If the software component is being purchased, then the material of Chapters 7 and 8 is used to evaluate prewritten software packages rather than to design and build a new software component from scratch. If the software component is being developed through prototyping, then the work of Chapters 7 and 8 evolves gradually as prototypes are tested and refined. Finally, if the software component is being developed through the detailed design method, then the work of Chapters 7 and 8 is finished and "frozen" before any programming begins.

Exactly when the final go/no go decision of a systems development project is made also depends upon circumstances. In a detailed design project, it is made after a review of the final programming estimate developed in Chapter 8. If the required resources, the schedule of deliverables, and final system features agree with the specifications made at the second go/no go decision, then the project proceeds to the Buy/Build Software Phase and beyond. If the detailed design uncovers errors or omissions in the second go/no go decision specifications, then the project team can either abandon the project or accept the new specifications and proceed to the Buy/Build Software Phase.

If the software component is being purchased, then the final go/no go decision might be made after some of the software tests presented in this chapter are applied to the package chosen at the end of Chapter 8. If the decision to proceed is positive, then a final purchase is made and the project team turns its attention toward the implementation issues presented in this chapter.

Developing the software through prototyping provides the greatest flexibility for the final go/no go decision. The decision could be made at any point in the process of developing and refining prototypes into a final operational software component.

The Horatio & Co. section discusses the final go/no go decision for the cost control system. The refining of the initial prototype of the software component is also presented, along with a discussion of user/management reaction to the system. The section continues with a discussion of the issues faced in implementing the completed system, and a final evaluation of supporting procedures. The section concludes with the project team's final report to management.

The What, How, and Why section of this chapter provides a detailed explanation of how to develop the deliverables presented in the previous section. The deliverables cover finalizing software acquisition/development, implementing the completed system, and evaluating the completed system.

The final section, You Do It, provides exercises, guidelines, and action documents to help you complete the acquisition/development of your software component and to implement and evaluate your completed system.

After completing this chapter you will

1.   make a final go/no go decision for your project
2.   understand the techniques of software development that go beyond programming, for example, software testing and team reviews
3.   know how to implement a completed system, taking into account its integration with the existing infrastructure
4.   know how to evaluate the completed system and report your findings to management

HORATIO & CO. COST CONTROL SYSTEM

The go/no go decision to proceed beyond the Design New System Phase for the cost control system project was straightforward, because no new discoveries came to light with the development of the initial prototype of the software component.

The Cost Control System
Prototypes

The version of the Horatio & Co. Cost Control System supplied on diskette with this book was the initial prototype developed by Pete and Betsy. This version and subsequent versions (there were four altogether) were used and evaluated by Sam Tilden and the engineers in the department.

Pete advised the reviewers to organize their responses according to system organization, completeness, accuracy, and ease of use. Figure 9.1 shows some of Sam's written comments on the initial prototype.

As the system builder, Betsy held team review meetings with the designers/users of the cost control system, namely, Sam Tilden and the engineers of the department. She used the written feedback from the prototype tests to guide these meetings.

Sometimes Betsy implemented changes requested in the written comments before the meetings. At other times, she implemented a change at the meeting so she could get immediate feedback. (Sometimes the designers/ users dropped a request when they saw it implemented in the working prototype.) Finally, Betsy rejected some changes because they went beyond the scope of the project or the capabilities of the software development environment.

The process of using the prototype, evaluating it, and refining it in light of the feedback continued until Sam and the engineers were satisfied that their requirements had been met.

Putting the Cost Control
System into Production

Pete called the fourth prototype of the cost control system an **operational prototype**, because it fulfilled the requirements of the users. This milestone, however, did not represent the completion of the project, because several issues from the final Designer's Tradeoff Chart, Figure 5.6, remained unresolved. These were the match with other company systems and the initial data conversion. In addition, the issues of user training and finalizing system documentation needed to be addressed.

The issues of merging new software into the firm's existing base of applications, converting the initial database, training users, and finalizing

System Organization

Main menu easy to follow in light of DFD for transaction processing and/or reporting system.

Will inactive jobs be included in the project to date the Job Cost Reports and Expense History Reports? If they are, is it possible to provide the option to eliminate them?

If I run an inquiry on the screen and decide to print it, I have to rerun the entire inquiry to get to the print option. Could we add a request to print at the end of a screen inquiry to avoid rerunning the inquiry?

Should be able to do more than one inquiry of a certain type before returning to the inquiries menu.

Completeness

Could use an option to print out all Job Budget versus Actual Reports instead of entering single job numbers. Keep Single Job option and add All Jobs option.

In engineers' activity analysis, we could use an analysis by activity, showing who did what activity, in addition to the analysis by engineer that shows what activities a person did. This would help with professional development plans.

Also, we could use an inquiry by description to look at who sold us what. This would help with the reorganization of the vendor base.

Could use a year to date Job Budget versus Actual Report in addition to the Monthly and the Project to Date Reports.

What about requests not available from the menus, like the average cost of engineering for office park construction projects?

Accuracy

How do I know inquiry by source includes all records? What if an entry is misspelled when it is entered? Then it would not be included.

Ease of Use

Would like the ability to page up and down through a long inquiry like a word processor.

Date of expense is missing from inquiries. Could we include it?

In a long report or inquiry could we have headings at the top of each screen or page? Right now, we get headings on the first screen or page only.

FIGURE 9.1
Sam Tilden's comments on the initial prototype

documentation must be faced by all development teams, regardless of the software acquisition/development methodology they choose to follow. The fact that Pete and Betsy developed the cost control system software through prototyping did not diminish their responsibilities regarding these issues.

Other Company Systems

The development team realized, early on, that much of the data processed by the cost control system was also stored in the central accounting system. Since the accounting system encountered the data first, the development team decided to transfer the data captured by the accounting system to the cost control system electronically, instead of entering it into the cost control system manually. It was now time to implement this transfer.

New data entry programs for Payroll and Accounts Payable transaction entry were written. These programs allowed the original accounting system data to be expanded to include the fields required by the cost control system. The programs were written in COBOL, the language of the central accounting system, and they were run on the central minicomputer that ran the accounting system (see Chapters 5 and 6). All validation processing was included in these programs. The necessary reference data files were set up on the central minicomputer (see Figure 7.6).

A daily transfer between the central minicomputer and the microcomputer network of the cost control system was instituted. Each day, Betsy **downloaded** fully processed Payroll and Accounts Payable transactions and added them to the cost control system's database.

Initial Data Conversion

The cost control system's prototypes were tested on a representative sampling of general ledger account, budget, and expense records. To put the software into production, reference data stores to validate SOURCE, JOB, and DESCRIPTN field entries had to be set up on the central minicomputer and BUDGET and EXPENSES records had to be added to represent all active jobs (see Figures 7.3 and 7.6).

The conversion process was carried out in a variety of ways. At the time of the conversion, ten jobs were active in the engineering department. This represented 480 monthly budget records. Sam Tilden compiled these records and entered them into the BUDGET file of the cost control system himself.

A review of the manual job cost ledger revealed 3,700 expense transactions for the ten active jobs. The manual job cost ledger contained full-text entries for the SOURCE and DESCRIPTN fields, for example, Aspen Engineering for SOURCE. In the automated system, data entry personnel entered codes that were validated against the reference data stores for these fields (see Sam's comments about spelling errors in Figure 9.1), so each manual record had to be reviewed to change the full-text entries for SOURCE and DESCRIPTN to codes. The modified manual records were keyed to diskette by a data preparation service and then appended to the EXPENSES file.

Training Users

Training for the cost control system covered menu-driven reports and inquiries for all engineering department personnel; file maintenance for Sam Tilden, Betsy Klein, the accounting department manager, the Accounts Payable supervisor, and the construction project managers; and ad hoc reporting for all personnel who requested it.

The accounting department manager, the Accounts Payable supervisor, and the project managers became involved when the reference data stores for the cost control system data entry procedures were implemented on the central minicomputer (see Figure 7.6). These individuals were assigned responsibility for ID, SOURCE, and JOB respectively. Responsibility for DESCRIPTN was assigned to Betsy Klein.

Training for the reference data stores was not included in the original budget, Figure 5.4, or schedule, Figure 6.8. Revisions to both the budget and the schedule were made accordingly.

Training for the menu-driven reports and inquiries was done briefly when Betsy introduced the early prototypes of the cost control system to Sam and the engineers. Betsy relied upon Sam and the engineers to teach themselves how to use this simple component of the cost control system, a decision which she based on the experience and interest of the group with similar systems. She also felt that self-teaching promoted a sense of experimentation that would enhance the feedback she received on the prototypes.

Training for the ad hoc reporting was more formal. The development team planned and scheduled a series of five four-hour workshops on ad hoc reporting for ten members of the engineering department. According to Figure 6.8, this training began with the development of the fourth prototype and continued almost to the end of the project. Pete developed the training program, and Betsy actually taught the classes.

Finalizing Documentation

With the completion of the cost control system software and the interface to the central accounting system, Betsy collected her notes on the operation of each program and the supporting manual procedures into a formal set of operator instructions. From the notes, she wrote Structured English descriptions for all procedures and organized them according to the processes of the cost control system's main menu. The operator instructions formed an important part of the training program Betsy delivered to the users of the cost control system.

Betsy also collected into a single volume the large amount of technical documentation that had been generated since the beginning of the project. The contents of this volume included the reports to management, the system analysis models, the Design DFD and the System E-R Model, the System Structure Chart, the GENIFER specifications, and all the dBASE programs of the system. Betsy's objective in collecting this material was to enable any information systems professional to work with the cost control system for either maintenance, enhancement, or interface with another application.

Evaluating the Cost Control System

Once the production version of the cost control system software was implemented, the members of the development team turned their attention to evaluating the final product in preparation for a final report to management.

The software and data components were evaluated for processing efficiency, and the procedures component was evaluated for timeliness, accuracy and completeness, and security and control. The evaluation provided an opportunity to make final adjustments to the original procedures and personnel specifications from the Design New System Phase of the project. At that stage of the project, these specifications were, by necessity, vague and general. Now that the hardware, software, and data components are complete, the development team can fill in the details of the final two components.

Processing Efficiency

Processing efficiency refers to how fast a system performs its tasks. During the Evaluation of Alternatives Phase, Pete used a rough estimate of the size of the database to judge the adequacy of dBASE III PLUS running on the department's local area network. He contacted other organizations with similar applications running in the same environment and observed performance. He also wrote some dBASE programs to generate test files of realistic size and ran some trials of various operations, such as reporting and reorganization.

Once the production version of the software was implemented, these test results were confirmed, and the cost control system software went into production running in the dBASE environment. Sometimes a development team embarks upon a prototyping project knowing full well that its CASE/ 4GL environment cannot provide the necessary processing efficiency in production. On these projects, the operational prototype is used as a final design document, and the production version of the software is programmed from it in a more efficient environment. In a sense, the operational prototype brings the project to the same point as the detailed design method, but with one important difference. The prototyping design is based upon user/designer feedback with a working product rather than responses to a paper-and-pencil design.

Timeliness

Chapter 7 discusses the design of procedures and personnel assignments from the final Designer's Tradeoff Chart, Figure 5.6. The specification of one-day-old data dictated daily data entry procedures, and in production, a daily data transfer procedure from the central accounting system to the cost control system. Operational procedures to generate and distribute the printed monthly reports, such as the Job Cost Reports to the project managers, also had to conform to the timeliness requirement of the firm.

Accuracy and Completeness

The cost control system development team evaluated the accuracy and completeness of the system along two dimensions: data entry and processing. An accurate and complete system should prevent as much inaccurate data from entering the system as possible, and once in the system, processed data in the form of reports and inquiries should be absolutely accurate and complete. Since the cost control system software was developed through prototyping, much of this evaluation was done before the implementation of the final production version of the software.

The team tested the accuracy and completeness of data entry by deliberately entering invalid data and observing whether or not the validation and verification procedures prevented such entries. Since Betsy had the most experience with data entry, she was the primary test data designer. She consulted the GENIFER Data Dictionary and constructed entries that tested every validation and verification condition specified for the database. She constructed entries containing common errors, and she also constructed entries with random data in an attempt to create erroneous conditions beyond those she knew from experience.

Betsy tested the accuracy and completeness of the cost control system's processing by comparing data in the system and reports and inquiries generated by the system to data and reports from other sources within the firm. For example, the cost control system's year-to-date G/L Budget versus Actual Report should agree with the central accounting system's Budget versus Actual Report every month. If they do not, then a comparison of each report with the files of budget authorization sheets and payment authorization vouchers, Figure 4.2, determines the inaccuracy.

Security and Control

The cost control system development team evaluated the security and control of the system along two dimensions: access and auditability. A secure system should provide access to the data each person needs to perform his or her work effectively, and it should restrict access to data that is beyond the scope of an individual's responsibilities. In a well-controlled system environment, an independent observer or auditor should be able to reconstruct the activity leading up to a given condition or state in the system. The auditor should be able to identify the individual responsible for each activity, and he or she should be able to reconstruct the activity without the use of documents controlled by the responsible individual.

The development team used the final Designer's Tradeoff Chart, Figure 5.6, to guarantee secure access to the database of the cost control system. In reviewing the data entry item under the Data Responsibilities heading of the Tradeoff Chart, the development team assigned responsibility for budgets to Sam Tilden and for everything else to Betsy Klein. The engineers needed access to the reports and inquiries function only.

A main menu was developed for each set of access requirements, and each group was instructed to begin running the system by calling the appropriate menu. In addition, the more comprehensive menus were protected with a password to prevent unauthorized use, either inadvertent or deliberate.

To provide an audit trail of expense transaction activity, the development team relied upon printed lists or journals. Betsy Klein reviewed her entries before updating by printing a proof list and comparing each line to the corresponding original or source document. During the update process, the central accounting system printed another list of the transactions, which was filed in the accounting department as the journal of original entry. The development team was satisfied that this design met the auditability criterion specified above.

Final Report to Management

The final report to management serves two purposes. First, it demonstrates what was accomplished in the project; and second, it sets the stage for future actions. Sam and Betsy worked together on the preparation of the report.

The report began with a recap of Sam's previous report to Mr. Chapin, Figure 1.2. The final or operational prototype met all system objectives. These objectives supported business tactics 1–3 to varying degrees. Sam and Betsy planned to begin work on tactic 4, reorganize the vendor base, after the presentation of this report. The budget presented in Figure 1.2 was exceeded by $2,500 (10 percent) due to the decision to use identification codes for the SOURCE and DESCRIPTN fields; the agreed-upon schedule of four months was satisfied.

The report continued with a section on system benefits. Sam was ready for the report preparer to transfer to another department (see Figure 5.2). He volunteered to supply Mr. Chapin with three reports before the end of the year, assessing the professional productivity gains and the improvements in budget control achieved by the operational prototype.

Sam related this plan to the systems development life cycle, Figure 1.4. At present, the project was in the Implementation and Evaluation Phase. Sam's progress reports would lead to a formal evaluation of the system at the end of the year in terms of the benefits outlined in Figure 5.2. This evaluation would continue throughout the following year as well.

Since Ed Henderson, the accounting department manager, worked on the project, Sam and Betsy sent him a draft of their report before submitting it to Mr. Chapin. Ed was satisfied with the report, and it was submitted to Mr. Chapin. A meeting to discuss the report was scheduled for the following Monday. In addition to Sam, Betsy, and Ed Henderson, Mr. Chapin invited Dan Klockner and Pete Willard to attend the meeting.

Mr. Chapin was satisfied with the work of the project to date. Benefits were achieved, budgets were observed, and schedules were met. His purpose in calling the meeting was to discuss the future of the cost control system at Horatio & Co. Remember that the project in the engineering department was undertaken as a pilot for a company-wide cost control system. "At this point, I think our efforts should focus on increasing the number of users of the pilot cost control system," he said. "What do you think, Sam?"

"I agree," said Sam. "At this time, the job cost reporting and monthly budgeting modules are farthest along in the development process. These are the top-paying modules of the system requirements model [see Figure 5.2]. The engineers' activity analysis module consists of two inquiries which use the job cost database. The reorganization of the vendor base module is still just a few ideas. I am excited about the activity analysis module. As we expand the cost control system to other users, I want to stay involved with the development of the last two modules."

"So how do we go about expanding the cost control system to other users?" asked Mr. Chapin.

Pete Willard offered his opinion. "The cost control system is one with a long life expectancy, regular utilization, and a stable environment. It is an ideal candidate for expansion to other departments. The microcomputer network can be extended in small increments to provide access to the system for a new group. The cost of adding a new group should be about the same as it was for the engineering department. Less analysis is required, but new hardware purchases are required in order to expand the network."

"What if the other departments cannot work with the design?" asked Mr. Chapin.

"We are approaching the last phase of the systems development life cycle, which involves the maintenance and enhancement of the cost control system," said Pete. "If necessary, we will continue to apply the prototyping cycle to enhance the operational version over time [2]."

"So Betsy will have to expand her duties as system builder and trainer," said Mr. Chapin.

"Yes," said Pete. "Someone will have to coordinate the technical side along with Ed. Betsy is the logical choice."

"Are you both willing to make that commitment?" asked Mr. Chapin.

"I'm anxious to do it," said Betsy.

"So am I," said Ed.

"What about you, Sam?" asked Mr. Chapin.

"Betsy, Pete, and I discussed this already," said Sam. "I will need some time to sit down with them to work out a realistic schedule to minimize the impact on our department."

"Fine," said Mr. Chapin. "I'll wait to hear from you before releasing a memo announcing the completion of the pilot cost control system to the entire staff. I'll invite the managers of the other departments to a demonstration of the system. Betsy, I want you to make a presentation about prototyping. The managers have been kept up to date with the progress of this project. My continued strong support and the success of the early users should encourage everyone to participate."

THE WHAT, HOW, AND WHY

The portion of the life cycle covered in this chapter involves the final go/no go decision, software development and testing, implementation of the completed system, and final evaluation [1]. The timing and duration of some of the earlier activities depends upon the chosen method of software acquisition/development.

Regardless of the software acquisition/development methodology, the implementation of the completed system and the final evaluation of the system components other than software—namely, hardware, data, procedures, and personnel—are carried out in essentially the same way. For a prewritten software package project, implementation and evaluation begin once the package is installed. For a prototyping project, they begin with the completion of the operational prototype. For a detailed design project, they begin when the programming is completed.

As you read the following sections on software development and testing, implementation of the completed system, and system evaluation, keep in mind the variations in timing and duration of the tasks that can occur, depending upon the project's software acquisition/development methodology.

Software Development and Testing

The typical means of developing software for detailed design projects is programming in a third-generation language such as COBOL; the typical means for a prototyping project is development in a CASE/4GL environment. In Chapter 8, you analyzed the software development environment for your project in terms of the seven fundamental transaction processing and/ or reporting functions.

Regardless of how it is developed, all software must be tested; and regardless of whether it is acquired or developed, all software must be reviewed to determine how well it satisfies the requirements of the system. These activities are discussed in the next two sections.

Testing Software

The testing plan used by Betsy Klein for the cost control system can be followed on any transaction processing and/or reporting project. The plan follows the seven fundamental transaction processing and/or reporting functions presented in Chapter 8.

Functions 1, Maintaining data and 2, Validating data, are tested first. In a CASE/4GL environment, validation and verification rules can be gathered from the data dictionary. For third-generation projects, a review of the design documents yields the data maintenance validation and verification rules. Test data should be processed to check that every validation condition is enforced accurately, that is, that valid records are accepted and invalid records are not accepted.

Validation and verification rules cannot detect all data maintenance errors. For instance, entering an expense of $100.00 instead of $1,000.00 in the cost control system does not violate any validation rules. To identify and correct such errors, the software developer relies upon effective data entry procedures. In the cost control system, Betsy instituted a procedure of printing a batch of transactions and reviewing the list against the original documents before releasing the transactions to the update procedures. Such **batch controls** are probably the most common way to detect nonvalidation errors.

After data maintenance and validation program units are tested and accepted, the software developer turns his or her attention to the remaining fundamental transaction processing and/or reporting functions. Updating, reorganizing, selecting, sequencing, and reporting can all be described as processing functions.

The primary test of processing program units is the **comparison-to-known-results method.** The developer begins by recording the contents of the test database, processing the data through the programs being tested, and comparing the results to results that are either derived manually or derived from another system and whose accuracy is known.

On many projects the comparison-to-known-results method is used to test the full system: hardware, software, data, procedures, and personnel. In a **parallel run**, the client runs both the new system and the original system for a short time after implementation of the new system. Comparing results detects not only errors in the software component but also errors in the other four components, particularly procedures.

Reviewing Software

Software should be reviewed by the entire development team working as a group. Such **team reviews** take different forms, depending upon the software acquisition/development methodology for the project.

For prewritten software package and prototyping projects, reviews are based upon hands-on use of a working product. Information systems professionals and members of the user/management group use the package or prototype, collect their impressions in writing, and share their observations in an open team review meeting.

Because of the resources required to program in a third-generation language, much of the software review for a detailed design project precedes the development of the working product. Such team review meetings are often called **walkthroughs**. Information systems professionals on the development team prepare mock-ups of system screens and reports on paper and simulate the operation of the system for the user/management group by displaying the appropriate mock-ups in response to user requests.

Recently, a number of software packages for preparing and running detailed design walkthroughs have been developed for the microcomputer market [3]. These packages greatly enhance the realism of the detailed design walkthrough.

No matter what the software acquisition/development methodology, the software component should be reviewed by both the information systems professionals and the user/management group. The review framework of system organization, accuracy, completeness, and ease of use is workable for each group. An action document based upon this review framework is presented later in this chapter.

Like all good user/developer communication, the purpose of the software team review meeting is a shared, complete, and accurate understanding of the product. All of the communication and creative problem-solving principles presented in Chapter 3 apply to these meetings. In addition, it is important to capture and share an accurate written record of the proceedings. One person at the review must serve as the recorder or scribe. It is this person's responsibility to take notes at the team review meeting and to prepare, distribute, and maintain an ongoing record of such proceedings.

Implementing the Completed System

No matter how a system's software is acquired or developed, the entire system—hardware, software, data, procedures, and personnel—must eventually be integrated into the existing infrastructure of the firm. The activities associated with implementing the completed system are establishing the interface with existing applications, initial data conversion, user training, and finalizing documentation.

Implementation is often confused with programming. This is incorrect. Implementation goes far beyond programming to include integrating the entire system into the existing infrastructure of the firm. Action documents to guide the implementation of your project system are presented in the You Do It section of this chapter.

Interface with Existing Applications

The work of establishing the interface between a new application and the base of existing applications depends upon the hardware and software environment of the firm. Several vendors are advertising distributed database capability, which means that each application accesses the one and only copy of the data it requires, regardless of where that data is stored.

Horatio and Co. did not maintain such an environment. The data stored on the minicomputer of the central accounting system was not directly accessible to the programs of the microcomputer-based cost control system and vice versa. An electronic file transfer procedure had to be implemented for the application to share common data.

Sharing data across applications in the firm involves careful data management. Someone in the firm must know what exists, who is responsible for it, who uses it, when, and how. In many firms the **database administrator** fulfills this responsibility.

If your project involves a "live client," you will take your directions from the person responsible for the data of the client firm. If you are using the written case for your project, then the necessary background information on sharing data is provided.

Identifying shared data requires a review of the organization-wide data dictionary. Many firms do not maintain such a dictionary formally, but store this information in someone's head. Needless to say, the more careful a firm is in managing its data resource, the more likely attempts at sharing data will be successful.

Initial Data Conversion

Recall the interpretation of master data stores as those that hold background and status information, and transaction data stores as those that hold day-to-day activity information. Before a completed system can be implemented, all master data stores must be complete and accessible, and all transactions that occurred since the last purge date must be entered into the database.

The person who was assigned responsibility for each data store during the design of the personnel component of the new system should supervise the initial conversion of that data store. Choices regarding the initial data conversion depend upon the state and condition of the source records and the availability of in-house resources for the tasks. Recall that the cost of the initial data conversion was estimated during the Evaluation of Alternatives Phase of the life cycle. New developments in the project since then may have an impact on the cost of data conversion or on the choices made regarding the issues mentioned above.

User Training

User training requirements are specified initially in the Learning section of the Designer's Tradeoff Chart, Figure 5.6. This specification is refined during the cost-benefit analysis, Figure 5.4, and during the planning of the tasks of the project, Figures 6.5 and 6.9.

Recall that the cost of training was estimated during the Evaluation of Alternatives Phase of the life cycle. New developments in the project since then may have an impact on the cost of training or on the choices made in the development of the training program.

Finalizing Documentation

Documentation serves both the user/management group and the information systems professionals of the organization. The user/management group looks to the documentation file for detailed operating instructions, and the information systems professionals look to the file for a complete presentation of the analysis, design, and implementation activities of the project.

Operator instructions describe both the operation of the system's programs and the execution of supporting manual procedures. A Structured English description of the operation of each program and supporting procedure should be included in the documentation file, along with the identification of responsible personnel. Refer to Chapter 4, and particularly to Figure 4.7, for information about Structured English descriptions. The organization of the operator instructions in the documentation file should follow the same pattern as the organization of processes in the system structure chart, Figure 7.7.

The greater the reliance upon CASE and 4GL tools in the development of a system, the easier it will be to collect and maintain accurate technical documentation for the information systems professional of the firm. Storage of documentation in electronic form also provides easier access for review purposes. Documentation maintenance was one of the early and most important benefits of computer-aided software engineering systems.

At a minimum, the technical documentation should include the database design, the system structure chart, and program and file specifications. Other items to consider are systems analysis and design models, budgets, schedules, the final Designer's Tradeoff Chart, and reports to management.

Evaluating the Completed System

A systems development project team carries out a series of evaluations and tradeoffs throughout the systems development life cycle. Once the completed system is implemented, a final evaluation of procedures and personnel is made to ensure that the new system provides timely, accurate, complete, and secure performance.

If the methods presented in this book are followed carefully, there should be no surprises for the development team at the final evaluation. One would certainly not expect to find a major requirement that was overlooked or a design choice that makes the primary users unhappy. An action document for the final evaluation of procedures and personnel is included in the You Do It section of this chapter.

Final Report to Management

A final report to management should be made after the implementation and evaluation of the new system is complete. In preparing this report, the project team engages in a critical assessment of both the successes and failures of their work.

This assessment allows the project team to synthesize their experience into usable capability that can be applied on the next project. An action document for preparing the final report to management is presented in the You Do It section of this chapter.

YOU DO IT

Use the cost control system material, the What, How, and Why section material, and the action documents of this section to guide your efforts in designing the new system for your project.

If your project involves a "live client," you will work with your client on the design until he or she is satisfied. If you are using the accompanying written case project (Chapter 10), you will develop your design according to the directions provided by your instructor.

Action Documents

The deliverables of the Buy/Build Software Phase and the Implement and Evaluate New System Phase of the life cycle are summarized in Action Document 9.1. Use Action Document 9.11 for planning and scheduling the software development and implementation tasks and the evaluation tasks, and for identifying the necessary inputs and outputs.

The final go/no go decision is listed as the first deliverable. As stated at the start of this chapter, the timing of the final go/no go decision and the information used to make it will vary depending upon the circumstances of your project.

Reviewing Software and Data

Use Action Document 9.2 for a review of the software and data components of the new system. Both the user/management group and the information system professionals should use this document as a guide to reviewing software and data according to system organization, completeness, accuracy, and ease of use. Remember that software must be reviewed regardless of the software acquisition/development methodology chosen for your project.

Use Action Document 9.3 to process feedback from this review.

Examine the feedback from the review and compare each item to the criteria, previous action documents, and sections listed below. Formulate a response to the feedback based upon this analysis.

Performance Efficiency

Use Action Document 7.4 to help identify design choices that affect processing efficiency. After you have made a list of these features, identify the corresponding menu items and test them for performance speed.

Collect your results on the form provided in Action Document 9.4. At the next team review meeting, review your findings and decide if modifications are necessary.

Implementation

Implementing the new system involves establishing the interface with existing company systems, doing the initial data conversion, training the users, and assembling the documentation that was developed throughout the preceding phases. Use Action Documents 9.5, 9.6, 9.7, and 9.8 to guide your implementation efforts.

Action Document 9.9 summarizes the typical issues in the final evaluation of procedures and personnel. Action Document 9.10 presents a checklist to help prepare for the final report to management. This report brings your project to a formal conclusion. Any and all of the issues listed in Action Document 9.10 could be raised at your presentation.

At the end of this phase, collect all relevant models, documents, and other materials, and use the cover sheet, Action Document 9.12, to submit your work as a progress report to your instructor.

References

1. Amadio, W. *Systems Development: A Practical Approach.* Watsonville, Calif.: Mitchell Publishing, 1989.

2. Jenkins, M. "Prototyping: A Methodology for the Design and Development of Application Systems." *Spectrum* Volume 2, Number 2 (April 1985): pp. 1–8.

3. Kozar, K. *Humanized Information Systems Analysis and Design.* New York: McGraw-Hill, 1989.

**IMPLEMENT AND EVALUATE NEW SYSTEM
DELIVERABLES**

1. Final go/no go decision.
2. Test software and data components.
3. Team review of software and data components.
4. Integrate completed system with existing infrastructure.
5. Initial data conversion.
6. User training.
7. Final documentation.
8. Final evaluation of supporting procedures and personnel.
9. Final report to management.

ACTION DOCUMENT 9.1
**Implement and Evaluate New System
deliverables**

User/Management Issues

IS Professionals Issues

Organization

Menus are consistent.

Screens follow a logical progression and conform to company standards.

Methods of data capture are consistent.

Provides flexible interface for multiple users.

Follows user preference for logical design of menu structure.

Future enhancements are possible.

Completeness

Outputs are timely and provide required information.

Instructions for operation of the system are clear.

Users have been trained in system operation.

Provides standard reports and inquiries.

Provides ad hoc reporting.

Fulfills user requirements.

Documentation provided.

Training provided.

Accuracy

Data entry controls are in place.

Audit trail.

Restricted access as prescribed.

Provides for backup, restore, security, updating, purging, data entry, and data transfer.

Ease of Use

Provides dates and times on reports.

Headings on all pages of reports.

Provides on-line help throughout.

Easily installed.

Easily integrated with other company systems.

Easily maintained and expanded.

If package, has good vendor support.

ACTION DOCUMENT 9.2
Reviewing software and data components

Criterion	Action Documents	Chapter
Scope of project	Objectives and tactics	1
Cost	Economic feasibility	5
Development environment capabilities	7 fundamental functions	8
Processing efficiency	Processing efficiency	9
Timeliness	Designer's Tradeoff Chart	5
Accuracy	Validation and verification specs	8
Completeness	Requirements model	4
Control	Procedures	7

R.T.C. LIBRARY, LETTERKENNY

ACTION DOCUMENT 9.3
Analyzing the software review

System Feature	Menu Item	Processing Speed	Accepted/ Rejected

ACTION DOCUMENT 9.4
Processing efficiency test document

INTERFACE WITH EXISTING SYSTEMS

Once the data to be shared among systems is identified, use the following questions to guide
the development of the interface:

1. How is this data captured and maintained?
2. How can our application access this data?
3. Are current maintenance policies, such as purging, compatible with our requirements?
4. Do current maintenance policies fulfill our application's timeliness requirements?
5. Who might need to share our data, and what are the consequences for our application?

ACTION DOCUMENT 9.5
**Checklist for establishing the interface
with existing systems**

INITIAL DATA CONVERSION

The issues to be addressed in converting a data store are:

1. Compiling source documents and/or records
2. Editing source records for conversion, for example, entering codes on manual records
3. Entering records into the database through maintenance programs using in-house personnel
4. Transferring records electronically into the database from other applications in the firm
5. Using a data preparation to key records to diskette and then transferring to the database

ACTION DOCUMENT 9.6
Checklist for initial data conversion

USER TRAINING

The issues to be addressed in developing and delivering user training are:

1. Who must be trained?
2. What must each person learn?
3. How long will the training last?
4. By what date must each person be trained?
5. What materials must be prepared? By whom?
6. How will the training be delivered? By whom?
7. What accommodation for relief from other duties must be made to accomplish the training?
8. Does the training plan provide redundancy in knowledge, so that no part of the system knowledge base is held by one person only?

ACTION DOCUMENT 9.7
Checklist for planning for user training

FINALIZING DOCUMENTATION

1. Operator instructions
2. Structured English descriptions of programs and supporting procedures
3. Identification of responsible personnel
4. Database design
5. System structure chart
6. Program and file specifications
7. Systems analysis and design models
8. Budgets
9. Schedules
10. Designer's Tradeoff Chart
11. Reports to management

ACTION DOCUMENT 9.8
**Checklist of items to include in final
documentation**

FINAL EVALUATION OF PROCEDURES AND PERSONNEL

1. Are the processes of the system—data maintenance, updating, reporting, and reorganization—performed frequently enough to satisfy the Timeliness requirements of the final Designer's Tradeoff Chart?

2. Have all validation and verification procedures been implemented? Have all batch controls, supporting journals, and comparisons to known results been implemented?

3. Has each person with potential access to the system been restricted or enabled at the proper level?

4. Is the system auditable?

POTENTIAL ISSUES FOR THE FINAL REPORT TO MANAGEMENT

1. Refer to Action Document 6.2 for general preparation guidelines.
2. Review previous reports.
3. Explain specifically how requirements were met, how tactics and objectives were supported.
4. Review requirements, tactics, and objectives not supported and explain why.
5. Present original and final Budget versus Actual Report and explain differences. Repeat for schedule.
6. Present a timetable for when system benefits will be realized.

ACTION DOCUMENT 9.10
Preparing for the final report to management

Deliverable 1: Final go/no go decision

Task	User/Mgt People	IS People	Documents Needed	Documents Produced	Estimated Duration

Deliverable 2: Software and data tests

Task	User/Mgt People	IS People	Documents Needed	Documents Produced	Estimated Duration

Deliverable 3: Team review of software and data

Task	User/Mgt People	IS People	Documents Needed	Documents Produced	Estimated Duration

ACTION DOCUMENT 9.11
Tasks for each deliverable (page 1 of 3)

Deliverable 4: Integrate completed system with existing infrastructure

Task	User/Mgt People	IS People	Documents Needed	Documents Produced	Estimated Duration

Deliverable 5: Initial data conversion

Task	User/Mgt People	IS People	Documents Needed	Documents Produced	Estimated Duration

Deliverable 6: User training

Task	User/Mgt People	IS People	Documents Needed	Documents Produced	Estimated Duration

**ACTION DOCUMENT 9.11
Tasks for each deliverable (page 2 of 3)**

Deliverable 7: Final documentation

Task	User/Mgt People	IS People	Documents Needed	Documents Produced	Estimated Duration

Deliverable 8: Final evaluation of supporting procedures and personnel

Task	User/Mgt People	IS People	Documents Needed	Documents Produced	Estimated Duration

Deliverable 9: Final report to management

Task	User/Mgt People	IS People	Documents Needed	Documents Produced	Estimated Duration

ACTION DOCUMENT 9.11
Tasks for each deliverable (page 3 of 3)

Date _____

To _____

From _____

Re: Buy/Build Software and Implementation Phases

The following documents are included in this analysis:

☐ Final go/no go decision

☐ Software and data test

☐ Team review of software and data

☐ New system integration

☐ Initial data conversion

☐ User training

☐ Final documentation

☐ Final evaluation of procedures and personnel

☐ Final report to management

☐ Other _____

_____

☐ Other _____

_____

☐ Other _____

_____

The following activities were carried out during this analysis:

☐ Interviews with _____

_____

☐ Written exercises with _____

_____

☐ Other _____

_____

☐ Other _____

_____

☐ Other _____

_____

**Action Document 9.12
Cover sheet for final-phase analysis**

CHAPTER 10

Written Case Project

This chapter provides a written case that you can use as your project for this course. Use of the written case should be considered as an alternative to a project involving a "live client." Use the material from this case whenever you work on a You Do It section in a preceding chapter.

Some of the You Do It exercises and action documents cannot be applied to a written case effectively. For these exercises, your instructor may ask you to do some research beyond what is presented here, either in the library, on your campus, or in your community.

Background Information

The Construction Trade Association (CTA) is the client firm for this project. Frank Chapin, president of Horatio & Co., is on the executive board of CTA, and he has recommended you to serve as systems development consultant.

CTA is a state-wide trade association for the construction industry. Jack Garrity is the executive director of CTA. Carol Bodnar is Jack's administrative assistant. Communication with the member firms is usually done through the company presidents.

Member firms pay annual dues to CTA. In return, CTA promotes the interests of the industry in the state capitol. These activities include representing the industry's point of view on pending legislation, such as new building codes, and advising legislators on regulatory issues, such as licensing of equipment operators. Jack Garrity spends 80 percent of his time on political activities.

CTA also provides direct services, such as educational seminars, to its member firms. Six months ago, the executive board decided to administer an employee health care insurance program in response to a mandate from the membership. The cost of covering employees with medical and dental insurance skyrocketed recently, and CTA discovered that by pooling the employees of the member firms into one large group, significant savings could be achieved. Even with the 3 percent service charge that CTA adds, the member firms are now paying less for employee health care insurance, with no reduction in coverage, than they were with their previous company plans.

In addition to her many other duties, Carol Bodnar is responsible for the administration of the insurance program. For the past six months, Carol has been processing the activity of the program manually. She and Jack knew that it would be difficult for her to handle the insurance program without some kind of assistance. The purpose of this project is to provide that assistance.

Carol and Jack are anxious to see what a computer can do for the insurance program. CTA already owns a PC clone with an 80286 processor, 1 megabyte of RAM, a 40-megabyte hard disk, and a color display. Carol uses the machine for word processing, spreadsheet analysis, and data communications. CTA also makes heavy use of their FAX machine in communicating with the member firms, the state capitol, and other construction trade associations throughout the country.

Administering the Insurance Program

Administrative activities for the insurance program include maintaining the rolls of insured employees, billing and collecting premiums from the member firms each month, and paying monthly premiums to the insurance company (called the carrier). Forty member firms participate in the program, enrolling a total of 2,000 employees.

Carol keeps a list of the enrolled employees in separate folders for each member firm. She calls this collection of folders the Insurance File. Figure 10.1 shows a portion of the list maintained for Horatio & Co.

The monthly premium for each employee depends upon his or her marital status and whether or not there are children in the family. The rate categories are single (no spouse, no children), husband and wife (no children), parent and child (at least one child under 21, no spouse), family (husband, wife, at least one child under 21). Figure 10.2 shows the current carrier rates for the program.

Carol keeps the Insurance File lists in pencil because they change often. Whenever a new employee is hired or leaves a member firm or whenever there is a change in category, such as a marriage or a child's 21st birthday, the member firm must notify Carol. Carol makes the adjustment on her list so that the change is reflected in the next month's bill to the member. She also notifies the carrier so that the bill from the carrier to CTA also reflects the change.

Member: Horatio & Co.

Employee	SS#	Date of Birth	Marital Status	# of Children	Medical	Dental	Last Change Date
Augustin, Felicita	103-29-3636	9-11-35	Single	0	yes	no	4-30-90
Long, Kim	534-32-1001	7-23-59	Married	0	yes	yes	4-16-90
Berg, Erika	393-54-2452	10-17-59	Married	1	yes	yes	2-2-90
Silva, Frances	636-42-6292	10-1-45	Single	0	no	no	6-15-90
Duvall, Sam	963-99-7363	4-3-40	Single	3	yes	yes	2-13-90
Kilpatrick, Mary	929-66-4732	1-30-49	Married	0	no	yes	3-15-90
Sindora, Joe	454-32-2886	11-27-47	Married	4	yes	no	5-4-90
Abelardo, Camille	040-32-0919	6-27-50	Single	2	yes	yes	6-22-90
Carlsen, Dana	342-26-8135	8-18-53	Married	3	no	yes	1-17-90
Chen, John	750-42-5484	8-24-54	Single	0	yes	yes	2-12-90

FIGURE 10.1
Insurance File: enrolled employees

Plan	Category	Monthly Premium	Effective Date
Medical	Single	117.65	1-1-90
	Husband & Wife	302.10	1-1-90
	Parent & Child	235.90	1-1-90
	Family	346.16	1-1-90
Dental	Single	13.57	1-1-90
	Husband & Wife	37.60	1-1-90
	Parent & Child	31.00	1-1-90
	Family	41.12	1-1-90

FIGURE 10.2
Insurance carrier rates

Because paperwork is sometimes delayed, adjustments in the rolls are reported with an effective date. It is not uncommon to report an employee deleted from the rolls with an effective date that is 2 months old. In such a case, the member firm is entitled to a credit of 2 months' premium for that employee. By the same token, if a firm reports an employee added to the rolls 2 months ago, then 2 months' premium is due from the member firm.

Carol records all adjustments on a log for each member firm. She keeps the logs with each firm's list of enrolled employees in the Insurance File of folders. Figure 10.3 shows the adjustment log for Horatio & Co.

When an adjustment is received, Carol records it on the log for the appropriate member firm and computes the premium adjustment, if any, for prior billings. She then records the change in status on the appropriate Insurance File list so that it is included in all future billings. Adjustments are always effective from the first day of a month, so that adjustment debits and credits are always multiples of full-month premium amounts.

On the first of every month Carol prepares an invoice for each member firm. The member invoice begins with the adjustments for the month. Each adjustment and the corresponding debit or credit is shown, and the amounts are totaled.

The regular billing section follows. The regular section reflects the current state of the member's employee roll as of the first of the month. Payment of the amount shown covers each employee for the coming month.

The member invoice ends with a final accounting of the member's account: previous balance, minus current payments, plus current premiums equals amount due. Member firms are not expected to maintain a previous balance in the insurance program for long.

Figure 10.4 shows a portion of a member invoice for Horatio & Co. Remember that CTA adds a 3 percent service charge to the carrier rates.

Member: Horatio & Co.

Date Reported	Effective Date	Employee	Adjustment	$ + or −
2-12-90	2-1-90	Chen, John	Add Dental	+ 13.57
3-15-90	3-1-90	Kilpatrick, Mary	Drop Medical	−302.10
6-15-90	5-1-90	Silva, Frances	Drop	−27.14
6-27-90	6-1-90	Abelardo, Camille	Drop 1 child	no change

FIGURE 10.3
Adjustments log

```
                          CTA Insurance Program
                             Member Invoice
Firm: Horatio & Co.                          Billing Date: 07/01/90

                               ADJUSTMENTS
```

Employee	Date reported	Effective date	Adjustment	$ + or -
Silva, F.	6/15/90	5/1/90	Drop	-27.95
Abelardo, C.	6/27/90	6/1/90	Child at 21	0.00
Total Adjustments				-27.95

```
                                 DETAIL
```

Employee	Marital Status	# of Children	Medical	Dental	Premium
Augustin, F.	S	0	Y	N	121.18
Long, K.	M	0	Y	Y	349.89
Berg, E.	M	1	Y	Y	398.90
Duvall, S.	S	3	Y	Y	274.91
Kilpatrick M.	M	0	N	Y	38.73
Sindora, J.	M	4	Y	N	356.54
Abelardo, C.	S	1	Y	Y	274.91
Carlsen, D.	M	3	N	Y	42.35
Chen, J.	S	0	Y	Y	135.16
Tilden, S.	M	2	Y	Y	398.90
.					.
.					.
.					.

```
Total Detail                                              9,784.16

Previous balance                                          9,646.70
Current payment (-)                                       9,646.70
Current premiums (+)                                      9,756.21

Amount due                                                9,756.21
```

FIGURE 10.4
Monthly member invoice

Before Carol mails the invoices, she makes a photocopy of each one. She files the copies in the folders that she collectively calls the Billings File. When payments arrive during the month, Carol marks the date and the amount of the payment on the copy of the most recent invoice. She reviews these entries to determine a member firm's previous balance during the preparation of the monthly invoice.

Soon after she mails the member invoices, Carol receives a monthly invoice from the insurance carrier. The format is similar to that of the member

```
                    XYZ Insurance Association
                            Invoice

To: Construction Trade Association
Plan: 86432                                    Billing Date: 07-01-89

                          Adjustments
                                Effective
Insured              SS#        Status  Date       Adjustment      Amount
-------------        ---------- ------   --------   --------------  --------
Robert Ilardi        472-11-8642 Family  06-01-89   Add insured     +346.16
Christine Ruch       547-21-8920 Single  07-01-89   Delete insured     0.00
Tamara Kops          548-71-1110 H & W   05-01-89   Add Husband     +368.90
Camille Abelardo     040-32-0919 P & C   06-01-90   Delete 1 child     0.00


                              Detail

Employee             SS#        Status                      Monthly Premium
-------------        ---------- ------                      ----------------
Tilden, Sam          002-43-3439 Family                              346.16
Allred, Joe          151-77-8641 P & C                               235.90
Klein, Betsy         231-21-3131 P & C                               235.90
      •                                                                •
      •                                                                •
      •                                                                •

Total this Plan                                                  498,247.36

Plan: 87351

                          Adjustments
                                Effective
Insured              SS#        Status  Date       Adjustment      Amount
-------------        ---------- ------   --------   --------------  --------
Frances Silva        636-42-6292 Single  05-01-90   Delete insured    -27.14
Camille Abelardo     040-32-0919 P & C   06-01-90   Delete 1 child      0.00
```

FIGURE 10.5
Monthly carrier bill

invoices generated by CTA. The adjustments section shows changes to the rolls reported during the month. The detailed billing section lists all employees in the plan by social security number. The final accounting section shows how the amount due was calculated.

Figure 10.5 shows a portion of the most recent carrier billing. Notice the carrier's reliance upon identification numbers: social security numbers for employees and plan numbers for the insurance plans. Plan 86432 is medical, and 87351 is dental.

When Carol receives adjustments from the members, she reports them to the carrier on special forms. New enrollments and changes to existing enrollees are reported on the Transmittal of Applications, Figure 10.6, and terminations are reported on the Transmittal of Deletions, Figure 10.7.

```
XYZ Insurance Association                                    Date: 06/30/90

FROM: Construction Trade Association                         TRANSMITTAL OF APPLICATIONS

Plan: 86432

                              Date                  New                            Effective
SS#            Name           of Birth   Reason     Addition?   Category           Date
-----------    --------------- ---------- ---------- ---------- ----------------   ----------
132-75-8761    Mann, Christopher  06-30-35  New hire    Y         Family            06-01-90
050-42-3439    Bisecky, Dianne    05-24-60  Marriage    N         Husband & Wife    06-01-90
```

FIGURE 10.6
Form to report additions and changes to carrier

```
XYZ Insurance Association                                    Date: 06/30/90

FROM: Construction Trade Association                         TRANSMITTAL OF DELETIONS

Plan: 86432

                                            Effective
SS#            Name            Reason       Date
-----------    --------------- ------------ ----------
147-68-2314    Lombard, Nancy  Retire       07-01-90
```

FIGURE 10.7
Form to report deletions to carrier

Daily	End of month
Record adjustments from members	Bill member firms
Issue ID cards	Settle carrier bill
Process cash receipts	Prepare control reports
Prepare bank deposit	Prepare general ledger transactions

FIGURE 10.8
Insurance program processes

Insurance Program Processes

Carol divides the processing activity of the insurance program into two categories: daily and end-of-month. Figure 10.8 summarizes the processes.

Record Adjustments from Members

Each day's mail brings a few insurance program adjustments from the member firms. Carol estimates that she receives 100 adjustments per month.

Each day Carol logs the adjustments and records the changes in the Insurance File. She mails the necessary transmittal forms to the carrier, and she files a copy of the transmittals in a folder marked Transmittal Forms Already Sent. This file is used to check the adjustment section of the carrier bill for accuracy.

Issue ID Cards

Each enrolled employee is issued an ID card upon enrollment. Some adjustments, such as the addition of dental insurance, require a new ID card. Carol receives such adjustments throughout the month. When she receives one, she mails the new card to the benefits manager of the firm that employs the insured. The benefits managers distribute the cards to the employees.

Process Cash Receipts

Each day's mail also brings payments from the member firms. Carol records the payments on the most recent invoice in the Billings File.

Recall that the most recent invoice reports current and past due amounts. With the receipt of a payment, Carol calculates a new total amount due. She calls any firm that maintains a balance due for more than two months to arrange a full payment plan.

Prepare Bank Deposit

Carol totals each day's cash receipts for the insurance program and deposits them into a checking account maintained expressly for the insurance program. In CTA's chart of accounts, all insurance program assets, liabilities, revenues, and expenses are recorded in separate accounts.

Bill Member Firms

The process of billing member firms is described above.

Settle Carrier Bill

This is the most time-consuming process in the system. Settling the carrier's bill means trying to match the amounts listed on the bill with CTA's files and with the amounts billed to the member firms.

From the carrier's point of view, all enrolled employees belong to the CTA group, so nothing in the carrier bill identifies an insured's employer. Since CTA's files are all organized by member firm, matching entries on the carrier bill with entries in files is difficult.

The rate at which the carrier processes adjustments is variable. Sometimes an adjustment appears on the very next bill, and at other times it does not appear for 2 or 3 months.

Carol checks her file of Transmittal Forms Already Sent against the carrier bill. Those transmittals that appear on the bill are removed from the file and placed in a file marked Verified Transmittals.

Unverified transmittals remain in the original file. If a transmittal remains there too long, Carol checks with the carrier to determine the cause of the delay. These delays point up the importance of the effective date in all transactions. The carrier honors all claims subsequent to the effective date, even if all of the processing is not complete at the time of the claim.

Prepare Control Reports

Once the carrier bill is settled, Carol reviews her files and prepares several control reports. The first report is a listing of all member firms and how much they owe CTA for insurance. Jack Garrity receives this report each month.

CTA is working on a very small 3 percent service charge, and Jack is worried about cash drain.

For the second report, Carol scans the Insurance File looking for employees who are approaching their 70th birthday. CTA's contract with the carrier requires employees aged 70 or over to name Medicare as their primary insurance carrier. The CTA program supplements Medicare by paying the portion of charges that Medicare does not pay.

Prepare General Ledger Transactions

CTA's chart of accounts identifies all insurance program items specifically. Carol must review each member bill to identify how much was billed for the medical insurance program and how much was billed for the dental insurance program. These amounts are posted to the appropriate revenue accounts in the general ledger.

The monthly carrier bill is separated into amounts due for the medical and dental programs. Carol picks up the general ledger expense postings for the insurance programs directly from this bill without any additional calculations.

APPENDIX

Other Software Development Environments

This appendix describes two alternatives to using the GENIFER/dBASE software development environment for student projects. The description consists of an overview of the documentation for each package along with a match-up of the documentation to the material presented in Chapter Eight.

RBASE for DOS

Microrim's RBASE has been a leading microcomputer-based database management system for quite some time. The version described here is RBASE for DOS, which made its appearance in 1987.

The system specification modules of RBASE for DOS are called EXPRESS modules. The correspondence with the components of GENIFER is shown below.

RBASE MODULE	GENIFER Component
Definition EXPRESS	Data Dictionary
Application EXPRESS	Menu screens under Screens and Reports
Forms EXPRESS	Data screens under Screens and Reports
Reports EXPRESS	Reports under Screens and Reports

The GENIFER notion of projects corresponds to the RBASE notion of databases. EXPRESS module users identify a database for a work session upon entry into the module.

RBASE databases consist of tables, the analog of dBASE files. RBASE does provide indexes (called keys); as an alternative, many of the commands allow a SORTED BY clause. The developer must trade off the display and processing efficiency of the index against the overhead required to maintain it.

A separate code-generation step is not required in RBASE for DOS, so there is no corresponding entry for the Program Generators option of GENIFER's Main Menu. There is also no separate feature corresponding to GENIFER's Documentation option. On-line Help is available by pressing the F10 key.

Definition EXPRESS

The RBASE Definition EXPRESS and the GENIFER Data Dictionary are, for all practical purposes, equivalent. RBASE tables correspond to GENIFER databases, which correspond to dBASE files. RBASE columns correspond to GENIFER fields.

The developer uses the Definition EXPRESS to create and maintain tables. The names, data types, computed expressions, and validation rules are all entered here. Key columns are also entered here. The material presented in the Maintaining Data and the Validating Entries sections of Chapter 8 corresponds to the RBASE Definition EXPRESS. Documentation on the Definition EXPRESS is presented in Chapter 2 of the RBASE for DOS User's Manual.

The Definition EXPRESS also allows the developer to specify a combination of columns from various tables as a database view. In GENIFER, views are created under the Data screens option of Screens and Reports.

Application EXPRESS

The Application EXPRESS is used to specify menu screen layouts and selections. Unlike GENIFER, table maintenance screens must be built, one option at a time, through the Application EXPRESS. The Forms EXPRESS and the Reports EXPRESS can be called from the Application EXPRESS.

The Chapter 8 material in the latter part of the Maintaining Data section, the material on purging, and the material presented in the Selecting Data, Sequencing Data, and Displaying Inquiries and Reports sections corresponds to the RBASE Application EXPRESS. Documentation on the Application EXPRESS is presented in Chapter 2 of the RBASE for DOS Building Applications and Command Dictionary manual.

Updating from transactions must be done with a developer-written program in RBASE. The Application EXPRESS allows the specification of such a program through the Template action. The technique is similar to that presented in the Updating from Transactions section of Chapter 8. The RBASE programming language is documented in Chapter 3 of the RBASE for DOS Building Applications and Command Dictionary manual.

R.T.C. LIBRARY, LETTERKENNY

Forms EXPRESS

The Forms EXPRESS is used to specify data screen layouts. The Chapter 8 material in the Maintaining Data, the Selecting Data, and the Sequencing Data sections corresponds to the Forms EXPRESS documentation. Documentation on the Forms EXPRESS is presented in Chapter 4 of the RBASE for DOS User's Manual.

Reports EXPRESS

The Reports EXPRESS is used to specify report layouts and actions. The Chapter 8 material in the Selecting Data, the Sequencing Data, and the Displaying Inquiries and Reports sections corresponds to the Reports EXPRESS documentation. Documentation on the Reports EXPRESS is presented in Chapter 6 of the RBASE for DOS User's Manual.

Other

Reorganization instructions to pack the database and rebuild the indexes are automatically included in GENIFER-generated maintenance programs. In RBASE, these must be included as a separate program using the Reload or Pack commands. These commands are documented in Chapter 8 of the RBASE for DOS User's Manual.

dBASE IV

Ashton-Tate's dBASE IV made its appearance in 1989. The material presented here was taken from the documentation for version 1.0.

The system specification modules of dBASE IV can be accessed through the Control Center panels. The correspondence with the components of GENIFER is shown below.

dBASE IV PANEL	GENIFER Component
Data and Queries	Data Dictionary
Applications	Menu screens under Screens and Reports
Forms	Data screens under Screens and Reports
Reports	Reports under Screens and Reports

The GENIFER notion of projects corresponds to the dBASE IV notion of applications. Uses of the terms *file*, *field*, and *index* are equivalent. The dBASE IV Applications Generator requires a code-generation step.

Data Panel

The developer uses the Data panel to create and maintain files. The field names, data types, and index key columns are all entered here. The Chapter 8 material in the Maintaining Data and the Sequencing Data sections corresponds to the dBASE IV Data panel. Documentation on the Data panel is presented in Chapters 2 and 6 of the dBASE IV Using the Menu System manual.

Queries

The Queries panel of the Control Center allows the developer to specify a combination of fields from various files as a database view. In GENIFER, views are created under the Data screens option of Screens and Reports.

The Chapter 8 material presented in the Selecting Data section corresponds to the dBASE IV Queries panel. Documentation on the Queries panel is presented in Chapter 7 of the dBASE IV Using the Menu System manual.

Applications

The Applications panel or Applications Generator is used to specify menu screen layouts and selections. Unlike GENIFER, file maintenance screens must be built, one option at a time, through the Applications generator. The Forms and Reports panels can be accessed during an Applications Generator work session, or the developer can choose to create all files, queries, forms, and reports before tying them all together through the Applications Generator.

The Chapter 8 material in the latter part of the Maintaining Data section and the material on purging correspond to the dBASE IV Applications Generator. Documentation on the Applications Generator is presented in the Using the dBASE IV Applications Generator manual and in Chapter 11 of the Using the Menu System manual.

Updating from transactions must be done with a developer-written program in dBASE IV. The Applications Generator allows the specification of such a program through the Batch Process action. The technique is similar to that presented in the Updating from Transaction section of Chapter 8. The dBASE IV programming language is documented in the Language Reference manual and in Chapters 1–6 of the Advanced Topics manual.

Forms EXPRESS

The Forms panel is used to specify data screen layouts. The Chapter 8 material in the latter part of the Maintaining Data section corresponds to the Forms panel documentation. Documentation on the Forms panel is presented in Chapter 8 of the dBASE IV Using the Menu System manual.

INDEX

Numbers in **boldface** type refer to pages on which terms are defined. Numbers in *italic* refer to pages on which relevant figures or action documents appear.